Frances de Paravicini

Early history of Balliol College

Frances de Paravicini

Early history of Balliol College

ISBN/EAN: 9783742855381

Manufactured in Europe, USA, Canada, Australia, Japa

Cover: Foto ©Thomas Meinert / pixelio.de

Manufactured and distributed by brebook publishing software
(www.brebook.com)

Frances de Paravicini

Early history of Balliol College

EARLY HISTORY

OF

BALLIOL COLLEGE

BY

FRANCES DE PARAVICINI

LONDON

KEGAN PAUL, TRENCH, TRÜBNER, & CO. LTD

1891

PREFACE

EVERY book is supposed to need a preface. For the following pages a very few words will suffice.

In love for the Foundress, and in reverence for the foundation, from the ample materials within my reach I have endeavoured to trace the Early History of Balliol College.

If the Members of Balliol College will be interested in it, and if Oxford Citizens will care for it, I shall be well repaid for the pleasant trouble and the happy hours it has cost me.

And here I would record my sincere thanks to the Reverend Benjamin Jowett, Master of Balliol, for his great kindness and courtesy in granting me access to the College Archives.

And I wish to express my gratitude to the friends who have, from time to time, always most readily, helped me with the translations of the Mediaeval Latin ; in most cases writing entire translations for me. All such help, in tasks where I, unaided, must have failed, has been invaluable. Especially my thanks are due to Mr. W. M. Geldart, Scholar of Balliol College, who has translated for me Dervorguilla's Statutes, and the Statutes of Sir Philip de Somervyle. And to Mr. G. W. Wheeler, M.A., of the College, and Assistant at the Bodleian Library, who has given me liberal help with the Latin Register.

I have given long extracts from the Manuscript of Antony à Wood, now preserved in the Bodleian Library (MS. Wood. F. 38) ; and also long extracts from the small book, *Balliofergus*, printed in 1668, written by Henry Savage, then Master of the College. And I have gleaned much, and quoted often, from the pages of Mr. Maxwell Lyte's most interesting and exhaustive *History of the University of Oxford*. Occasional references to the *Fourth Report of the Royal Commission on Historical Manuscripts* imply that I have adopted Mr. Riley's words for the description or translation of a document.

With the exception of documents given in modern Latin, instead of the abbreviated type, I have endeavoured, in all quotations, whether from ancient records or modern writers, to follow the originals in every detail of words, spelling, and punctuation. This plan, strictly right and consistent in itself, has caused many seeming inconsistencies in the pages of this volume.

FRANCES DE PARAVICINI.

OXFORD : *June* 1891.

CONTENTS

CHAPTER I.

CHAPTER II.

CHAPTER III.

CHAPTER IV.

Page 64, l. 26. *For* Hertipoll, *read* Hertilpoll.

This translation was made from a modern Latin transcript of the Statutes, which may have been incorrect in some minor details.

Page 88, l. 21. The date 1219 seems to refer to the older foundation, before Dervorguilla built Dulce-Cor, commonly called New Abbey.

Page 92, l. 9. I am told that there is doubt about the walls of the Master's dining-room being the original walls of Dervorguilla's Chapel.

Page 97, l. 24. Antony à Wood wrote 'Urban 6,' which appears to be a mistake for Urban 5.

Page 228, last line. The letter from Pope Eugenius probably is in the College archives ; but it did not come under my notice.

Page 242, l. 10. *For* Octoboni, *read* Octobonus.

Page 291. In this extract, through a mistake in transcribing, the abbreviations have not been given.

Page 307, last line. I have been unable to find any trace of the note Henry Savage speaks of, adding that it was 'torn off.' But at the end of one (perhaps more) of the manuscripts of Duns Scotus, in the College Library, is a note which says that Duns was educated at Merton College.

Page 338, l. 23. 1,100*l.* seems to be a large sum. There may be some mistake.

EARLY HISTORY

OF

BALLIOL COLLEGE

CHAPTER I.

IF we stand to-day in the Broad Street at Oxford,
and look at the modern buildings of Balliol College,
it is hard to realize that the ground they cover,
and the name they bear, have an history, old, rich,
closely mixed with the annals of learning, and mingling continually with Ecclesiastical and University
interests. The range of gothic [1] stonework which
faces the Street ; the Master's house, men's rooms,
and lecture rooms, the porter's lodge, and the square
tower above it, replaced an older building, and an
older tower, in about the year 1868. Pieces of oak
from the interior of the ' Old Tower,' as it has since
been called, were bought up by enterprising carpenters and fancy-dealers, and made into cabinets and

---

[1] Called *Modern Gothic*.

B

boxes ; and then were sold again to Balliol men, at an increased value. And the ' New Tower ' stood, white and fresh from the stone-masons' hands, to witness to the vitality of Dervorguilla's foundation.

Passing round Fisher Buildings, we come again upon gothic work, and another tower, above a less important gateway. The ground here has its history also ; and these buildings, together with the front part of a comparatively old dwelling-house, hide from us the new dining hall, a quite modern block of masonry and brickwork, at the north end of the garden quadrangle.

Broad Street, obviously so called, is the old Horsemonger Street of the twelfth and thirteenth centuries, which reached from North Gate to Smith Gate ; and the length and general outline remain almost the same, though the appearance of the Street has been continually changed by successive altera-tions. We are told that ' the Reason of its attaining this Name was from a Market of Horses sometime kept there ; for the Prior of St. Frid. by a Patent from K. H. I. had it granted him to be kept from North Gate to Holywell, and so to the North East Corner of the City Wall, and it was called the Horse and Horsemonger-Street Market ; but at length, when Merton College had that Manor in their hands, some Strife happened between them and the said Priory, who told them they were not to keep any such Market there in alieno solo ;—it was therefore left off.—The Place afterwards was wholly known and written by the Name of Canditch, Candida fossa, because of the clear Stream that formerly ran under all the North Wall.' [1]

The line of the City Wall is so well known, we need hardly linger over any description of it. Some portions of the Wall still remain, at the end of the gardens at the back of houses in Broad Street, not far from St. Michael's Church. Thence it continued to Turl Gate and to Smith Gate. Under this Wall, on the north side of it, ran the clear stream, which gave the Street its name. This stream was divided into Fish Ponds, one of which, lying farther on towards East Gate, was 'for the Mayor's Table, and his own Use.' That this ditch, or stream, was originally a part of the trench, or moat, round the City Wall, there can be no doubt ; and also that, in times of even slight rain, it would easily fill with water, is a natural supposition. There is no record of the depth, or width, of the trench ; but we read that the people, to whom the Fish Ponds were leased, neglected the cleansing of them, and the current of the stream was in several places stopped ; and 'they came by Degrees to be dried up ; and at last, by Conveyance of Dirt and other Filth of the City, and of Earth

[1] *City of Oxford*, Peshall, p. 239.

from Foundations of Colleges, were in a manner levelled with the other Ground.'[1]

Canditch has sometimes been spoken of as the ' King's Highway of Canditch.'   And, indeed, such a Street as it was in those days, and such as we see it now; though now despoiled of much of its beauty, and disfigured by our modern shops and houses, a cobble road, and patient cab-horses ; it well deserves the regal appellation.   The broad level space, which was all road and gravel, with its borderings of grass, and its large trees, began near St. Mary Magdalen's Church ; and extended eastward to the little Chapel by the City Wall, near to Smith Gate, built—history does not tell us by whom—in honour of our Lady, and known as ' Our Lady's Chapel.'   Canditch was wider than the present Broad Street.   On the north side stood the small Halls and Hostels, where Students lived and learned : and all along the length of the Street, on the south side, was the running stream, soon to degenerate into a ditch for rubbish ; and the grand City Wall, with its bastions, of that sad greyness peculiar to the Oxfordshire stone.

On the north side of Horsemonger Street were several Halls ; but, from the meagre records we have, it is not easy to learn their origin, or to trace their exact position.   It must always be regretted that no contemporary account has been preserved for us of

[1] *City of Oxford*, p. 202.

the numerous Halls which existed in Oxford at that time. There are no trustworthy narratives, and very few traditions, concerning them ; but only a long list of their names, and we have some know-ledge of the Streets and localities where they stood. Mr. Anstey, in his introduction to the *Munimenta Academica*, says it is possible that some MSS. may even now be lying in the Bodleian Library, or in Muniment Rooms of Colleges, which would throw light on the history of the Halls ; but, he adds, it is more probable that such MSS. may be found, if they exist at all, hidden away, their value not under-stood, in private Libraries. In the City Archives, there certainly were once valuable documents, relating to the history of the University ; but even these cannot now be discovered. The records of the Halls are, virtually, lost ; unless we accept, as a last resource, the suggestion that at Rome might be found particulars of appeals from Oxford, which would give us some insight into the obscure details of Oxford life in those early days.

In speaking of the Halls in Oxford, we must be careful not to confuse them with the Colleges. The Halls, known simply as Halls, Hostels, or Entries, were—as far as we can ascertain—merely lodging-houses, or boarding-houses, for Scholars ; and were unendowed. A boy, sent to Oxford, went to one of the Monasteries, and that would be with a view to

his becoming a Religious ; or he went to one of the
boarding-houses, and became, in course of time, a
secular Clerk ; or he remained a Laic.   But, both
Clerks and Laymen were spoken of as Scholars
and Students ; that is, they were studying, and
were under the rank of Bachelor ; while the title
of Master implied having taken the highest degree
in any Faculty.   It is uncertain when these
boarding-houses and Halls were first established ;
but we know of their existence in early days, from
the accounts of disputes about rent.   In 1213,
the Townsmen, who had suffered much from the
severe interdict which had been laid on the Town,
applied to Nicholas of Tusculum, the Papal Legate,
for protection and forgiveness.   And we find that
the Legate, in 1214, remembering all the grievances
of the Scholars, decreed—among other things—that,
for a certain number of years, only half the rent
agreed upon should be paid for the Halls and Inns.
Besides these Halls, there were Schools in Oxford,
which were distinct from the Schools in the Religious
Houses.   It has been computed that there were not
less than thirty-two in School Street.[1]   And this
seems to be no great number ; for a School merely
meant the house, or room, where public lectures
were given, and where Disputations took place.
Each Master, lecturing, was obliged to have his own

[1] *Munimenta Academica*, vol. i. p. 240.

lecture room. The Masters rented the Schools; and each School, or house, had, in all probability, two or three lecture rooms.

Mr. Maxwell Lyte, in his *History of the University of Oxford*, does not attempt any minute description of the locality of early foundations. About Balliol, he only tells us, that ' the Scholars of Balliol lived for some years in a hired house situated in the northern suburb of Oxford, in Horsemonger Street, near the church of St. Mary Magdalen. Thence they removed to another house a few yards eastward in the same street, known as Mary Hall, which, with three adjoining plots of ground, was purchased for them by the Lady Dervorguilla in 1284.'[1]

That 'hired house' was the original Balliol Hall, which has since grown into Balliol College.

But, before beginning to speak of the foundation of the College, we must take a rapid glance at Oxford as it then was; that we may recognize the work that John de Balliol meant his ' House at Oxford' to do, and the need there was for such an endowment.

---

[1] *Hist. Univ. Oxford*, Maxwell Lyte, p. 86.

CHAPTER II

THE origin of the University of Oxford must always remain an open and doubtful question. There are the old legends, now rejected, which tell us how Alfred the Great built here three Halls, which formed the nucleus of the future University ; and, at the same time, linked his name with the foundation of University College. But it is well known, that the University, with the help of money given by William of Durham for the support of poor Clerks at Oxford, established a Society of Clerics ; and the building they inhabited came, by degrees, to be recognized as the Great Hall of the University, or University Hall. And, later on, what is now University College was known, and spoken of, as the ' Hall of Master William of Durham.'

We know that King Alfred ' legatos præterea ad Gallias direxit et inde Sanctum Grimbaldum, sacerdotem et monachum ac virum in disciplinis ecclesiasticis eruditum, nec non et Johannem presbyterum et monachum bonis moribus adornatum ; ex ultimis etiam Walanorum finibus, de monasterio Sancti

David, Asserum ad suum accivit consortium, ut horum omnium sapientia et doctrina regis desiderium cresceret, qui et in brevi ita profecerunt, quod librorum omnium notitiam haberet perfectam.'[1]

[*Translation.*—Moreover, he directed messengers into Gaul, and thence called into his company St. Grymbald, Priest and Monk, a man learned in Ecclesiastical disciplines; and also John, Priest and Monk, adorned with good moral virtues; and from the farthest confines of Wales, Asser, from the Monastery of St. David; so that by the wisdom and learning of all of them, the desire of the King might be advanced: and in a short time they succeeded so well that he had a perfect knowledge of all books.]

The story that Grymbald and John were brought to Oxford, that they might teach, and establish Schools, would tend to prove that there were Schools and Scholars here before Alfred's time. The story goes on to say, that the Students in Oxford refused to accept the Forms of Reading, and the Institutions, which Grymbald and the learned men who accompanied him from France wished to introduce; and so sharp was the dispute between the two parties, that Alfred hastened to Oxford, to induce them to come to amicable terms. But Grymbald, not satisfied by the King's attempt at a compromise, left Oxford, and retired to the newly-founded Monastery

[1] *Matthew Paris*, ed. Luard, vol. i. p. 407.

at Winchester. We are told how ' Sanctus Grim-
baldus migravit ad Dominum.' In the year 904,
' Sanctus presbyter Grimbaldus, magnæ vir sancti-
tatis, et unus magistrorum Alfredi regis, gaudia con-
scendit regni cælestis.'[1] Also we hear of St. Neot, a
Professor of Theology ; and Asser, the Monk ; and
John, the companion of Grymbald, whose lectures
King Alfred often attended.

Unfortunately, around the truth of the story about
Grymbald there has been much entanglement and
controversy ; and it is now generally believed to have
been inserted into Asser's *Life of King Alfred*, by
an unknown hand, in the time of Richard II. ' But
here we do come to at least real persons, Alfred and
Grymbald, and the rest, though acts are ascribed to
them which we may safely affirm they never performed.'[2] We would like to think that with these
names, perhaps, the real tangible history of education at Oxford begins. Alfred's presence in the City,
and his efforts to encourage a love for learning, not
unfrequently shown by his listening to the teaching
given by those whom he had placed here, forms a
bright picture of Saxon times. The fact of Grymbald's sojourn in Oxford seems to be secured to us
by the account of the local jealousy, which would not
acknowledge his superior attainments ; and his name

---

[1] *Matthew Paris*, ed. Luard, vol. i. p. 437.
[2] *Munimenta Academica*, Introduction, p. xxviii.

lives with us still, in the dark Crypt under St. Peter's Church, known as ' Grymbald's Crypt,' built for his last resting place. It can be seen any day. There are two rows of short pillars in it; the vaulting is composed of semicircular arches of hewn stone ; and, at the east end, are indications of an Altar having once been there. These are fascinating pictures ; but the mist of myth and legend that encircles them, bids us look at them for not too long, lest our love for the Saxon King, and his saintly associates, should tempt us to trust to what are, apparently, only forged fables.

The most that can be said on this subject has been ably stated by an eminent authority.—' Thus whatever we know at all, by tradition, by documents (suspected or unsuspected,) or by the evidence of general probability,—converges to the same result,— that the Oxford Schools are as ancient as King Alfred. And the same authority argues, with a directness of thought which is unanswerable, that when we find ' undoubted proofs, that a School existed at Oxford in the middle of the eleventh century (*v.* Ingulf.) and since then, without interruption ;—when we cannot find any epoch to which we could reasonably ascribe the foundation of these institutions, except that at which Alfred lived ;—all sound historical judgment would lead us to ascribe the foundation to Alfred.' [1]

---

[1] Huber's *English Universities*, trs. by Newman.

After Alfred's time there is a singular dearth of names of note in connection with the Oxford Schools. We hear of no eminent Teacher after Grymbald left; and the study of Theology died with St. Neot. In 1133, Robert Pulein came to Oxford, and began to lecture on the Bible, and to preach on Sundays. St. Bernard of Clairvaux, in one of his letters (CCV), alludes to a request he had made about him, ' ob sanam doctrinam quæ apud illum esse dignoscitur'; and further describes him, as 'fultum gratia amicorum, quorum in curia non minima auctoritas est.' Henry I., attracted by the accounts of this great Scholar, and of the good doctrine he taught, and his devout life, offered him a Bishopric; but this he refused, 'having food and raiment,' and only accepted the Archdeaconry of Rochester. The fame of his piety and learning reached Rome, and he was sent for by Innocent II. Pulein was made Cardinal in the Pontificate of Celestine II.; and, afterwards, he was Chancellor to Pope Lucius VII.

The next great Teacher at Oxford was Vacarius, who came here a few years after Pulein had been called to Rome. The presence of Vacarius marks an epoch in the progress of studies at Oxford, for he introduced the study of Roman Jurisprudence, at that time unknown in England; but which he had followed at the University of Bologna. He came to England at the invitation of Theobald, Archbishop of Canterbury ; and he became very popular at Oxford, where Students crowded to his lectures, eager for the new kind of knowledge. Nothing is known of the Teachers immediately following Pulein and Vacarius ; nor is it known in what part of Oxford lectures were then delivered. The Students were under the jurisdiction of the Bishop of Lincoln ; and, therefore, it has been concluded that they were independent of the neighbouring Priory of St. Frideswide, and the Abbey of Oseney ; and that the public lectures were delivered in the City.[1] But hardly anything is known about the teaching in Oxford, after the time of Vacarius, until 1186, when Giraldus Cambrensis, one of the Chaplains to Henry II., visited the City, and read his *Topography of Ireland* to the inhabitants. His own account of this visit, and of his public readings, is better than any description we can give. When the *Topographia* was finished,— lucernam accensam non sub modio ponere, sed super candelabrum ut luceret erigere cupiens, apud Oxoniam, ubi clerus in Anglia magis vigebat et clericatu præcellebat, opus suum in tanta audientia recitare disposuit. Et quoniam tres erant in libro suo distinctiones, qualibet recitata die tribus diebus continuis recitatio duravit ; primoque die pauperes omnes oppidi totius ad hoc convocatos hospitio suscepit et

[1] *Hist. Univ. Oxford,* Maxwell Lyte, p. 12.

exhibuit. In crastino vero doctores diversarum
facultatum omnes et discipulos famæ majoris et
notitiæ. Tertio die reliquos scolares cum militibus
oppidanis et burgensibus multis. Sumptuosa quidem
res et nobilis, quia renovata sunt quodammodo
authentica et antiqua in hoc facto poetarum tempora ; nec rem similem in Anglia factam vel præ-
sens ætas vel ulla recolit antiquitas.'[1]

[*Translation.*—Not desiring to put the candle he
had lighted under a bushel, but wishing to set it on a
candlestick, that it might shine ; he determined to
read his work before a large audience at Oxford,
where the Clergy were more numerous than elsewhere
in England, and excelled in all clerkly qualities. The
book was divided into three parts ; and, as he read
one part each day, the reading lasted three successive days. On the first day, he hospitably entertained all the poor of the whole Town, whom he
invited for the purpose. On the next day, he received, in like manner, all the Doctors of the various
Faculties, and their more distinguished Scholars. On
the third day, the other Students, with the Knights
of the Town, and many of the Burgesses. It was a
costly and splendid affair, truly ; for the occasion was
a genuine revival of the good old times of the Poets.
There never was anything like it seen in England,
either in present days, or in past antiquity.]

[1] *Giraldus Cambrensis*, ed. Brewer, vol. i. p. 72

In 1209, all lectures at the University were interrupted and all studies arrested, in consequence of a serious quarrel between the Clerks and the Townsmen. A Student in Arts murdered a young girl, and the Townsmen, in their haste for vengeance, not being able to secure the guilty man, put to death two Students who were entirely innocent of the crime. The University, as has been stated, was under Ecclesiastical jurisdiction; and the Clerks and Masters at once joined together to resist this unjust interference on the part of the civil authorities, which was an infringement of their right to be tried and punished by lawful superiors, and in Ecclesiastical courts. Pope Innocent III. had laid England under an interdict; and little sympathy for Church authority, or support for the Clerks, could be expected from King John. The Scholars, terrified at the bold assumption of power on the part of the Townsmen, and fearing also the anger of the King, fled from Oxford in great numbers. One account says that not a single Student remained in the City. In the *Chronicon de Lanercost*, we find the following account of the migration from Oxford :—

' Unde multipliciter, et quoad seculares et quoad religiosos, illo tempore persequebatur rex prædictus ecclesiam Anglicanam, unde clerici, timentes regis tyrannidem, Oxoniam fere omnes reliquerunt, aut si autem remanentes non multo tempore post, propter

unius suspendium, ex toto villam interdicendo reces-
serunt, partim apud Redyngs, partim Parisius diver-
tentes.　Hoc credo accidisse propter oppressionem
et necem secutam unius puellæ, quæ fuit turpiter
reperta apud Maydenhal.'

[*Translation.*—So, at that time, the aforesaid
King was persecuting in various ways the Clergy of
the English Church, both secular and regular ; and
so the Clerks, fearing the King's tyranny, nearly all
deserted Oxford.　And the few that remained, not
long after, on account of the hanging of one of them,
departed, laying the City under a total interdict :
some went to Reading, the rest to Paris.　I believe
this happened on account of an outrage on a girl,
and her subsequent death.　She was found in a
shameful condition at Maydenhal.[1]]

When the Scholars left Oxford, the Church laid
a still more severe interdict on the City, which
was not removed until 1213 ; when the repentant
Burghers appealed to the Papal Legate, promising
to accept his judgment, and to do penance for their
rash deeds.　Then the Scholars were allowed to return to Oxford.

The letter of the Pope's Legate is worth inserting in full ; for it shows, not only the severity of
Ecclesiastical punishment, but is also an illustration
of the wise economy that, while reproving the arro-

' Maiden Hall.

gance of the Townsmen, introduced new laws, which would secure some privileges to the University, and tend to promote peace between the rival parties. It is to the decrees of this Legate, Nicholas, Bishop of Tusculum, that we trace the origin of some of the now existing University laws, which make all resident members of the University, to a certain extent, free from civil jurisdiction.—

' Littera N. Legati de pœna Burgensium propter suspendium clericorum ab eis commissum.

' N., Dei gratia Tusculanus Episcopus Apostolicæ sedis legatus, dilectis in Christo filiis Burgensibus Oxoniæ salutem in Domino.

' Cum propter suspendium clericorum a vobis commissum mandatis Ecclesiæ per omnia stare jurassetis, Nos, volentes agere misericorditer vobiscum, statuimus quod a festo S. Michaelis, anno ab incarnatione Domini millesimo ducentesimo decimo quarto usque in decem annos sequentes, Scholaribus Oxoniæ studentibus condonetur medietas mercedis Hospitiorum omnium locandorum clericis in eadem villa, mercedis inquam taxatæ communi consilio clericorum et nostro ante recessum Scholarium propter suspendium prædictum clericorum : Finitis vero prædictis decem annis, aliis decem annis proximo sequentibus locabuntur Hospitia sub mercede cleri, ut prædictum est, taxata.

' Hæc de Hospitiis constructis et taxatis ante

præfatum clericorum recessum : constructa vero post-
modum vel construenda aliaque prius constructa sed
non taxata arbitratu quatuor Magistrorum et quatuor Burgensium taxabuntur, et prædicto modo per
utrumque decennium locabuntur. Communia quoque
ejusdem villæ annuatim dabit quinquaginta duos
solidos dispensandos in usus pauperum Scholarium
per manus Abbatis de Osneya et Prioris ecclesiæ S.
Frideswydæ de consilio venerabilis fratris Hugonis,
tunc Episcopi Lincolniensis et successorum suorum
vel Archidiaconi loci sive ejus officialis aut Can-
cellarii, quem Episcopus Lincolniensis Scholaribus
ibidem præficiet, ita scilicet quod viginti sex solidi
solventur annuatim in festo Omnium Sanctorum et
viginti sex solidi in Capite Jejunii.   Præter hoc etiam
eadem Communia pascet centum pauperes Scholares
in pane, cerevisia, potagio, et uno ferculo piscium vel
carnium singulis annis in perpetuum die S. Nicholai
quos Episcopus Lincolniæ vel Archidiaconus loci seu
ejus officialis aut ipse Cancellarius vel alius ab hoc
Episcopo Lincolniæ deputatus providerit.   Jurabitis
etiam quod victualia et alia [Scholaribus] necessaria
justo et rationabili pretio vendetis, et ab aliis vendi
fideliter procurabitis, et quod in fraudem hujus
provisionis graves non facietis constitutiones vel
onerosas, per quas conditio clericorum deterioretur.
Si vero contingat amodo clericum capi a vobis, statim,
cum fueritis super eo requisiti ab Episcopo Lincolniæ

seu Archidiacono loci vel ejus officiali vel a Cancellario seu ab eo qu<s>m Episcopus Lincolniæ huic officio deputaverit, captum ei reddetis, nec aliquo modo machinabimini in his vel in aliis quod præfati Lincolniæ Episcopi jurisdictio elidatur, vel jus suum vel ecclesiæ suæ in aliquo minuatur. Jurabunt etiam quinquaginta de majoribus ex vobis pro se et Communia et hæredibus suis, quod hæc omnia supradicta fideliter observabunt, et hoc juramentum quolibet anno renovabitis ad mandatum Episcopi Lincolniæ per quot idem Episcopus voluerit citra numerum prætaxatum. Cartam quoque sigillo communi signatam sub prædictis articulis facietis ascribi, et venerabili fratri Hugoni nunc Episcopo Lincolniæ liberabitis, cui voluerit in custodiam committendam ; hoc autem vos et hæredes vestri facietis, ut honor et reverentia clericis eo exhibeatur abundantius quo magis per vos fuerant dehonestati. Magistri vero, qui post Scholarium [recessum] irreverenter legerunt Oxoniæ, suspendentur per triennium ab officio legendi ibidem. Omnes autem, qui de suspendio clericorum fuissetis confessi vel convicti, venietis, ad mandatum venerabilis fratris Hugonis nunc Episcopi Lincolniæ, cum interdictum fuerit laxatum, ad sepulcra clericorum discalceati et discincti, sine capis et palliis, sequente vos Communia, et ipsorum corpora differetis in cœmeterio sepelienda ubi clerus providerit, præstito sibi, ut prædictum est, a vobis juramento ; et, carta

communi confecta et venerabili fratri Hugoni nunc
Episcopo Lincolniæ liberata, licentiam habeant
Scholares et Magistri Oxoniam redeundi et ibidem
legendi, exceptis his qui per triennium sunt suspensi,
de quibus est præmissum.

' Si vero contra statuta nostra et proprium vene-
ritis juramentum, ex ipso facto sciatis vos excom-
municationis vinculo innodatos, et venerabilis frater
Hugo nunc Episcopus Lincolniæ et successores sui
vos et villam vestram reducant in pristinam suspen-
sionis sententiam.   Vobis igitur auctoritate legationis
qua fungimur mandamus in remissionem peccatorum,
firmiter injungentes quatenus hanc constitutionem
nostram recipiatis ad mandatum venerabilis fratris
Hugonis Lincolniæ Episcopi fideliter adimplendam.

' Datum apud Rameseiam septimo kalend. Julii.' [1]

[*Translation.*—Letter of Nicholas, Legate, concerning the punishment of the Burgesses, on account
of the Clerics whom they hanged.

Nicholas, by the Grace of God, Bishop of Tusculum, Legate of the Apostolic See, to his beloved
sons in Christ, the Burgesses of Oxford, Health in
the Lord.

Since, on account of the Clerics whom you
hanged, you have sworn to stand, in all things, by the
commands of the Church ; We, being willing to deal
mercifully with you, decree that, for ten years from

---

[1] *Munimenta Academica*, vol. i. p. 1.

the Feast of St. Michael, in the year of the Incarnation of our Lord 1214, the moiety of the rent of all Hostels let to Clerics in the same Town shall be remitted to the Scholars studying at Oxford; the rent, that is, rated by the common counsel of the Clerics, and our own, before the withdrawal of the Scholars, on account of the hanging of the Clerics. When these ten years are ended, for another ten years, next ensuing, the Hostels shall be let as rated under the clerical rent, as aforesaid.

So far respecting the Hostels erected and rated before the withdrawal of the Clerics: as to those erected afterwards, or to be erected, and others erected but not rated, they shall be rated at the arbitration of four Masters and four Burgesses; and shall be let, in the same manner, throughout the two terms of ten years. The Community of the same Town shall also give 52s. a year, to be spent for the use of poor Scholars, by the hand of the Abbot of Oseney, and the Prior of the Church of St. Frideswide, with the counsel of our Venerable Brother, Hugh, now Bishop of Lincoln, and his successors, or of the Archdeacon of the place, or his official, or the Chancellor whom the Bishop of Lincoln shall set over the Scholars here; so that, to wit, 26s. be paid yearly on the Feast of All Saints, and 26s. at the beginning of Lent. Besides this, also, the Community shall provide bread, beer, pottage, and one dish of fish or flesh, every year in perpetuity, on St. Nicholas' Day, for an hundred poor Scholars, whom the Bishop of Lincoln, or the Archdeacon of the place, or his official, or the Chancellor himself, or another deputed by the Bishop of Lincoln, shall appoint. You shall also swear that you will sell, and will procure to be sold faithfully by others, victuals, and other necessaries, [for the Scholars], at a just and reasonable price, and that you will not, in fraud of this provision, make grave or burdensome regulations, by which the condition of the Clerics may be made worse than before.   But if it happen from henceforth, that a Cleric be arrested by you, forthwith, when you are required concerning him by the Bishop of Lincoln, or the Archdeacon of the place, or his official, or by the Chancellor, or by him whom the Bishop of Lincoln shall have deputed to this office, you shall hand over the prisoner to him, nor in anywise shall you desire, in these or other matters, that the jurisdiction of the Bishop of Lincoln be eluded, or his or his Church's right be impaired in anything.   Also, fifty of the elders of you shall swear, for themselves, and the Community, and their heirs, that all these things shall be observed ; and you shall renew this oath, every year, at the mandate of the Bishop of Lincoln, by as many as the same Bishop shall will over the above-rated number. You shall also have recorded, and sealed with the common seal, a Charter under the aforesaid articles, and deliver it to our Venerable Brother, Hugh, now Bishop of Lincoln, to be committed into the keeping of whom he may will : and this you and your heirs shall do, that the honour and reverence due to Clerics may be the more abundantly shown, the more it has been disgraced by you. And those Masters, who irreverently lectured at Oxford, after the [withdrawal] of the Scholars, shall be suspended for three years from the office of lecturing there. And all who have confessed to, or been convicted of, hanging the Clerics, shall, at the mandate of our Venerable Brother, Hugh, now Bishop of Lincoln, when the interdict shall have been relaxed, come to the graves of the Clerics, shoeless, and ungirded, without caps and cloaks, all you of the Community following, and carry their bodies to the Churchyard, to be buried where the Clergyman shall provide, the oath being taken by you to him, as is above said : and when the common Charter has been made, and delivered to our Venerable Brother, Hugh, now Bishop of Lincoln, let the Scholars and Masters have licence to return to Oxford, and read there, except those who are suspended for three years, as aforesaid.

But if you go against our Statutes, and your own oath, know that you are bound, *ipso facto*, with the chain of excommunication; and let our Venerable Brother, Hugh, now Bishop of Lincoln, and his successors, bring back you and your Town under the former sentence of suspension. We, therefore, command you, by the Legatine authority which we discharge, in remission of your sins, firmly enjoining that you receive, at the mandate of our Venerable Brother, Hugh, Bishop of Lincoln, this our constitution, to be faithfully fulfilled.

Given at Ramsey, the 7th day before the Kalends of July.]

Migration from Oxford appears to have been a not unusual course of action for aggrieved or offended Scholars, and even Teachers, to pursue; not, necessarily, always from fear, but sometimes only ' of malice.' We read that, in the year 1287, ' the Universite of Oxforth chose a Chauncelere, Maister William Kyngeston. Thei sent on the bischop of Lincoln for his confirmacion : the bischop seide it was his deute to com himselve. Thei answerd that this was her elde privylege ; and this wold thei kepe. The bischop was inflexibil, and thei were obdurat. And so of malice thei left her redyng, and here teching. Many scoleres went away ; thei that abode were evel occupied. But at the last the bischop condescended to her elde custome.'[1]

To give any description of the neighbouring

---

[1] Capgrave's *Chronicle of England*, ed. Hingeston, p. 168.

Monasteries, is quite beyond the scope of this small history. Among the Abbeys then existing in England, the Benedictine House at Abingdon was, perhaps, one of the best known. The fact of its nearness to Oxford, at a time when numbers of Clerks and Scholars were continually flocking hither, must have added to its reputation ; as, undoubtedly, the position of the Town, between Oxford and the Capital, favoured the trade and commercial interests of the inhabitants. Reinald Rich was one of Abingdon's most successful merchants ; but the fame of the merchant has died away, and he is known in history only as the father of the afterwards celebrated Edmund Rich, who is the first person recorded to have taken a degree at Oxford.

Although Edmund's life must have been a contrast to the ordinary lives around him, yet it affords some illustration of the time he lived in, and the state of Oxford when he studied and taught here. Brought up under the shadow of the great Benedictine Monastery at Abingdon, all his childhood was passed in the midst of religious and intellectual surroundings, which greatly influenced his young days, and his after life. As a child, he grew to love and reverence both saintliness and learning : all his early associations fostered his desire for holiness, and strengthened his ambition for knowledge. His mother, Mabel, was distinguished for her extreme piety, and she used all her mother's influence and gentle art to train the character of her favourite son. A touching vision rises before us when we read, that ' Edmund was, under his mother's training, all that even such a mother could desire, or hope. He was diligent in his juvenile studies, and showed little inclination for those manly sports, which would have qualified him to do battle in the world. His abstinence, however, from such pursuits gladdened his mother's heart. When he saw Mabel, having discharged her household duties, kneeling on the cold hard pavement of the Abbey Church ; mingling tears with enthusiastic devotions ; the sympathising child would creep to her side, and impart the only kind of comfort, which to her heart was acceptable, by uniting his prayers with hers.'[1] At the age of twelve Edmund was sent to Oxford, to study Grammar. Afterwards he went to Paris, to continue his education at the University ; and when he returned to Oxford, we hear of him as a Teacher, and one of those who, at that time, were noted for their eager desire to restore the fame of Oxford, and to stimulate the religious and intellectual life here. The well-known story of his early piety is, perhaps, best related in the words of the Chronicler, who tells us that, A.D. M.CC.XXVIII. Master Stephen Langton ' a præsenti luce ad gloriam translatus est octavo

---

[1] *Lives of Archbishops of Canterbury*, Hook.

idus Julii.'—' Cui successit sanctus Edmundus, de
Abyndon oriundus, ac magister in Logica et Theolo-
gica, vir eximiæ munditiæ, abstinentiæ et vigiliæ,
sicut aliqua exempla de singulis inferius ponenda
comprobabunt.

' Nam in exemplum munditiæ illibatæ istud
primo occurrit, quod puerulus intendens Oxoniæ
grammaticalibus, gloriosæ Virginis imaginem, quam
sæpe, et una cum tota Universitate, vidimus, clam
desponsavit, imposito digito Virginis aureo annulo,
quod multi postea oculis conspexerunt.' [1]

[*Translation.*—A.D. 1228, Master Stephen Langton was taken from this world to the light of
glory, on the 8th of July.—To whom succeeded St.
Edmund, of Abingdon ; a Master in Logic, and
Theology ; a man of special purity, abstinence, and
wakefulness, as certain instances to be quoted hereafter will prove.

As an example of his innocent candour, we may
mention that, when he was a small boy, studying
Grammar at Oxford, he betrothed to himself secretly
an image of the Glorious Virgin; which we, and the
whole University, have frequently seen. On the
Virgin's finger he placed a golden ring, as many
persons afterwards saw with their own eyes.]

And the same simple and devoted faith, which
characterized his early years, marked several of his

[1] *Chronicon de Lanercost*, ed. Stevenson, p. 36.

practices as a Teacher, and made his life at Oxford both remarkable and noteworthy. One of his first objects was to assist the Friars in their efforts to make Oxford celebrated, as a place of study and learning, for Theology and Philosophy; and he soon became a popular and attractive Teacher. His modern Biographer, who shows little appreciation for Catholic devotion and sanctity, is constrained to tell us, and we can readily believe, that 'the expression of his countenance was always cheerful, and there was a peculiar grace in his manner.'[1] With no great effort of the imagination, we see him, in his long gown of grey cloth, passing abstractedly by the buildings in School Street, as he hastened in the early morning to Mass at St. Mary's, or at St. Peter's; and to our ears, almost, the voice is audible, which thrilled his hearers in the lecture room, or broke into pleading admonitions to his much-cared-for pupils. He was, what we moderns would call, 'generous to a fault,' for his fear of hurting the susceptibilities of his poorer Scholars led him to desire all to make only what payments they liked, or to consider his lectures free. And it was not 'scholarly pride,' but simple humility, that prompted him to say with a smile, as he placed the uncounted money on the window-sill, 'Earth to earth, ashes to ashes, dust to dust.'

[1] *Lives of Archbishops of Canterbury*, Hook.

Simple, loving, and beyond dispute is the testimony of Chroniclers and Historians to the saintliness and genius of this great Teacher.

'ye said S. Edmund was borne at Abendon in
Berkshire, at wch place was (and is still as I think)
a lane called S. Edmunds lane wherein probably he
receiued his first breath.' Antony à Wood wrote.
And, besides the facts we have mentioned about his
life and work here at Oxford, much more might be
gathered from historical documents, manuscript and
printed, to tell us of his work in the world, beyond
the limited circle of his Oxford friends and pupils ;
of his intrepid plain-speaking ; and of his heroic self-
sacrifice. The Chronicles we turn to, in our desire
to learn more about this wonderful man, point always
to his deep humility, his profound knowledge, and
his untiring zeal. There is a fascination for us in
the picture of that quiet Teacher, whose voice drew
hundreds to his lecture room in School Street, where
his ' School' lent glory to our University. The man
who had no thought for life ; who never heard the
heedless remarks, nor the impertinent questions ;
and who ignored, alike, the rewards and the rebuffs,
the praises and the censures of this world ; drew
around him those who were to build up the intellectual greatness of Oxford ; and by his wisdom, and
his learning, and his gentle influence, he guided and
taught them. It was a work incalculably great.

Never again has Oxford known such a Teacher.
Through the silence of centuries, and the darkness
of years forgotten, still are we attracted to the story
of that earnest life, which, even in our days, has its
visible results. We love the details of his saint-life;
his early devoutness; his daily Mass; the beautiful
Form, which stood by him as he taught; how he,
who was 'courted by the greatest schollers of that
age both for his piety and learning, did often according to his manner convers in privat with God,
especially in his walkes of recreation in the feilds
neare Oxon.' And we reverence his vast learning;
and the noble use he made of it.

In Wharton's *Anglia Sacra* is the concise
summary :—' Edmundus de Abendoniâ, consecratus
est in Archiepiscopum anno Domini MCCXXXIV.
Iste sanctissimus fuit. Ortâ autem inter ipsum &
Regem Henricum gravi dissensione super jure &
libertatibus Ecclesiæ Cantuariensis, Monachisque
suis alias commoventibus, post intolerabiles injurias,
habito super hoc Suffraganeorum consilio, excom-
municavit occupatores injustè & perturbatores juris
& libertatum Ecclesiæ Cantuariensis generaliter; &
quosdam, de quibus legitimè constabat, specialiter.
Nolens autem cum Rege contendere, sed magis
maliciis cedere, mare transivit. Obiit autem ibidem,
cùm sedisset sex annis; requiescitque apud Pontiniacum, anno Domini MCCXL.'

[*Translation.*—Edmund of Abingdon was consecrated Archbishop, in 1234. He was a very holy
man. A serious difference arose between him and
King Henry, concerning the rights and liberties of
the Church of Canterbury. After suffering intolerable injuries, under pressure of his Monks, and
previously taking the counsel of his Suffragans in
the matter, he excommunicated by a general sentence
the unjust intruders and the infringers of the rights
and liberties of the Church of Canterbury. But a
few of them, with regard to whom he had juridical
proof, he excommunicated by name. However, he
did not wish to have contentions with the King;
but, preferring to give place to evil, he crossed the
seas. There he died, after a sojourn of six years,
in 1240; and he lies buried at Pontigny.]

Capgrave, in his *Chronicle of England*, gives a
simple and straightforward account of the dispute as
to the succession to the See of Canterbury. He
states, that ' In the XVI ȝere of Herry felle a new
contraversie at Cauntirbury: for summe chose the
prioure of the Trinite Cherch, and summe chose
Maystir Jon Blundy. Whan this eleccion cam to
the Pope, he cassed it; and than the prioure of the
Trinite resined his ryte; and the Pope refused
Maister Jon Blundy, because the bischop of Wyn-
chester wrot onto the emperoure for his promocioune.
This cause was alleggid ageyn him, that he had too

benefices, with cure of soule, withoute leve of the
Cort. Than were the munkis at her lyberte to have
a new eleccion; and thei chose Maistir Edmund
Abyngdon, a holy man, whech was thanne tresorer
of Salisbury.'

And by other Chroniclers this 'holy man' is
mentioned. Matthew Paris relates how he used his
influence as a peace-maker;[1] and also speaks of
him as a man 'honestæ conversationis et bene lite-
ratum.'[2] The account of his death is in keeping
with the many characteristics of his life: ' Beatus
Edmundus . . . Pontiniacum aliquandiu moraretur,
orans et plorans pro statu ecclesiæ Anglicanæ.'[3]
And, later on, we find our King Henry III.
'veniens apud Pontiniacum infirmatus, ad feretrum
beati Edmundi oravit, et sanitatem recepit.'[4]

Although it is beyond doubt that St. Edmund
had Schools in Oxford, it is impossible to say for
certain where they stood. Antony à Wood seems to
think that they might be 'that house, afterwards
called St. Edmund's Hall in Schoolstreet, and in the
Parish of St. Mary.' And he adds a list of the
' divers famous persons [who] were his auditors and
admirers in the said Schools, among which were
Robert Grosteste, who afterwards wrote several
Epistles to him, in one of which he mentions his

Matthew Paris, ed. Luard, vol. iii. p. 290.   ¹ Ibid. p. 244.
³ Ibid. ed. Madden, vol. iii. p. 282.   ⁴ Ibid. p. 341.

" serpentina prudentia," and "columbina simplicitas. &c." Then, Robert Bacon, Rich, Fishacre, the eminent Dominican : Roger Bacon, with others mentioned elsewhere.'[1]

These names bring with them other memories. Now a new vista opens before us. School Street, with its thirty-two Schools, and many Masters and Teachers of various merit and importance, in the better neighbourhood of St. Mary the Virgin and St. Peter in the East, gives place to the poorer locality of St. Frideswide and St. Ebbe, where the foundations were being laid for the new generation of Teachers and Schoolmen, who were to take their part in the making of Oxford, and lend their names to her wide-spread fame. The now dingy and almost unknown Paradise Square, was the garden of the Franciscans ; and owes its name to the traditions of holiness and peacefulness, that are ever associated with the followers of St. Francis.[2] Near where the City gas-works are now, close to the river, on ground now covered with narrow Streets and Courts, and thronged by the poorest of the City's people, stood the fine Dominican Friary, with its grand Church. No trace of the Franciscan House remains, and it is almost impossible to learn what was its exact position. But a local His-

---

[1] *Antony à Wood,* ed. Gutch, vol. ii. pt. ii. p. 738.
[2] This may be only report, from the fact that the site of Paradise Square was within, or adjoining, the Franciscan walls.

torian has saved for us some facts about St. Dominic's Church. He tells the sad story of sacrilege and destruction, in quaint but touching words.

'Their Dissolution came with the general and common Fate of all such under H. VIII.

'Then that House, which by the Learning and Piety of these Friars had attracted many, even Prelates, to lay down their Honours and Preferments and become one of them, with all the Inclosure of Ground, containing 3 Acres in Compass, towards the East; the Grove on the West, with all Appurtenances, likewise the Messuage aforesaid adjoining their Gate, and the neighbouring Seat of the Grey Friars, was by King H. VIII. 31st of his Reign, sold for 1094£. to R. Andrews, of Hayles in Co: of Glouc. Esq; and J. How, Gent. Soon after they sold them to W. Freer of Oxford, and Agnes his Wife, and their Heirs; who demolished the Church and most of the Monastery, selling the Stone, Lead, Glass, Bells, &c at a very cheap Rate, unless we allow for the Sacriledge of it.

'This Island, now converted chiefly into a Garden, is in the different Occupations of T. Tredwell and Ann Castell; and the House, called the Prior's House, as though detached from the rest of the Friary, consisting of good large Rooms, fit for the Quality of such prime Person, and of a monastic Form, is at present demised to —— Polston.

'Their Church was built by them, and dedicated to St. Nicholas on the Day of St. Vitus and Modestus, Anno 1262, by R. or Benedict Gravesend, Bishop of Lincoln.

'Here have been buried; Walter Malclerk, a famous Author.

'Piers Gaveston, Earl of Cornwall.

'Sir J. Golafre, of Fyfield, Berks, Knt. Aug. 1378, with great Pomp.

'Sir Peter Besills, Knt. of Besills-Lee, Berks, in 1426.—He is reckoned among the principal Patrons of the said Church; the South Wing whereof he also built, and is said to have bequeathed 120£. for making of six Windows in the same.

'Stephen Wall, Bishop of Meath, in Ireland, buryed 1376.

'Besides these have been found, at the dissolving this Monastery, many Tombs, Stone Coffins, with the Bodies of Men in them; Rings on their Fingers, Chalices on their Breasts, Coins about their Necks, and Parchment Deeds with their Seals to them ;— Hearts wrapped up in Lead; one of which, with an Inscription, being dug up in 1644, by a Gardener, and brought to King Charles I. then at Oxford, was in the Presence of the King taken out of the Wrapper ; and, which was much admired, appeared almost fresh and uncorrupted.

'Mr. Wood mentions, very imperfectly, twelve

Priors of these Dominicans; of whom, Simon de Bonil, in 1238, was Chancellor of the University.'[1]

These Houses have perished; but the work that the Friars did is the true memorial of their greatness. They taught piety to the Oxford people, and they made the Oxford Schools. Adam de Marisco was the first Franciscan who read lectures at Oxford, and his School was in great repute. ' Lyons, Paris, and Cologne were indebted for their first professors to the English Franciscans in Oxford. Repeated applications were made from Ireland, Denmark, France, and Germany for English Friars; foreigners were sent to the English School as superior to all others. It enjoyed a reputation throughout the world for adhering the most conscientiously and strictly to the poverty and severity of the Order; and for the first time since its existence as a University, Oxford rose to a position second not even to Paris itself. The three Schoolmen of the most profound and original genius, Roger Bacon, Duns Scotus, and Occham, were trained within its walls. No other nations of Christendom can show a succession of names at all comparable to the English Schoolmen in originality and subtilty, in the breadth and variety of their attainments. Italy produced its Aquinas, a great organizer, like the Roman himself; its Bonaventure, in whom St.

[1] *City of Oxford*, Peshall, p. 265.

Francis reappears in a shape more learned, if not more spiritual; Germany its laborious Albertus Magnus; Spain its Raymund Lully, the representative of Spanish adventure and Spanish genius. But no nation can show three Schoolmen like the English, each unrivalled in his way, and each working with equal ability in opposite directions. The influence of the English school was consequently more profound, more brilliant the reputation of its Teachers.'[1]

And when the Lady of Balliol set her hand to carry out her husband's wishes, she went for counsel and help to a Franciscan Friar; her object being to found an House at Oxford, which should be an home both for piety and learning.

[1] *Monumenta Franciscana*, ed. Brewer, Preface, p. lxxxi.

CHAPTER III.

The early Chroniclers liked best to tell us about those, who, while worldlings were wrangling and fighting, laboured to promote study, and to diffuse the love of learning.   In Mediaeval pages, the prominent names are not those of Kings, and their Captains and Courtiers ; but the names of men like St. Hugh of Lincoln, and Bishop Grosseteste; whose work, steady though noiseless, whether pursued in the Bishop's Palace or the Friar's Cell, must ever be counted in the Wealth of Nations.   Yet Chroniclers do not neglect other matters ; and always, as the noble deeds of good men are related with a proud fidelity, so the misdeeds, even of people of importance, are told with unflinching courage.   The Monk of St. Alban's, who has, it may be said, saved English History, gives us details of King Henry III. demanding a subsidy, in 1244 ; and certain persons were appointed to consider the demand.   They were all men of great reputation, and high position ; whose wisdom, judgment, and integrity, could be relied upon.   And

among them we find the name of John de Balliol.
And Balliol's name is again mentioned when a Charter
of the King of Scotland was sent to the Pope for
confirmation.[1]

John, Lord of Balliol, in his magnificent Castle,
high above Tees, and commanding a far view
over surrounding woods and vales, was a Baron of
great importance. His riches were considerable ;
and included, besides his own property, the large
possessions which his wife inherited from her father,
Alan, Prince of Galloway. An attempt had been
made to deprive the three daughters of Alan of their
inheritance ; but it was unsuccessful. Alan's daughters were,—Helen, who married Roger de Quinci,
Earl of Winchester ; Dervorguilla, who married John
de Balliol ; and Christian, who married William de
Fortibus, afterwards Earl of Albemarle. Christian
died childless ; and her share in her father's property
was given to Dervorguilla. And thus John de
Balliol's wealth was greatly augmented.

In the finely written pages of the *Chronica
Majora*, with their quaint and beautiful illuminations
—for Matthew Paris was Chronicler and Artist—we
learn how Balliol was able to purchase peace with an
angry King.—[1255.] ' Tempore quoque sub eodem,
Johannes de Bailloil, miles, dives et potens, cujus

[1] *Matthew Paris*, ed. Luard, vol. iv. pp. 362, 384.

pater in armis strenuus regi Johanni in arcto posito
multum servierat et in dubiis casibus sæpe contulerat
adminiculum, cum graviter, sicut et Robertus, accu-
saretur, sibi pecunia, qua abundavit, regis necessitati
satisfaciendo, caute pacem comparavit.'

[*Translation.*—About this time also, John de
Balliol, Baron, rich and powerful, whose father, an
ardent Warrior, had done King John good service
when he was in difficulties, and had often helped him
in doubtful chances, was accused with Robert on a
grave charge.   However, by spending some of the
money in which he abounded, and thus occurring
to the King's necessity, he cannily obtained a
peace.]

But the sins of this rich and powerful Baron, the
report of whose wealth made King Henry pause in
his wrath and act with a cunning kindness, are
chronicled in very plain words.—

 ' Eodem anno, facta est concordia inter epi-
scopum Dunelmensem Walterum et Johannem de
Bailloil militem super pluribus controversiis inter
ipsos motis.   Similiter est pax reformata inter pri-
orem de Thynemue et dictum Johannem.   Ipse enim
J[ohannes], supra quod deceret et animæ suæ expe-
diret, avarus, rapax, et tenax, tam ecclesiam de
Thynemue quam ecclesiam Dunelmensem diu ac
multum injuste vexaverat et enormiter dampnifica-
verat.   Nec non et alias ecclesias ac viros ecclesias-

ticos ac milites, causis excogitatis et inventis, sibi
vicinos læserat fatigatos, juxta illud,

> "Omnisque superbus
> Impatiens consortis erit."

Similiter autem et avarus, cui sua non sufficiunt,
alienis inhiabit. Cognoscens autem dominus rex,
quod idem Johannes multis denariis abundaret,
quæstionem gravem contra ipsum, ut prædictum est,
[intendit]; sperans pro pace redimenda thesauri sui
cumulum mutilare.'[1]

[*Translation.*—In the same year, an agreement
was come to by the Bishop of Durham and John de
Balliol, Baron, on many points of difference which
had arisen between them. Likewise peace was
restored between the Prior of Tynemouth and the
said John. For this John who, more than was
becoming or safe for his soul, was covetous, rapa-
cious, and grasping, had for a long time, unjustly and
severely, molested both the Church of Tynemouth
and the Church of Durham, and had done them in-
calculable damage. Moreover, on pretexts devised
and framed by himself, he had worried and harried
other Churches, and Ecclesiastics, and Barons, of his
neighbourhood, according to the saying,

> 'No proud man will ever brook a fellow.'

In the same way a miser, who is not content with his
own goods, will open his maw for other men's. Now

---

[1] *Matthew Paris*, ed. Luard, vol. v. p. 528.

the Lord King, knowing that this same John possessed a large quantity of specie, started, as I said before, a serious matter of debate with him, in hopes that, in negotiating peace, he would be able to mutilate somewhat his treasured pile.]

It was difficult to spoil Matthew Paris. Pages might be filled with accounts of the special favour shown to him by King Henry III. Once, at a solemn public feast, the King, recognizing Matthew Paris, sent for him, and made him 'sit on the middle step between the throne and the floor.' And, when visiting at St. Alban's, the King would 'have him at his table and in his chamber.'[1] Yet the kingly favour, probably appreciated, did not hinder Matthew Paris from 'remonstrating boldly with the King,' perhaps on more occasions than one. Nor did it prevent his breaking into quiet laughter over his patron's weaknesses. 'O regem mirabilem,' he wrote, 'cui impensa officia quasi nebulæ pertranseunt matutinales, offensæ autem per tot tempora thesaurizantur!'[2]

[*Translation.*—O wonderful King! Services done him vanish from his mind like a morning mist, while slights are treasured up so many years.]

And history has other tales to tell us sometimes

---

[1] *Matthew Paris*, ed. Madden. Preface.
[2] *Ibid.* ed. Luard, vol. v. p. 569.

about Oxford, besides the often-repeated story of work, and industry, and success.

About the first notice we find of a Scotch Scholar at Oxford is,—' The K. at the request of Ralf arch-deacon of Chester, the Chancellor of Oxford, and others, masters of the University, commands the Sheriff of Oxford to deliver up to them Alan of York, August' of Devon, Nigel the Scot, and two other clerks, who were found with bows and arrows in the K.'s forest of Shotover, and for that offence seized and detained in the K.'s prison at Oxford.' [1] And among the Clerks, who were accused of joining in the riot against the Pope's Legate, at the Abbey of Oseney, in 1238, we find several Scotsmen,— ' John Curry, Roger the Scotsman, Peter the Scots-man ; and Reginald of Cuningham is freed by showing an alibi; while Engelram de Balliol and others are mainperned by Henry de Balliol.' [2]

There must have been ' sets ' in Oxford, even in those days. The conflicts between the Northerners and Southerners were only signs of national antago-nism ; an antagonism, which, in spite of University authority, would insist on breaking out occasionally. In the history of our Oxford City, there is one May Day so blackened by outrage and murder, that all the sweet thorn-blossom of centuries has

---

[1] *Close Roll*, 15 Hen. III. m. 9.
[2] *Calendar of Scotch Documents*. Preface.

not bleached its memory yet. On May 1, 1248, Gilbert of Dunfermline, a Scotch Student, of some position in his northern home, was passing near Carfax, in the afternoon, when a number of Towns-men suddenly attacked him; and, as he fled in haste down the High Street, they pursued him, throwing stones at him, and pelting him with offal from the butchers' stalls. He managed to get to All Saints' Church, and there, staggering to the door for shelter, he fell down, overcome by the blows of his pursuers; and some days afterwards, he died from the effects of the ill-treatment he had received. And, doubtless, there were many incidents of the same kind that passed unrecorded. Indeed, it may have been a thought to improve the social standing of the Scotch Clerks, as well as to facilitate their chances of coming to the University, that prompted the good Bishop of Durham to make John de Balliol give, as part of his penance, a 'sum of fixed maintenance' to Scholars studying at Oxford. John de Balliol, in fulfilling the injunction, was sure to think about the poor Scotch boys, who had to come so far to seek their education. Perhaps in his heart there lurked some sympathy for the trespassers in Shotover forest; and the reckless youths, who were mixed up in the fray at Oseney, when the cook was shot. If poor Scholars were to be maintained at Oxford, might not an 'House' be established? And might

not some from his ' ain countree ' find home, and
lectures, and a scholarly position, within its walls ?
John de Balliol himself had sporting proclivities,
which were more easily passed over than were the
misdeeds of the unimportant Students. From the
Close Rolls, Henry III. we learn that ' The King
lately gave John de Balliol three bucks in Shirewood
forest, which he says he has not got; and he took
by chance (a casu) a stag, a hind, and a buck therein
without the King's leave. The King pardons said
offence.'

But more serious sins had come to light, two
years before, and the Church had not dealt quite so
leniently with her ' truant son.'

In the year 1260, ' Dominus Walterus de Chirkham, Dunelmensis episcopus, ex hac luce plenus
dierum profectus est, vir mitis et mundus, corpore
exiguus sed mente liberalissimus ac pius, qui non
dilexit saltus lustrari sed psalmos. Tantæ autem
erat in exercendo officium auctoritatis ut potentissi-
mis honori esset et timori, ac rebelles ecclesiæ rigide
refrænaret. Contigit enim baronem suæ diœcesis,
totius Angliæ nominatissimum, cervicisse contra
honestatem sui gradus, et ecclesiæ reverentiam aliud
perperam commisisse. Accepta vero temeritatis
illius audacia, pius pastor admonet de emenda ;
verum quoniam superbia citius eligit confundi quam
corrigi, addit ille temeritati contemptum. Sed

episcopus, erectis animis, ita sagaciter fugitivum filium reduxit ad sinum, ut solemniter ad ostium Dunelmensis ecclesiæ, inspectante omni populo, de manu antistitis vapularetur, ac summam certæ sustentationis scholaribus Oxoniæ studentibus assignaret perpetuo continuandam.' [1]

[*Translation.*—The Lord Walter de Chirkham, Bishop of Durham, departed this life full of days, a gentle and pure man, in person little, but in mind very large and devout, who loved to traverse, not the woods, but the psalms. He was of such authority in the exercise of his office that he was honoured and feared by the mightiest, and sternly checked those that rebelled against the Church. Now it happened that a Baron of his diocese, the most famous in the whole of England, had gotten himself drunk with beer, quite contrary to the fair esteem beseeming his rank, and had done other evil disrespectful to the Church. When he heard of the audacity of that effrontery the good shepherd admonished him that he should make amends ; but inasmuch as pride chooses rather to be confounded than to be corrected, he added scorn to effrontery. But the Bishop, strengthening his heart, so shrewdly brought back his truant son to his bosom, that with much ceremony at the entrance of Durham Cathedral, before the eyes of all the people, he suffered scourg-

---

[1] *Chronicon de Lanercost* ed. Stevenson, p. 69.

ing at the hands of the Bishop, and assigned a sum of fixed maintenance to be continued for ever to Scholars studying at Oxford.]

This was the penance of John de Balliol, and was the origin of Balliol College.

In the nine remaining years of his life, Balliol seems to have fulfilled his obligation of 'maintaining Scholars' at Oxford; for we find the King (June 22, 1266) commanding 'his Mayor and bailiffs of Oxford from the farm of their Town at next Michaelmas, to pay to John de Balliol £20, that the King has granted him in loan for the use of the Scholars whom he maintains in said Town.'[1]   Henry III. had received, in his time, money that was no 'loan' from John de Balliol's coffers; and now the King might graciously lend him £20 for the support of his Scholars.

As far as we can ascertain, an House was established, known as the 'House of Balliol,' where poor Scholars were received; and a sum of eight pence a week was allowed to each of them, towards the expenses of a common table.   But the House appears to have had no rules for self-government, and it was not in Balliol's lifetime definitely endowed.   John de Balliol died in 1269, at Barnard Castle, and Dervorguilla continued the maintenance of the Oxford Scholars, until she was able to give a

[1] *Calendar of Scotch Documents.*

more distinct character to the 'House of Balliol,' by endowing the Community which bore her husband's name, with permanent buildings, and substantial funds. And then she gave to the Scholars those beautiful Statutes, which, in their wisdom, charity, and simplicity, and in the evidence of tender care for all her poorer Scholars, must ever be prized as the best and richest of her gifts, who was 'mulier magna opibus et prædiis tam in Anglia quam in Scotia ; sed multo major ingenuitate cordis.'

Dervorguilla, the eldest of the three daughters of Alan, Prince of Galloway, was born in 1213. From her father she may have inherited some of her gifts for administration, and the management of her large properties. Alan of Galloway was Prince of a lawless and reckless people, who needed the hard hand of a stern and warlike master to keep them in control. One notice of the almost savage race is interesting, for its own sake, and because of its allusion to John de Balliol.

A.D. M.CC.XXXII. 'Tunc temporis Alanus dominus Galwydiæ moritur, circa purificationem beatæ Virginis ; cujus aspera gens ad mala prompta, post obitum domini non per duos annos manus a malo continentes, et a subjectione regis Scottorum recedere volentes, filium ipsius Alani illegitimum, Thomam nomine, filias abhorrendo, sibi dominum et quasi regem constituerunt. Adjuncto quoque sibi quodam facineroso,[1] Gilleroth, et fines suos egressi, terras regis, baronum et militum, circumjacentes ferro flammaque depopulati sunt. Igitur rex, coadunato exercitu, ipsos bello aggressus est, et interfecta infinita multitudine miserorum, ac capto duce sceleris, terram filiabus Alani, justis heredibus, pacificam reddidit et quietam. Postea domino Johanne de Bailliol seniorem sororem illarum ducente, Derforgoyl nomine, traditus est insimul dictus spurius Thomas ejus custodiæ, qui usque ad decrepitam ætatem inclusus erat in interiori parte Castri Bernardi.'[2]

[*Translation.*—At that time, towards the Purification of the Blessed Virgin, Alan, Lord of Gal loway, died. His savage clan, always ready for mischief, could not withhold their hands from evil as much as two years after the death of their Chief. Wishing to shake off their subjection to the King of the Scots, and scorning girls, they made to themselves Lord and almost King, the illegitimate son of Alan, Thomas by name. They also leagued with a certain scoundrel called Gilleroth, and, sallying from their boundaries, laid waste with fire and sword the surrounding country belonging to the King, and his Barons, and Knights. The King, therefore, mustered an army, and attacked them. He made an infinite slaughter of the caitiffs, and took the chief of the

---

[1] *Sic.*   [2] *Chronicon de Lanercost*, ed. Stevenson, p. 42.

conspiracy prisoner.   Then he restored the land in peace and quiet to the daughters of Alan, the lawful heirs.   Later, Lord John de Balliol married Dervorguilla, the eldest of these sisters, and the aforesaid misbegotten Thomas was handed over to his ward, and was confined up to an extreme old age, in the donjon of Castle Barnard.]

Dervorguilla may have inherited some characteristics from her father ; but, at least, all her thoughtfulness, her tender devotion, and her steadfastness of love and purpose, were more probably the rich heritage of one, who could, on her mother's side, claim descent from St. Margaret of Scotland, and her son, David.   After her mother's death, Dervorguilla was brought up by her grandfather, David, Earl of Huntingdon (grandson of David, King of Scotland), at Fotheringay.   In 1233, she married John de Balliol.

A very simple, and apparently quite accurate, account of the Balliol family is given in the Notes to *Wyntoun's Chronicle*, edited by David Laing.—

' It is most probable that the family of Bailleul, or Balliol, came to England with the Conqueror from Normandy, where some of the name still remain. *Guy de Baillol*, who possessed lands in Northumberland and Durham in the time of William II., is believed to be the first of the name upon record. (*Dugd. Mon.*, vol. i. p. 388 ; *Blount's Tenures*, v.

Biwell.)   *Bernard*, apparently son of Guy, was one
of the English barons who defeated King David I.
at the battle of the Standard, and distinguished
himself in the skirmish wherein King William was
made prisoner.   His sons were Engelram and
Eustace, of whom the former appears by Dugdale
to have had no issue ; but according to Crawfurd
(*Officers of State*, pp. 253, 260) he was the first of
the Balliols in Scotland, being Lord of Reidcastle
by marrying the heiress of Walter de Berkley,
by whom he was father of Henry Chamberlane
of Scotland, and great-grandfather of King John.
According to Dugdale, Eustace was father of *Hugh*,
whose son *John* married Dervorgil, the daughter of
Alan Lord of Galloway by Margaret eldest daughter
of David Earl of Huntington, whereby he got vast
estates in many parts of England, and in Scotland
first a third, and on the death of her sister, a half of
Galloway, with an eventual title to the crown for his
posterity.   Children of this marriage were *Hugh*,
Alan, *Alexander*, who all died without issue, JOHN
who became King, and apparently Marjory, married
to John Cumin, Lord of Badanach.   The sons of
King John by Isabel, daughter of John de Warren,
Earl of Surrey, were *Edward*, who for some time
acted as King of Scotland, and Henry, who both
dying without issue, there remained no male heir of
the chief family of the Balliols.'

We do not hear much about Dervorguilla's married life; but Wyntoun, in his delightful *Cronykil*, tells us of her piety; and one chapter is entirely about,—

> ' How Dervorgill that Lady
> Spendyt hyr Tresoure dewotly.'

The first two lines explain,

> ' Now to rehers it is my will
> Sum wertws dedis off Derworgill.'

And the chapter ends with an account of some of her generous foundations.

> ' Scho fowndyt in to Gallway
> Off Cystews ordyre ane Abbay ;
> Dulce-Cor scho gert thaim all,
> That is Swet-Hart, that Abbay call :
> And now the men off Gallway
> Callys that sted the New Abbay.
> Howssys off Freris scho fwndyt tway :
> Wygtowne, and Dundé [war] thai.
> In ekyng als off Goddis serwyce
> Scho fowndyt in Glasgw twa chapellanyis.
> And in the Unyversyté
> Off Oxynfurde scho gert be
> A Collage fowndyt.   This lady
> Dyd all thir dedis devotly.
> A bettyr lady than scho wes nane
> In all the yle off Mare Bretane.
> Scho wes rycht plesand off bewté,
> Here wes gret taknys off bownté.'

And, indeed, the Balliol College Statutes bear testimony to her doing 'all thir dedis devotly.' In them, she specially provides that her Scholars shall be present at Divine Office on Sundays and

Festivals ; that there shall be Masses said for her husband's soul ; that the richer Scholars shall live so temperately, that the poor shall not be hurt by heavy expenses ; that the food left at table shall be given to some poor Scholar ; and she begs her Scholars to keep faithfully, and never part with, the Portitorium,[1] which she gave them, for the good of her husband's soul.

Dervorguilla must have lived an active life, in a troublous time. From the Scotch Records, we glean many interesting facts about her, which all tend to prove her application to business, and her ready attention to the management of her property ; while her liberal endowments, all wisely planned for the good of Church and Nation, are the many monuments of her large-minded charity.

We must not here attempt to enumerate her good works. We must not stop to speak about the Wigton Friary, built for the Dominicans ; nor the House of the Grey Friars, at Dumfries ; nor, though it tempts us much, must we linger to look at the ruins of Dulce-Cor, the Abbey built by

---

[1] It would seem that this was a Monstrance, or Ciborium ; a sacred Vessel for the Altar, in which the Consecrated Host was reserved, or carried. Du Cange gives, Portitorium, or Portatorium, as *Lectica*, that in which anything is carried. Antony à Wood says, it was a 'corporeis case, wherein the Body of Christ, or the host, is kept.'

Henry Savage describes it, as 'a Corpore's Case (such as Will: Wright the Master gave in the Raign of Phil: and Mary. See the Register) wherein the Priest carryed the Host.'

Dervorguilla to the 'Greater Glory of God, and Saint Marie,' and in memory of the husband she loved so well. We must pass at once to the work she did for us in Oxford; a work undertaken in loving fulfilment of her husband's last desires.

CHAPTER IV.

1282 is the date of the foundation of Balliol College ; that is, the date when the ' House of Balliol ' was permanently endowed, and received its Statutes for self-government.   The first tenement rented for the College was the house in Horsemonger Street, which John de Balliol's Scholars had for several years occupied ; and which was, later on, called Old Balliol Hall.   It was also known as Sparrow Hall ; and, afterwards, as Hamond's Lodgings.   In 1379, this Old Balliol Hall, sometimes called Sparrow Hall, was leased by the University to the Master of Balliol, and the following description of its situation is gathered from the wording of that lease.

' Old Balliol Hall, with its Garden and Appurtenances, was scituate between a Tenement of Saint Frideswids on the West part, and a certain Garden of the Master and Scholars on the East, and extended itself from the Kings-street, or Kings Highway of Candych on the South, to the Garden of the said Tyrwhit Master of the House on the North.   The

area whereof (Garden and all I suppose to be meant)
was 96 Foot in length from North to South, and
47 Foot in breadth at the South end, and 41 at
the other.   The name of Sparrow-Hall, which the
University calls it by, might be given it before our
Founder first took it of them, or else since, by some
under-Tenant of that name, who used it for a place
of entertainment for Students, the Colledge having
no longer use for it in that kinde.' [1]

Another account of Old Balliol Hall tells us, that
—' It stood next, on the West side, to Balliol Coll:
—and on the East side of the said Lodging, near it,
was another named Mary's or Mary-Hall, mentioned
in a certain Charter in the Year 1266, whereby the
Prior and Canon of St. Frid. did grant to J. de Eu
their whole Right and Claim of 6*s*. per Ann. which
they were wont to receive from the Hands of the said
John, for a Messuage, with its Appurtenances, called
Marye-Hall, situated between the Lands of Philip
de Ewe on the East, and Jeffry de Sawcer on the
West, called by some therefore Sawcer Hall, in
Horsemonger-Street in Magdalen Parish. It appears
to have had its Situation near or on the Scite where
the Forefront of that College now stands.   Near it
St. Margarets Hall was standing within the limits
of Balliol.' [2]

' On or near the Scite where the Forefront of that

---

[1] *Balliofergus*, p. 7.   [2] *City of Oxfora*, Peshall, p. 239.

College now stands' is rather a vague description of the situation of a small house, which stood on some portion of the ground now occupied by the long line of buildings, which reach from Fisher Buildings at the west end of Broad Street, to where the College joins the Trinity front quadrangle. But another history comes to our aid, which states, that 'The Scholars of this Society first inhabited Old *Baliol* Hall, on the Area whereof was lately built a Dwelling House call'd *Hammond's*-Inn; after that *Devorgilla* (as aforesaid) had them translated to St. *Mary* Hall, then situated near the South-west Corner of the present Quadrangle; to which, by a Purchase of three Acres of Ground she added a Hall, Kitchin, and other out-Buildings, with pleasant Walks and Groves. Soon after the Fellows of *Baliol* purchasing several Parcels of Ground (two of which lay in *Horsemangerstreet*, and a third between *Baliol* Land on the West, and Land belonging to *Slatter* of *Ensham* on the East:) *John*, Son and Heir of *Walter de Fetteplace*, conveyed both these Spots of Ground to *Tho. de Hevorth*, and *Tho. de Pontefract*, Fellows of this College, who soon after gave the same to the Society.'[1]

So we find the Scholars living first in Old Balliol Hall, and afterwards in an house a little eastward of it, called Mary Hall, which was 'then situated near the south-west corner of the present quadrangle.'

[1] *Ayliffe*, v. 1. p. 269.

Dervorguilla purchased this Mary Hall in 1284, and also three plots of land adjoining it; and there were built the hall, kitchen, and other buildings; and there she had made the 'pleasant walks and groves.' St. Margaret's Hall was 'a certain messuage called "Seinte Margrete halle" in the suburb of Oxford, in the parish of St. Mary Magdalen, between the tenement called "Baylolhalle the New," on the one side, and the tenement called "Old Baylolhalle" on the other.'[1]

The College still preserves several deeds relating to St. Margaret's Hall. One is 'a parchment deed, in Latin, being a grant by William Cnaresburg and Agnes, his wife, to William Kyrnesale, John de Notyngham, John de Suttone, and John de Craunce-wyk, Clerks, of a messuage situate between the tenement of the University of Oxford, "which is called Old Balliolshalle," on the west side, and the tenement of the Master and Scholars of the Hall of Balliol, "which is called New Balliolshalle," on the east side. "Given in the suburb and hundred aforesaid, on the 20th day of May, in the 11th year of the reign of King Edward the Third." The two seals are in fair condition.'[2]

And there is a 'Record of a fine levied thereon between the above parties, (tr.)—"In the Hustings of Oxford, on Monday before the Feast of the

---

[1] *Hist. MSS. Com.*, Fourth Report, p. 447.   [2] *Ibid.*

Annunciation of the Blessed Virgin Mary," in the
12th year of the reign of King Edward the Third,
"before Henry de Stodelegh the Mayor, Richard de
Selewode and John Peggy, then Bailiffs, William de
Burcestre, Richard Cary, Andrew de Normenhale,
and Stephen de Adynton, then Aldermen ; " as to a
messuage called "La Margerethalle," situate between
the tenement called " La Niwebaillolhalle," on the
one side, and " La Oldebaillolhalle " on the other.' [1]

St. Margaret's Hall, therefore, evidently occupied
the space between the house, known sometime as
Sparrow Hall, sometime as Hammond's Lodgings,
which John de Balliol's Scholars first inhabited, and
was consequently called Old Balliol Hall ; and the
house known as Mary Hall, which was situated in
the south-west corner of the present quadrangle,
where Dervorguilla established them in 1284. That
is, St. Margaret's Hall stood where the east part of
the Master's house now stands. Together with the
documents which relate to St. Margaret's Hall, is a
writing on paper, in a hand of the seventeenth century, which states that the Hall was ' the 7 tenement
from the south east end of the College.'

But it was before the Scholars were moved to
Mary Hall, and before the hall, kitchen, and other
buildings were erected for them, that Dervorguilla
gave them Statutes, and formed them into a distinct

---

[1] *Hist. MSS. Com.*, Fourth Report, p. 447.

Society. The poor youths, who were glad to accept—
what in those days was a liberal support—the eight
pence a week ; and to be lodged in Balliol Hall, and
known as John de Balliol's Scholars, were living in an
hired house when Dervorguilla gave them their first
Statutes. The house, which appears to have been a
tenement of some importance, must have been of
sufficient size to lodge many Scholars ; and it must
have given rooms large enough to serve for hall, and
lecture room. This Old Balliol Hall was, as late as
1379, again hired for the Scholars, when their numbers increased, and New Balliol Hall was found to
be not large enough to take them all in. Therefore,
nearly one hundred years afterwards, the College
rented from the University the old original building
in which John de Balliol's Scholars had first lived
together, and where they received their first rules for
self-government.

Chief among the many valuable and interesting
documents kept in the College Archives, are the
original Statutes, written in Latin, which have been
very carefully preserved. They are on one sheet
of parchment, very clearly written. The large seal,
which is nearly quite perfect, is in red wax, vesica-
shaped. The impression on it is distinct. The
figure, stately and striking, is supposed to represent
Dervorguilla. She has on a plain robe, and a veil
across her forehead. In her right hand she holds an

escutcheon, with an orle upon it, as being Lady of
Balliol; and in her left hand is the Lion of Galloway.
The face is clearly cut; and, despite the diminutive
size, there are traces of fine features, and a certain
dignity of expression. The inscription round the
seal is 'S. Dervorgille de Balliol filie Alani de
Galewad'.' On the reverse of the seal are the arms
of Balliol and Galloway impaled, with the inscription,
'S. Dervorgille de Galewad'. Domine de Balliolo.'

The exact words of Dervorguilla's Statutes are,—

'Deruorgulla de Galwedia dña de Balliolo: dilc̄is
in xp̄o Fri? Hugoni de Hertilpoꝉ ꞇ Magr̄'o Willõ
de Menyl Slm̄ in dño sēpiꞇnam. Vtilitati filiorꝑ ꞇ
scolariũ nr̄.orꝑ Oxonie ꝯmoranciũ / affc̄tu maꞇno
ꝑuidere cupiētes omĩa inf̄ʔius annotata volum⁹
mandam˵ ꞇ p̄cipim⁹ ab eis inuiolaƀiliꞇ obs̄uari.
Ad honorēꝯ gꞟ dñi nr̄.i Ihũ xp̄i ꞇ glõse matꞌs sue
Marie nᵉñõ ꞇ sc̄orꝑ oĩm. In pꞟmis volum˵ ꞇ
ordinam⁹ / q̨ scolares nr̄ i onĩs ꞇ sĩgꞒi teneantʳ diebȝ
dñicis ꞇ festis pꞟncipalioribȝ diuino intēe officio nᵉnõ
ꞇ sermõibȝ seu p̄dicaꞓibȝ in eisdē festis ꞇ diebȝ /
nꞟ ꝯtĩgat aliq̨ ex eis impediri ꝓpꞒ vrgētē nēc̄itatē
vꞒ euidētē vtilitatē ceꞒis vᵒ diebȝ diligñꞒ scolas
exᵉc̄ceāt ꞇ studio intēdant scd̄m statuta vniũ-
sitatis Oxonie ꞇ scd̄m forᵃm inf̄ ius annotatam.
Ordinam⁹ ꞇ̃ q̨ scolares nr̄ꞌi teneantʳ nr̄.is ꝑcuratoribȝ
obedire in omĩibȝ꞉ q̃ ex nr̄ a ordinacõe ꝯcessione
ꝯmissione ad eorꝑ regim̃ ꞇ vtilitatē ꝑtin꞉e noscũtur.

Itẽ volum⁹ q̃ scolares nr̃i ex semetip̃is eligant vnũꝰ
p̃ncipalem cui cet̃i om̃s humilit̃ obediant in hiis que
officiũ p̃ncipalis ꝯtĩgũt scd̃m statuta ꞇ ꝯsuetudines
int̃ ip̃os vsitatas ꞇ appbatas . Predc̃s autẽ p̃ncipal̃
p⁹q̃ᵃ legitieꝰ fũit elect⁹ / nr̃is proc̃atorib3 p̃sẽtẽ .
nᶜ a꞉d de suo officc̃o exc̃ceat / añq̃ᵃ ab eis autoritate
nr̃a in p̃fato officc̃o fũit institut⁹ . Cet̃ũ statuim⁹ q̃
scolares nr̃i ꝑc̃ent tres missas celebrari singl̃is annis
sollẽpnit̃ / ꝓ ãĩa dilecti mariti nr̃i dñi . J . de Bal̃l̃ . ꞇ
ꝓ ãĩab3 p̃decessor꞊ nr̃or꞊ omniũq̃ꝏ fideliũ defũctor꞊ .
nᶜnõ ꞇ ꝓ nr̃a salute ꞇ ĩcolũitate ita q̃ p̃ma missa
celebret̃ʳ in p̃ma epdomada aduẽtus dñi ꞇ scd̃a in
epdomada septuag꞉ . ꞇ t̃cia ꞉ in p̃ma epdomada post
octauas pasche ꞉ ꞇ fiant p̃dc̃e misse de scõ sp̃u vel
de beata vgie꞉ . vel ꝑ defũctis scdm̃ dispõm ꝓcurator꞊ .
singl̃is t̃ dieb3 tam in p̃ndio q̃ᵃ in cena dicãt
bñdicc̃õm añq̃ᵃ ꝯmedãt ꞇ post ref c̃õm gr̃ias agãt . ꞇ
orẽt spãlit̃ ꝓ ãĩa dilc̃ti mariti nr̃i sr̃꞉ius nõĩati . ꞇ ꝓ
animab3 õm̃ p̃decessor꞊ nr̃or꞊ nᶜnõ ꞇ liberor꞊ de-
fũctor꞊ . ꝓ ĩcolũitate ꞇ nr̃a t̃ liberor꞊ cet̃or꞊q̃ꝏ amic-
or꞊ nr̃or꞊ viuor꞊ . nᶜñ ꞇ ꝓ nr̃is ꝓcuratorib3 scd̃m
antiq̃꞉t⁹ vsitatam . Et vt melius ꝓuideat̃ʳ sustẽtacõi
paup̃ꝰ ad quor꞊ vtilitate꞉ intẽdim⁹ laborare ꞉ volum⁹ q̃
dic̃õres in societate scolariũ nr̃or꞊ ita tẽpate studeant
viũ . ut paupꞇores nl̃lo modo g̃uẽt̃ʳ ꝓpt̃ expẽsas
oꞇlosas . Et si ꝯtĩgat totam ꝯmũitate꞉ scolariũ
nr̃or꞊ in expẽsis ꝗ̃ib3 aliq̃ᵃ septimana excedere
porc̃õm a nob̃ eis ĩpẽsam ꞉ volum⁹ ꞇ p̃cipim⁹ dist̃cte

q̴ ad soluc̃om illarꝑ expẽsarꝑ excedẽciũ nichil õino
recipiatʳ vltᵃ vnũ denariũ ĩ vna septimana ab eis qⁱ
scᷟm disꝺcom ⁊ arbitⁱũ ꝑcuratorꝑ nꝛ̃orꝑ indicãtʳ
impotel̃tes vel insufficiel̃tes ad totalẽ illarꝑ expẽsarꝑ
soluc̃om faciel̃dam . si eqᵃĩ porc̃o deberet ab oñibꝜ
sociis exhiberi . p̾ⁱdc̃a tñ nolum⁹ ad magnã vacac̃om
q̃ durat a tᵃnslac̃oe b̃i Thome martiris vsꝗ ad festũ
beati luce . nᶜ ⁊ ad septimanas illas in qⁱbꝜ occurrũt
festa Natiuitatis d̃ñice . cⁱcũcisionis . ephphaniẽ .
pasche . ⁊ pẽtecostes . nᶜ in aliis casibꝜ in qⁱbꝜ
ꝑcuratores nꝛ̃i indicau̾ĩt illᷟ omittẽᷟ . Volum⁹ ⁊
ꝑcᵃatores nꝛ̃os diliḡntẽ habere examinac̃om sꝛ̃
p̾fata scolariũ nꝛ̃orꝑ ĩpotẽcia . ⁊ q̴ scolares iꝓi ad
ꝑcuratores nꝛ̃os accedant cũ oñi ꝯfidé̾cia ꝓ eorꝑ
necessitate intimanda . Et si ꝯtĩgat aliq̴m vel aliquos
de scolaribꝜ nꝛ̃is c̃otᵃ ordinac̃om istam murmᵛare .
aũ occasione istius ordinac̃ois pauꝑiores v̾bo vel
signo aliqᵒ ꝓuocare꞉ volum⁹ q̴ scolares nꝛ̃i teneantʳ
sb̃ iuram̃to nob̃ p̾stito nõ̃a taliꝑ murmᵛanciũ aũ
ꝓuocanciũ nꝛ̃is ꝑcᵃatoribꝜ reuelare . qⁱ q̾ⁱdẽ ꝑcuratores
h̃ita sꝛ̃ʼ hoc sufficiel̃ti ꝑbacoeꝺ : autoritate p̾sẽciũ sũ
spe redeñdi iꝓm vel iꝓos eiciant indilate . Statuim⁹
⁊ q̴ scolares nꝛ̃i c̃omuniꝑ loqᵃtʳ latinũ ⁊ qⁱ passim
ꝯtrafec̃it a p̾ncipali corripiatʳ . ⁊ se bis vel ter
correptus se nõ eñdau̾it a comunione m̃se seꝑetur ꝓ
se comedẽs ⁊ vltĩo oñium ꞔuiatʳ . Et si incorrigibiꝉ
manserit ꝓ epdomadam꞉ a ꝑcuratoribꝜ nꝛ̃is eiciatʳ .
Volum꞊ ⁊ q̴ qᵃlibet altera epdomada inꝑ scolares

nr̃os in eort́ domo dispute͛ vnũ sophisma ꝷ de-
t́minet͛ ꝷ h̄ fiat c̓cularit̃ . ita ū sophiste opponant
ꝷ rñdeant ꝷ qⁱ in scoł det̃iãũit : det́minẽt . Si v°
aliqⁱs sophista ita ꝓuectus fũit ꝗ m̃ito possit in breui
in scolis det́minare : tũc ei dicat͛ a pⁱncipali ꝗ pⁱus
det̃iet domi int̃ socios suos . In fine ꝷ cuiˢlib꜔
disputacõis p̃figat pⁱncipał dié̃ disputacõis seꝗtis .
ꝷ disputacõm regat ꝷ garrulos cohibeat ꝷ assignet
sophisma ꝓxi° disputand̃ . opponé̃té̓ . respõdét̄ē ꝷ
det̃iatoré̃ . vt sⁱ melius valeant ꝓuidere . Consimili
modo fiat qⁱlib꜔ alt̃a epdomada de questione . Pre-
cipimᵍ ꝷ scolarib꜔ nr̃is fⁱmit̃ iniũgétes ut portitoriũ
qd̃ eis ꝑ ãĩa dilcti mariti nr̃i cõcessimᵍ diligñt̃
custodiant . n͛ aliquo modo ꝑmittant illd̃ inpignorari .
vel quocũꝗ titulo alienari . Hẽant ꝷ scola res nr̃i
vnũ paupé̓ scolare̓ ꝑ ꝓcuratores nr̃os assignatũ .
cui singłis dieb꜔ reliqⁱas m̃se sue teneant͛ erogare .
nⁱ ꝓcuratores nr̃i illd̃ det́ũint omittéd̃ . Vt auté̓
omĩa ꝷ singła p̃dcta a nr̃is scolarib꜔ tépe ꝓcuvatoré̃
quort́cũꝗ inviolabilit̃ obseruét̃͛ ⸴ p̃sens scⁱptũ
sigilli nr̃i munim̃ie roborauimus . Dat̃ apd̃ Botel
in octauis assũpcõis głose virg̃s Marie . anno gr̓e .
ᴍ° . ᴄ°ᴄ° . octogesimo scdõ.̓

[*Translation.*—Dervorguilla of Galloway, Lady
of Balliol, to her beloved in Christ, Brother Hugh
de Hertipoll, and Master William de Menyl, everlasting Salvation in the Lord.   Desiring, with a
mother's affection, to provide for the well-being of
our sons and Scholars dwelling in Oxford, we will,

ordain, and prescribe, that they do keep inviolate all that we hereinafter make known. Therefore, to the Honour of our Lord, Jesus Christ, and of His Glorious Mother, Mary, and of all the Saints. Firstly, we will and ordain that our Scholars, each and all, be bound on Sundays and the chief Feast Days to be present at Divine Office, and likewise at the sermons, or discourses, held on those days and Feasts, unless it chance that any one of them be hindered, by reason of some urgent necessity, or matter of evident utility; but that on other days they do diligently attend the Schools, and give heed to their studies, according to the Statutes of the University of Oxford, and according to the manner hereinafter made known. Also we ordain that our Scholars be bound to obey our Procurators, in all matters that, according to our ordinance, grant, and commission, are known to concern their order and well-being. Also we desire that our Scholars do choose, from among themselves, a Principal, whom all the rest shall humbly obey in those matters which concern the office of Principal, according to the Statutes and customs used and approved among them. And the aforesaid Principal, when he shall have been lawfully chosen, shall be presented to our Procurators, and shall in no way exercise his office until he shall have been invested with the aforesaid office by them, and by our authority. Also we decree that our Scholars

F

have three Masses celebrated solemnly every year, for the soul of our beloved husband, Sir John de Balliol, and for the souls of our predecessors, and for all the faithful departed. And likewise for our salvation, here and hereafter. And, of these, the first Mass shall be celebrated in the first week of the Advent of our Lord, and the second in the week of Septuagesima, and the third in the first week after the octave of Easter; and the aforesaid Masses shall be of the Holy Ghost, or of the Blessed Virgin, or for the faithful departed, according as the Procurators shall appoint. And on every day, both at breakfast, and at supper, they shall say the benediction before they eat, and after the meal they shall give thanks. And they shall pray in particular for the soul of our beloved husband aforesaid, and for the souls of all our predecessors, and likewise for the souls of our children that are dead; and for our security, and the security of our children, and all our friends that are yet alive; and also for our Procurators, according to ancient usage. And that better provision be made for the sustenance of the poor, for whose advantage it is our intent to labour, we desire that the richer members, in the Society of our Scholars, be zealous so temperately to live, that the poorer be in no way oppressed by the burden of expense. And if it chance that the whole Community of our Scholars in any week exceed, in their common expenses, the sum granted to them by us, we

desire and prescribe strictly that, for the payment of
expenses thus in excess, not more than one penny
be received in any week from those who, according
to the discretion and judgment of our Procurators,
shall be deemed to have no means, or means not
sufficient, for the payment in full of such expenses,
if an equal portion were exacted from each member.
Yet we do not desire that the aforesaid be extended
to the Long Vacation, which lasts from the Translation of Blessed Thomas, the Martyr, till the Feast of
Saint Luke ; nor to those weeks in which occur the
Feast of the Nativity or Circumcision of our Lord, or
of the Epiphany, or of Easter, or of Pentecost; nor in
other cases in which it shall seem good to our Procurators to omit the enforcement of this rule. Also
we desire that our Procurators make diligent examination concerning the above-mentioned matters.
And the Scholars themselves shall go to our Procurators, with all confidence, to inform them of their
necessity. And if it chance that any one, or more,
of our Scholars murmur against this ordinance ; or,
on the occasion of this ordinance being enforced,
provoke the poorer Scholars, by word or sign ; we
desire that our Scholars be bound, under oath sworn
to us, to reveal to the Procurators the names of those
that are guilty of such murmuring, or provocation.
And the Procurators, if they have sufficient proof of
the matter, shall, by the authority of these presents,

immediately expel such person or persons without
hope of return. We also do appoint that our
Scholars shall in common speak Latin, and he who
shall chance to have acted in contravention hereof,
shall be reproved by the Principal. And if, when
reproved twice or thrice, he shall not amend himself,
he shall be put away from their company at table,
and eat alone, and shall be served last of all. And
if he shall remain incorrigible throughout a week, he
shall be expelled by our Procurators. We desire
also that in every other week one Sophism shall be
discussed and determined among our Scholars, in
their House, and this shall be done in turn, in such
manner that the Sophists shall introduce and reply,
and they shall determine who shall have determined
in the Schools. But if any Sophist shall have made
such progress that he shall shortly have the right to
determine in the Schools, then the Principal shall
bid him first determine at home among his fellows.
And at the end of each Disputation, the Principal
shall post up the day of the next Disputation ; and
he shall order the Disputation, and restrain them
that speak overmuch, and appoint the Sophism to be
next discussed, and them that shall introduce, reply,
and determine, in order that they may be the better
able to make provision. In like manner shall they
discuss a question every other week. Also we ordain, and strictly enjoin upon our Scholars, that the

Portitorium, which, for the soul of our beloved husband, we have granted to our Scholars, they do diligently keep, nor permit it in any wise to be pledged, or by any means alienated. Also our Scholars shall keep one poor Scholar, appointed by our Procurators, for whom they shall be bound every day to save the remnants of their table, unless our Procurators shall decree that this be omitted. And that the above ordinances, each and all, be kept inviolate by our Scholars, obeying the Procurators, whosoever they shall at any time be, we have confirmed this writing with the corroboration of our seal. Given at Botel, in the octave of the Assumption of the Glorious Virgin Mary, in the year of Grace one thousand two hundred and eighty two.]

There is also, on a small piece of parchment, a letter from 'Dervorguilla de Galwith, Lady of Balliol,' to Brother Richard de Slikeburne. It has been photographed for the Scottish National Collection of Manuscripts. Brother Richard was a Friar Minor, a Priest, and probably one of those who made the House of the Grey Friars at Oxford so celebrated. There are two traditions about his connection with the College. One, that he was Dervorguilla's Confessor, and that he used his opportunities of giving advice, to urge her to found the College in memory of her husband. The other, that Dervorguilla, wishing to follow out her husband's desires, purchased the tenements in

Horsemonger Street, and gave them to the Scholars she had helped to support at Oxford. Then, having endowed the College, she sought counsel and advice from Brother Richard de Slikeburne about the organization, and the perpetuation of it.

Mr. Maxwell Lyte, speaking of the Students who had been maintained at Oxford by the alms of Sir John de Balliol, says,—' It appears that for some time after his death they received their allowances regularly from his widow, Dervorguilla ; but there is no proof of their existence as a distinct community earlier than the year 1282, when a formal ordinance was issued for their government. In this, Dervorguilla committed the supreme authority to her two proctors, or agents, Friar Hugh de Hertilpol and Master William de Menyl, who, though members of the University, did not live in the house with the Scholars. The ordinance does not explain how future proctors were to be appointed after the death of the foundress, and it is only by examining a very imperfect list of these officers, who were also described as " Rectors," or " Extraneous Masters," that we are led to believe that one of them was to be chosen from among the Franciscan friars, and the other from among the secular Masters of Arts. Such a belief, however, receives considerable support from an ancient tradition, which points to Friar Richard de Slikebury as the confessor of Dervorguilla, and the person who persuaded her to carry out the wishes of Sir John de Balliol with regard to the Scholars at Oxford.'[1] Friar Richard de Slikeburne may have been Dervorguilla's Confessor ; but the tenor of her letter to him would rather prove that the College was founded before she went to him for advice about the government of it. The great esteem in which the Friars Minor were then held, and their celebrity for learning, and for the strictness of their lives, made it natural that Dervorguilla should turn to one of their Order, probably a man well known in the University, to aid her in her work. Dervorguilla's letter is one of the most valued of the documents in the College Archives ; and it is here given exactly as it is written.

'Veñande Religiõis viro ac patri suo In xp̄o km̄o Fratri . R . de Slikeburñ de Ordine Frm̄ Minoʒ D. de Galwitħ Dña de Balliolo Salm̄ & Deuocõis augm̄tũ in Sp̄ũ Sc̃õ . Qm̄ elemosinam paupũ Scariũ Dom⁹ ñr̃e de Ballõ Oxoñ studenciũ p̄ deuocõnem bone memorie Dñi Joħis de Ballõ quondam sponsi ñr̃i dudũ inchoatã ac p̄ nos post ei⁹ decessum acten⁹ continuatam ad diuine Laudis honorem & toci⁹ Ecclħ̃e militantis utilitatē ñ modicã testat̄ ᵱfic̃e viroʒ illust'um assertõ fidedigna / Hinc est qd̃ ad tantoʒ tam religiosoʒ qᵘm seculariũ instantiam õi fauore dignissimam / elemosine p̄dc̃e ᵱpetuacõnem Sp̄ũ Sc̃õ sugg'ente affectare qᵘmplĩmũ excitamʳ / Quappᵗ de vſã discrecõne deuocõneq₃ plenam g'entes fiduciam / a veñabili Patre Ministro ᵥ̃rõ ppetuacõnis eiꝰdem execucõnem voɓ cõmitti ꝓcʳauimꝰ finali effectuj mancipanɗ. voɓ prece qᵃ possum⸴ attente supplicantes / qᵘtinꝰ assistente voɓ consolacõne diuina dc̃ãm ppetuacõnem satagatis adimplere ꝑut melius noꞔitis diuine cõsonũ volũtati Sc̃ẽ Matris Eccl̃iẽ utilitati & dc̃õr₂ Scolariũ cõmoditati aptũ & ꝑficuũ . Et nos qᵘntũ in noɓ est in omnib₃ & ꝑ õĩã ratũ & gratũ ɦꝛ̃ẽ ꝑmittimus quicquid vos cⁱca negocia Scolariũ ꝓ̃dc̃õr₂ ordinarꝰ . faꝛe . mutar⸴' . seu ꝑcurare decreꞔitis . et quociens attornatis indigemꞔ ad quascũq̥ saysinas capiendas seu donandas ad opꞔ Scolariũ ꝓ̃dc̃õr₂ . siue de domib₃ siue de ᷑tris siue de aliis quibuscũq̥ ẽptis emendis ũt cõmutandis . iꝑos ex nũc ordinamꝰ facimꝰ & cõstituimꞔ ñrós attornatos & ꝑcuratores / quos vos nõĩẽ ñró nõĩandos dux᷑itis seu assignandos . Et oñiia & singula ꝓ̃dca̋ vniꞔsis Sc̃ẽ Matris Eccl̃iẽ filiis tenore ꝑ̃senciũ significamꝰ . In cuiuꝰ rei testimoniũ has l̃rãs ñrãs patentes voɓ tᵃnsmisimꝰ ñró sigillo cõsignatas . Daᵗ apɗ Fodring̋ In Octauis Pascĥ . Anno Dñĩ . Mᵒ. CCᵒ . Octog̋ qᵃrto.'

[*Translation.*—Dervorguilla de Galwitha, Lady of Balliol, to the Venerable Religious, and her most dear Father in Christ, Brother Richard de Slikeburne, of the Order of Friars Minor, Health, and increase of devotion in the Holy Ghost,

The credible assertion of illustrious men bears witness that the alms, which were given by the devotion of our late husband, John de Balliol, to the poor Scholars studying at Oxford, of our House of Balliol, and which we have continued to give from the time of his decease until now, are of no small utility to the Honour of God, and of the Church Militant. On this account we are greatly moved, at the instance of many men of great consideration, both Religious and secular, the Holy Ghost this inclining us, to continue to bestow the aforesaid alms. Wherefore, as we have entire confidence in your discretion and devotion, we have obtained of your Venerable Father Minister, that the bestowal of the same should be committed to your charge ; begging you with all the earnestness we can, that with the help of Divine Consolation, you will fulfil this task as you shall best judge it to be according to the Divine Will, and apt and profitable for the utility of Holy Mother Church, and the advantage of the Scholars aforesaid. And we promise, as far as in us lies, to ratify and approve, in all and through all, whatever you shall decide to order, do, change, and provide, concerning the business of the said Scholars. And whenever we need attorneys to take or give seisin, whether of houses, lands, or whatsoever other things that are bought, or to be bought, or exchanged, in the business of the said Scholars, we from this time ordain, make, and appoint, as our attorneys and Procurators, those whom you, in our name, shall have chosen or assigned. And by the tenor of these presents, we signify all and each of these things aforesaid, to all the children of Holy Mother Church. In witness of which we have sent you these our letters patent, sealed with our seal. Given at Fotheringay, on the octave-day of Easter, in the year of our Lord twelve hundred and eighty-four.]

This letter of Dervorguilla's is written on a small piece of parchment ; the writing is irregular, and not good ; and the seal has been lost.

In 1668 a 'Commentary' on the College was written by Henry Savage, who was then Master. This history, called *Balliofergus*, says,—

' The Office of Procurators, [in whose hands had been the Government of the House from the very first Foundation till now] did not upon the choice of a Principal cease ; the said Principal and Scholars being strictly obleiged to obey them, as you may observe in the perusal of these Statutes of *Dervorgille*, two years after the publication wherof, which was 1284, did she under her Seal, put a final establishment to the House for perpetuity, by Letters full of Piety and Publick-spiritedness, directed to *R. Sclikebury* a Minorite : to whose discretion she thereby committed the choice of her Attornyes and Procurators to be made in her Name ; the Scholars, before this, having chosen *Walter Fodringheye* to be Principal according to the Statutes. Whereupon *Dervorgille* and the rest of the Executors of *John de Balliol* had made a Grant to the said *Walter Fodringheye*, Principal, and the Scholars, of all the Goods of *John de Balliol* for the perpetuation of the House. *Ad perpetuationem domus* de Balliol *quam ille feliciter inchoavit & perpetuare decreverat, si mortis auctor & vite sibi concessisset suum adimplere propositum*, are the very words of the Grant, dated *Anno* 1282. Whereupon divers obligations were now Sealed to the said *Walter Fodringheye* and the Scholars, for the payment of moneyes due to *John de Balliol*: whereof one was from *Walter Balliol* Rector of *Wickford*, for the payment of 59 *pounds sterling* 1282 : and another from *Stephen de Eure* Rector de Milford,[1] for the payment of 44 *pounds* 13 *shillings* 4 pence, part of the 100 *pound* assigned to him by *John de Balliol's* Executors of the debt of *Alan Fitz* Count [*ex debito Alani Filii Comitis*]. This Bond was dated *in festo Sancte Margarete* 1285.'[2]

This Grant was confirmed by Oliver, Bishop of Lincoln. The confirmation, written in Latin, is on a small piece of parchment, and only two fragments of what must have been a large seal are left. On one fragment of the dark green wax is a very

---

[1] Mitford ?   [2] *Balliofergus*, p. 17.

fine face, with a quite beautiful expression. The Bishop's vestment, just below the head, is still distinct. The writing commences,—

'The noble woman, and devout unto God, Dervorguilla, of Gallewyth, Lady of Balliol, having newly ordained, to the honour and praise of the supreme and undivided Trinity, of the most glorious Virgin Mary, Mother of the only Son of God, of the Blessed Virgin and Martyr, Katherine, and of the whole Court of Heaven, and for the advantage of the whole Church militant, and the stablishment of the University of Oxford, for the soul of the noble man, of pious memory, John de Balliol, her late husband . . . a certain place, with buildings and all appurtenances, which she determined should be named 'the House of the Scholars of Balliol.' . . . Given at Lidington, on the Ides of June, in the year of our Lord 1284.'[1]

There is a copy of this deed, in larger writing. The seal, in white wax, is even more fragmentary. The lower part of the vestment only can be distinguished.

There is another deed, written in Latin, which is well worth noticing. It was signed at Crealawe, in Northumberland, on Trinity Sunday, 1287. The five or six seals, which were originally attached to it have all been lost. It begins,—

---

[1] *Hist. MSS. Com.* Fourth Report, p. 442.

' " To all the faithful in Christ, who the present letters shall see or hear, Hugh de Eure and Stephen, his brother, and other the executors of the testament of Sir John de Balliol, greeting in the Lord. Bearing in mind the pious affection, which our dearly beloved Lord, Sir John above-mentioned, had towards the Scholars of the House of Balliol, which at Oxford, by inspiration of the divine Spirit, he happily began, and had determined to make provision for the lasting maintenance thereof, if the Author of life and death had granted him to fulfil his purpose." In order to carry out his wishes, and those of " the Lady Dervorgulla de Galewitha," they give to the Scholars of the said House of Balliol all the debts which were due to the said Sir John de Balliol at the time of his death, and appoint Master Walter de Fodringeye, Principal of the said Scholars, or any other his successor, their attorney to gather in the same.' [1]

In another deed, Brother Richard confirms this Grant; but reserves therefrom £100 which was due to the estate from Sir Robert Fitz-Roger, as also the monies which were due from the Monks of Rievalle. Yet, in spite of this generosity to Sir Robert and the Monks, for which in all probability there was some good reason, Brother Richard seems to have been worthy of the confidence that Dervor-

[1] *Hist. MSS. Com.* Fourth Report, p. 442.

guilla placed in him when she begged him to promote the perpetuation of her House, as is proved
by two deeds still preserved in the College Archives.

‘A small parchment deed, in Latin, five of the
seven seals originally appended to which, are left,
and in fair condition. It states that, on Saturday
after the Feast of St. Mark the Evangelist, at
Wygeton, in the year 1285, in presence of L.
Bishop of Whithern, and the Abbots of Dundreynan
and of Tungeland, of Sir Dovenild [Donald] Fitz-
Cane, Sir Martin Clerk, Thomas Maculaitch,
Ronuauld, and others, it was agreed that Thomas
Maculaitch should deliver 120 cows into the hand of
Rouland Ascolock, according to the will of Sir Alan
Fitz-Comte ; to be kept by him till the Feast of the
Assumption then next ensuing, and then to be
delivered in full payment of the sum of 100 pounds
due to the executors of Sir John de Balliol, and
demanded by Brother Richard de Slekeburne, on
their behalf. This delivery to be in full satisfaction,
if so deemed by John de Tesedale, and if not, then
the complement, still due, shall be added thereto.
One of the seals, that of the Bishop, has on it a
hand and a pastoral staff.’

And ‘ A small parchment deed, in Latin, whereby
Hugh de Euer, Knight, acknowledges himself bound
to Master Walter de Fodringey, Principal, and his
Fellows, Scholars of the House called "De Balliolo,"

in Oxford, in a sum of 22 li. 10 s. 10 d., part of 100 pounds, due to the executors of the testament of John de Balliol by Sir Alan Fitz-Comte, and assigned by him and his co-executors in aid of the perpetuation of the said House ; the same to be paid, by counsel of Brother Richard de Sclyke-bourne, without further delay.   For payment thereof, he binds himself and his heirs, and his goods, movable and immovable.   " Given at Engleby, the Thursday after the Feast of St. Valentine, A.D. 1286."   Part of the diminutive seal is left.' [1]

Thus we gather that Brother Richard, not only advised and helped Dervorguilla in the work of establishing the House of Balliol ; but was also active in collecting the debts due to Sir John de Balliol, and seeing that such monies were applied to the good of the House.   The Scholars of Balliol had ' in addition to the endowments given to them by the foundress, acquired from the executors of the will of Sir John de Balliol the right to collect and retain all the debts owing to him at the time of his death.' [2] In another instance, when the £100 due from Alan Fitz-Comte was paid, some portion of it having been previously received, there was a remaining sum left over ; and this was given to the Scholars ' by counsel of Brother Richard de Slikeburne.'

---

[1] *Hist. MSS. Com.* Fourth Report, p. 444.
[2] *Hist. Univ. Oxford,* Maxwell Lyte, p. 87.

In the *Calendar of Documents relating to Scotland*, this £100 is mentioned.—

'The K. to Master Thomas de Hunsingouere. Writ of "dedimus potestatem" to receive the attorneys of Dervergulla de Balliol and Thomas Randolf, in the plea before the K.'s justices itinerant at York, between the said Dervergulla, Thomas, Hugh de Eure, and Stephen, parson of the Church of Midford, executors of John de Balliol's testament, and Alan son of the Earl (fiz le Cunte), regarding a debt of £100 claimed by the executors from Alan. Gloucester, 4ᵗʰ April, 8ᵗʰ of his reign.'

Edward I. appears to have been anxious on many occasions to render assistance to Dervorguilla, or at least to show a friendly spirit towards her. Little instances of his good will are discovered, here and there, amid the mass of Scottish documents preserved for history.—

'The K. wishing to do a special favour to Dervergulla widow of John de Balliol, grants to her for this turn, freedom from common summonses of the justices errant in the counties where her lands lie, both common pleas, and of the forest.'[1]

And, Oct. 7. 1285. 'The K. notwithstanding the statute against mortmain, wishing to do a special favour to Dervergulla widow of John de Balliol, grants leave to her to give a messuage in the suburb

' *Patent.*   8. Edw. I. m. 5.

of Oxford to the Master and Scholars studying in the House of Balliol there, *in perpetuum.*'[1]

Somewhere about 1288, we find that among the goods arrested for the King of Scotland's debt to John 'le Macune,' the goods of 'the Lady de Baylloll, and some others to the value of £10 in the realm of Scotland were arrested, and by the King's writ were entirely delivered.'

There is a curious deed, which will interest Oxford readers, for it tells us how Headington reapers were paid in those days; and reminds us of the pennies due to St. Mary Magdalen's Church.—

' Inquisition . [in virtue of writ, dated Bristol, 29th December previous, directed to the Sheriff of Oxford], made by Robert de Heyford [and 11 others] jurors of the hundred outside of the north gate of Oxford, who say that the Lady Dervergulla widow of John de Balliol, may enfeoff Master Walter de Foderingeye and his Fellows, Scholars of the House of Balliol, Oxford, Students, of a messuage in the suburb of Oxford; that it consists of three fees, united by the purchase of John de O., one whereof was William Burge's and owes 1*d.* of annual rent at the F. of St. Martin, and 1*d.* of hidage at " Hocke-dai," and the service of a day in August to reap at Hedindon, worth 1*d.* Another fee was John le Wepere's, and owes 4*d.* of annual rent at the F. of

[1] *Patent*, 13 Edw. I. m. 3.

G

St. Martin, and 2*d.* of hidage at " Hockedai," and
suit of hundred from 3 weeks to 3 weeks. That
suit may be redeemed yearly for 12*d.* It also owes
a day's service to make hay in Northam, value 1*d.*
and the service of a man reaping for a day in August
at Hedindon, value 1*d.* Also 4*d.* to the high Altar
in the Church of the Blessed Mary Magdalene. The
third fee was Nicholas de Kingeston's, wherein he
enfeoffed John de Eu with Johanna his daughter in
frank marriage, and it owes no service. The whole
tenement is held *in capite* of the K. *Note,* that the
suit of the hundred aforesaid is due at three terms,
viz. when the K.'s writ comes to be pleaded in the
hundred—when a robber is to be tried in the hundred
—and when they are summoned to enclose the court
for trial. Thus should the suit be held. And if
they neither attend nor make essoin, they must not
be heavily amerced. The jurors append their seals.
Dated at Oxford, on the morrow of Epiphany, in
the 13th year. [seals gone.]' [1]

To Oxford people several of the names in this
deed will be familiar ; and the thoughts of many
will turn quickly, from the people mentioned, to the
modern localities which bear their names. On rising
ground, just beyond Iffley, is the pretty country
house, known as '*Heyford* Hill,' which looks
down upon the river and Kennington Island ; and

' *Inq.* p. m. 13. Edw I. No. 127.

on the other side of Oxford, is the well known
'*Kingston* Road,' a rather important Street, with its
row of fancy cottages. 'Hedindon' is unmistak-
able; and when we find, in the College Archives,
deeds witnessed by Robert de Wormenhale, Thomas
Wormenhale, and Adam de Chisilhampton ; and in
one deed a shop described as 'next to the shop of
Nicholas de Gersingdone ;' we stop for one minute
to wonder, whether these men originally took their
names from the near hamlets, or whether from a
cluster of huts round the landowners' homes have
grown the picturesque Villages, which help to make
the near neighbourhood of Oxford so especially
beautiful.

Two more of the many Balliol deeds must be
spoken of here, because of their historical interest.
In one, we find Hugh de Balliol, 'son and heir of
the late Sir John de Balliol,' acknowledging that he
owes the sum of 10 marks sterling to his father's
executors, for two horses bought of them. He pro-
mises to pay the 10 marks at 'Foderinghe,' before
Pentecost, 1289, on pain of ecclesiastical censure.
The other is 'a Latin deed, on parchment, somewhat injured by damp; whereby John de Balliol,
son of John de Balliol, having seen the writing of
feoffment and of perpetuation of the House of the
Scholars of Balliol in Oxford, confirms the same.
It has a small seal attached. There is another and

a very similar, deed, in the archives of the College, attested by the same witnesses, but written in another hand.   In this latter John de Balliol is called "son and heir" of John de Balliol; it being evidently executed after his elder brother, Hugh's, death.   This last-mentioned deed has only a fragment of its seal. Hugh Gobyun ["Gubyun" in the second deed], and Robert Bertrain of Bothale ["Bottalle" in the second deed] are among the witnesses.   There is no date to either; but, having the same witnesses, they were probably executed within a few days of each other.'[1]

This John de Balliol was Dervorguilla's youngest son; the same John de Balliol, Lord of Galloway, who claimed the Scottish throne, and was by Edward I. adjudged King of Scotland, in right of his descent from her.   Yet when Balliol tried to assert the judicial independence of his kingdom, Edward marched into Scotland, and then followed the fall of Berwick, and the terrible massacre, which did not cease until a procession of Priests carried the Sacred Host into the King's presence, and prayed for mercy. Then Edward burst into tears, and called his troops off; but the slaughter had done its work, and the Town was ruined for ever.   Balliol made one more effort for the freedom of his people; but his attempt was fruitless, and he had to implore peace, and promise submission.   'Edward disdained to treat with

---

[1] *Hist. MSS. Com.* Fourth Report, p. 446.

him in person, but informed him, that he intended, within fifteen days, to advance to Brechin ; and that on Balliol's repairing to the castle there, the Bishop of Durham would announce the decision of his lord superior. This was none other than that of an absolute resignation of himself and his kingdom to the mercy of his conqueror ; to which Balliol, now the mere shadow of a king, without a crown, an army, or a nobility, dejectedly submitted. In presence of the Bishop of Durham and the barons of England, he was first stript of his royal robes ; after which they spoiled him of his crown and sceptre, and compelled him, standing as a criminal, with a white rod in his hand, to perform a humiliating feudal penance. . . . . After this humiliating ceremony, Balliol delivered his eldest son, Edward, to the King of England, as a hostage for his future fidelity ; and this youth, along with his discrowned father, were soon after sent by sea to London, where they remained for three years in confinement in the Tower.'[1]

The Scots, however, still continued to regard John de Balliol as their rightful King. Philip of France tried to make it one of the articles of his truce with Edward, that Balliol should be released from prison ; but this Edward refused. Afterwards, at the request of Pope Boniface, the King consented to deliver Balliol from his imprisonment in the

[1] *Hist. Scotland*, Tytler, vol. i. p. 118.

Her body was brought in state to Sweetheart Abbey. There is no trace of her tomb remaining now; but tradition says that she was buried near to the High Altar.

About Sweetheart Abbey, we read,—

' SWEETHEART (*Abbacia Dulcis-cordis*), in Galloway, called by Lesly *Suavi-cordium*, was an abbey, founded in the thirteenth century, by Dervorgilla, daughter to Alan lord of Galloway, niece to David earl of Huntington, and spouse to John Baliol, lord of Castlebernard, who died in the year 1269, and was here buried. Andrew Winton, prior of Lochleven, informs us, that after his death his lady caused take out his heart, and spice and embalm it, and putting it in a box of ivory, bound with silver, and enamelled, closed it solemnly in the walls of the church, near to the high altar; from whence it had the name of Sweetheart, which was afterwards changed into that of New Abbey.

' The first abbot of this place was Henry, who died in his journey to Citeaux in the year 1219. He was succeeded by " Ericus magister Conversorum ejusdem domus." Afterwards, John abbot of this place swears fealty to Edward Langshanks in the year 1296, according to *Prynne*, p. 552, and he is there designed "Johan abbé de Doux-quer." There is a charter by another John abbot of this place, dated at New Abbey, the 23d October 1528, and granting "Cuthberto Broun de Cairn, in emphyteosim, totas et integras quatuor mercatas terrarum de Corbully, in baronia sua de Lokendolo, infra senescallatum de Kirkcudbright ; reddendo annuatim summam octo mercarum usualis monetae regni Scotiae, ad duos anni terminos, viz. Pentecostes, et Sancti Martini in hyeme."

' Gilbert Brown, descended of the family of Garsluith, is among the monks that assent thereto. He was the last abbot of this abbey. Calderwood, in his History informs us that he sat in Parliament the 17th August 1560, whilst the Confession of Faith was approved ; and in the year 1605, he was apprehended by the Lord Cranston, captain of the guards appointed for the borders, and was sent to Blackness, and after some days was transported to the castle of Edinburgh, where he was kept until his departure out of the kingdom. He died at Paris, 14th May 1612. Sir Robert Spotiswood, president of the Session, and secretary of State to King Charles I., was designed Lord New-Abbey, being then in possession of this dissolved abbey.' [1]

---

[1] *Religious Houses in Scotland*, Spottiswoode, p. 424.

CHAPTER V.

In reading the account of the ' Buildings ' of Balliol College, given by Antony à Wood, in his *History of the Colleges and Halls in Oxford*, we have to bear in mind that he wrote about the College as it was two hundred and twenty years ago ; and, in following his description of the buildings, we must forget for a time the quite modern Balliol, and try to realize the front quadrangle, and the garden quadrangle, and the different buildings, as they were in those days. With the exception of the change made when the new dining hall was built at the north end of the garden, and the old dining hall made into a Library and Reading Room for the Undergraduates, the general plan of the College has remained the same ; though the many new buildings, near to the back gate and the hall, have added considerably to its size, and to its structural importance.

Balliol College, almost the oldest foundation in Oxford, has none of its original walls and rooms remaining ; but the ground-plan of those buildings, and also the outlines of the various plots of ground belonging to them, have been preserved. Merton College, a foundation as old as Balliol, or even older, can point to its beautiful Chapel, which, 'if not erected before the Founder's death, was erected immediately afterwards, perhaps under the direction of his executors, out of his residuary bequest to the College;'[1] and to the dining hall, 'of which the main walls have been preserved in subsequent restorations.'[1] Worcester College can show, on the south side of the quadrangle, the quaint old lodgings, with their original doorways, and separate roofs, which were Cells to different Benedictine Abbeys. Worcester Undergraduates, even now, inhabit the very rooms lived in by Monks, who came from St. Albans, and from Abingdon, and from other Benedictine Houses, to study at Oxford. Over the doorways are still the arms, now worn and defaced, of the Monasteries. Yet we recognize the Cross of Norwich, and the Griffin of Malmesbury. And very old, also, is the magnificent Chapter-room at Christ Church, formerly belonging to the Augustinian Canons of St. Frideswide; and now used as vestry to the Cathedral. At St. John's College, men still pass under the square tower, where, on a niche, high up, is the old Statue of St. Bernard, placed there when the College was Cistercian, and the Monks followed the teaching of their great Master-Saint.

---

[1] *Memorials of Merton College*, Brodrick, p. 13.

St. John's men dine to-day in an hall, the walls of
which formed the Monks' refectory. But the original
buildings of Balliol, unimportant and unsubstantial,
as they probably were, only served their time ; and
the College can now show nothing older than the
Library. There is some doubt about the first Chapel,
or Oratory ; but all evidence seems to prove that it
was the large hall, which is now the Master's dining
room. If this be so, the walls are probably the
original Chapel walls, built about the year 1293.

The following description of the ' Buildings ' of
Balliol College is taken, word for word, and letter
for letter, from the original manuscript of Antony à
Wood (the one written in double column) now kept in
the Bodleian Library. The edition, by John Gutch,
of Antony à Wood's *History and Antiquities of the
Colleges and Halls in the University of Oxford*,
which is the ordinary and well-known copy of Wood's
writings about Oxford, differs from the manuscript
in some slight particulars ; and, in many instances, it
destroys the beautiful simplicity, and the attractive
quaintness of Antony à Wood's style.

Passing over all that he says about the foundation of the College, we come to—

' The firſt place then yᵗ this Society inhabited,
was old Balliol hall before mentioned, on yᵉ ground
of wᶜʰ yᵗ late building was erected, wᶜʰ is now called
Hammonds Lodgings, afterwards yᵉ Lady Deruorguill

remoued them to Maries hall, wch stood where y^e
S.W. Corner of ye Colledge quadrangle now ſtands,
& on w^{ch} & ye 3 acres of land adioyning, wch she
purchased as before is deliued, she added & built
seuall conuenient places, as refectory kitchen out-
houses & walkes, afterwards were added these
seuall plotts of ground, viz two plotts in Horsemonger ſtreet, one of wch lay betweene ye land of y^e
house of Balliol, wch I suppose was y^t belonging to
Maries hall wch was on ye W. side of ye said plott,
& ye land of John le Slatter of Ensham on ye eaſt, &
ye other plot layd between ye land somtimes of ye said
Jo: le Slatter & ye land of John de Sewy ; both w^{ch}
being conueyed by John ye Son & heir of Walter
Feteplace, to Mr Tho: de Heworth & Mr Tho: de
Pontfraict Clerks & fellowes of this Society 31. Ed. I.
a° 1303 were by them soone after giuen & conueyed
to ye Colledge : ye next two plotts y^t were added,
joyned to ye other two on ye eaſt side, & reacht to ye land
of ye Monks of Durham, wch is ye now entrance or
alley leading to Trinity, somtimes Durham, Colledge,
conueyed to ye house of Balliol by Gilb^t de Pontfraict
& Tho: de Humbleton (fellowes then or before of y^e
same house) 4. Ed. 2. 1310 . hauing before obtained
them of John le Feteplace Burgeſſe of Oxōn : ye 3^d
peice of Ground was St Margarets hall lying between old & new Balliol hall, conueyed to ye said
house or hall by William de Brockelesby & Tho: de

Caue clerks somtimes fellowes therof 16. Ed. 3.
1342, soe y^t ye said land being ₚcured (besides another portion wch extended from ye way leading unð
ye eaſt end of Magdalen Church to ye land of y^e
Monks of Durham to enlarge their walkes, wch was
conuey ed by John ye son & heire of Geffry le
Sawcer burgesse of Oxōn, to Walt: de Foderingey
ye firſt Principall & Will: de Bonkis clerk & fellow
a^o 1291 . or therabouts) wch now containes all y^e
front of ye Colledge & ye void peice of ground on y^e
W. side (on wch stood St Margarets hall) & moſt
of ye Land behind ye said front (wch reached to y^t portion beforementioned, bought of Joh: le Sawcer w^{ch}
was as a head land to it) ye Colledge enlarged their
buildings for ye reception of their Students (hauing
soe many y^t they were forced to lodge in halls or
Hostles adioyning) but after such a way void of all
Vniformity, notwithſtanding ye Coll: had Benefactours
towards them, y^t some being pulled downe in y^e
raigne of H. 6. most part of ye present quadrangle
was built ; as firſt ye eaſt part by seuall of ye nobility
(as I suppose) y^t had bin nursed up here, among
wch was Georg Neuill Archbishop of York, whose
arēs as I remember are in one or more of ye windowes
looking eaſtward : ye North part (excepting y^e
chapple) was, (some of it) built then, & some afterwards, as I shall shew when I come to speak of y^e
library, wch taketh up ye cheif part of y^t side ; ye weſt

side wch containeth part of ye lodgings belonging to
ye Mafter, Buttery and refectory or Coṁon hall,
was built with ye moneys of William Grey Bishop of
Ely Georg Neuill Archbishop of York & others as
their armes on ye stone walls & in ye windows of
ye said buildings doe shew ; and ye South part wch is
ye forefront of ye College was not built till ye time of
H. 7. to w^ch, w^t benefactours were numbred, I cannot yet discouer, unleff Mr. Will: Bell who was then
Mafter was one, for on ye top of ye tower ouer y^e
gate, are carued in stone under ye ridge wch parts y^e
upper chamber and roofe 2 bells & another at ye top
of ye Taƀnacular work ouer ye pedeftall arguing y^t y^e
said will: Bell was either a Benefactor to y^t building,
or else y^t ye cheifeft part was erected in his time,
though began in his prædiceffors Rob: Abdy, who
ɡbably might be a Benefactour also as he was to
this library.

   ' soe much for those buildings y^t are now for y^e
most part imployed as lodgings for ye Master, Fellows
& Scolars ; as for ye other places viz ye Chapples
hall & Library with those matters to be obserued of
& in them, I shall speak of in order, and firft for y^e
chappells or places wherin ye Society haue celebrated Seruice & ye memories dayly of their pious
Benefactours, haue bin seũall ; ye first was in an
Isle adioyning S. Marie Magdalens Church, in whose
parish ye Colledge is situated.   Y^e 2^d in an Oratory

dedicated to St Katherine wch was built by ye Society about ye year 1293 with ye moneys cheifly of ye Lady Deruorgill wch she left at ye time of her death ; for then viz a^o 1293 as it appears from record the fellowes or Scolars pcured license of Oliuer Bishop of Lyncolne, y^t they might noe more celebrate seruice in their parish church but in ye Oratorie built within their owne Colledge soe y^t they visited ye said church on ye greater Solemnities of ye year as othor students were obliged to doe to ye churches of those parishes wherin they liued, in wch license noe pmission was allowed them for ye Celebrating ye Sacraments wch was ye matter they cheifly desired, not onely as a great conuenience, but also an aduantage to them, though afterwards granted by ye authority of ye pope : in this Chapple (by ye name of St Katherines Chapple) did Mr Hugh Warkenby & Mr Will: de Gotham (whome I haue mentioned before) setle a chapleine with maintenance for him issuing out of of seūall meffuages in Scooleftreet. 4 Ed. 2. a^o 1310 wherby y^t duty y^t lay upon ye fellowes or scolars was then taken off. Afterwards ye Colledge being minded to make ye said chapple more elegant or rather erect another (hauing bin incouraged therto by Benefactours,) one Adam le Poleter Burgeffe of Redyng who had deliūed 20^{li} into ye hands of Nicholas de Querppelad Abbot of ye monastery at y^t place to be bestowed by him on pious vses for ye health of

ye said Adams soule was by ye said Abbot at y^c in-
treaty of certaine persons giuen to ye said Colledge
a^o 1327 for ye building of ye chapple of St Katherine
there, with 10 marks of his owne, a glaffe window
worth 10^li, & some timber besides at ye same time, with
a desire alsoe y^t w^t he had done, might be recorded
y^t twas not his vtmost charity to ye world but
had intentions for more & greater : and now as y^c
Colledge who had before obtained license from Oliuer
Bishop of Lyncolne to celebrate diuine offices within
their owne oratory because of ye frequency of disputations & lectures wch hindred them from attending diuine offices in ye parish Church, & ye same
obtained from & appued by his succeffors John Dal-
darby Hen: Burwash & Thomas Becke as appeares
in a writing under ye seal of ye said Thomas A^o d.
1346. soe also was ye like license upon ye same conditions as ye former were, granted by Joh: Boking-
ham Bishop of Lyncoln a^o 1368. in wch their oratory
is ftiled a chapple & in none of those going before,
but as in ye former there was a tacit soe in this laft
license an expreffe exception of administring y^e
Sacraments ; in wch ye Society acquiesced till upon
their petition, Pope Vrban 6. in ye 2 year of his pontificate granted license to performe ye same.

' This Chaple or Oratory whersoever it stood I
know not (though there be not wanting some of this
house y^t say it was ye larg hall two story high be-

H

longing to ye Master (w^ch, as is before said was built in Bishop Greys time, as his armes cut in stone under ye great Bay-window looking eaftward, shews,) wch cannot agree with y^t deliůed before concerning ye chapple because ye said hall was built in H. 6. his time) continued in vse till ye raigne of H. 8. & then this comely & decent chapple wch now stands on ye N. side of ye Quadrangle was built : / it was begun in ye 13 year of ye said Kings raigne 1521 & compleatly finished 1529 to wch diůs Benefactors freely gave, but w^t their names were I know not, as for those y^t gaue ye windowes are from ye inscriptions therin apparent as they thus follow

· In ye Eaft window (wherin is represented in liuely Colours ye paffion resurrection & ascension of Christ, for wch Nich: Wadham offered 200^li to make an Eaft window for his Colledge chapple) is this written

Orate pro anima m^ñ Laurentij Stubs Sacre Theologie Profefforis et istius Collegij specialis Benefactoris qui hanc fenestram procurauit sumptibus suis A^o.D. MDXXIX.

· Vnder ye said inscription is ye effigies of ye said Laur. Stubs kneeling before a deske, with his crowne tonsured and Doctorall formalities on him . & on each side these armes or rather rebuses belonging to his name.

Ar. a trunk or stump or stub . of a tree couped

& eradicated pp peirced through with an arrow in feſſe of yᵉ 1ˢᵗ.

S. on a cheu : ingrail'd betweene 2 lylyes & a phæon ar : 3 lyons faces B. on a cheif G. 2 keys in Saltire betw : 2 like trunks of trees. o.

'In yᵉ firſt or upper window on yᵉ N. side of y
    chapple, this at yᵉ bottome

Mr. Tho : Leson hanc fenestram vitrari fecit An. D. 1530.

'his picture is there also kneeling as Laur Stubs is, with shaued Crowne & formalityes on.

'in yᵉ 2ᵈ· window

Thomas . . . . Dʳ et subdecanus Eboracensis hanc fenestram vitrari fecit an. dni 1530.

'his picture is there as Tho : Lesons is.

'in yᵉ 3ᵈ· window

Mʳ Johañes Hygdon S. T. Dʳ et olim Collegij Magdalenensis P'ſses hanc feneſtram vitrari fecit Ano Dñi 1530.

'his picture is there also as yᵗ in yᵉ 2ᵈ window.

'in ye 4. window.

Rich : Atkins Armiger Com : Glouc : et huius Collegij socio Com : D.D.

'painted by Abr : Vanling an. 1637.

'In yᵉ upper or firſt window on yᵉ South side

where is yᵉ martyrdome of Sᵗ Katherine liuely represented, is this inscription.

Opus pium Magistri Laurentij Stubbs Sacre Theologie profefforis et Magistri Ricardi Stubbs Sacre Theologie Bacalaurei et huius Collegij Magistri et Benefactoȓ suoȓ. An. Dñi MDXXIX. vndneath wᶜʰ inscription wᶜʰ runs through yᵉ middle of yᵉ window, are yᵉ pictures of yᵉ said Laur : & Rich Stubbs kneeling againſt Deskes with their formalities on them & their armes as before by them.

'in yᵉ 2ᵈ window.

Petrus Wentworth sacræ Theologiæ profefforis et huius Collegij Soc : D.D. 1637.

'in yᵉ 3ᵈ window

Willelmus Compton miles cum pia consorte sua hanc fenestram vitrari fecit A᷄ dñi 1530.
ouer wᶜʰ inscription are yᵉ pictures of yᵉ said sʳ Will : & his Lady kneeling, with their childrē behind them & their armes on & between, them, wᶜʰ being already represented in a copper cut by another hand I shall omitt any further speaking of them.

' The next place to be veiwed is yᵉ hall wᶜʰ as I haue said before was built with moneys of Bish Grey, Archb : Neuill & Tho. Chace somtimes Master of this place & afterwards Chancellour of yᵉ Vniu̇sitie & others ; in yᵉ windows of wᶜʰ were

lately these armes, viz those belonging to y^e
Vniũsitie & this Colledge, then Tho : Chaces w^{ch}
are Ar: a cheuron betweene 3 Talbots heads erased
sab : & another borne by the Citty of York wch is
Ar. on a crosse G. 5 lyons passant gardant or, all
wch with diuers more hauing bin anciently set up
& afterwards defaced, were renewed as I suppose
in Dr Lawrence his time.

      ' on y^e Wainscot these

a lyon rampant within a Bordure charged with flowers
de liz.

   ' 3. Bells belonging either to Mr Will or Dr Joh.
Bell in whose times & by whose money pbably y^e
Wainscot was at firſt set up

impaled $\begin{cases} \text{party p pale on a cheu : p pale 2} \\ \text{lyons Combatant on a cheif 3} \\ \text{mullets} \\ \text{a lyon ramp : crowned} \end{cases}$

Quart: $\begin{cases} \text{France} \\ \text{\&} \\ \text{Engl.} \end{cases}$

  ' Soe much for y^e hall, as for y^e library (wch is reputed one of y^e beſt in Oxon y^t are priuat, if y^n haue
a regard to its building, beautifull windows y^t are not
too light, & other conueniences) it was built by
seũall persons, viz y^e lower or west part containing
half of it, was built by ye aforesaid Dr Tho Chace a°
1431; & ye vpper half by m^r Rob. Abdy, som-

times Mafter of this house about ye year 1477 assisted therin by ye moneys of W. Grey Bishop of
Ely, wch part of Chaces being finisht, as also yt of
Abdyes, ye said Bishop inriched it with choice &
pretious Manuscripts amounting to ye number of
about 200 (I speak at ye leaft) on moft of wch if not
all, his armes painted on velame, were faftned, &
defended by peices of cleer horne nayled ouer them:
ye said Exemplars it seems or at leaft moft part of
them, were by him bought and procured among those
seuall libraryes wch he purchased as well in England
as in Italy, for there in his trauells viz at Florence
Venice & other places, he spared neither labour
nor coft to pcure them, wch after seuerall years of Collection, (rather for his country sake, then himselfe)
freely gaue them upon ye enlargment of this library
by ye aforesaid Rob: Abdy; but alas with resent-
ment let it be spoken, diuers of them wch smelt of
supftition or yt treated of Schoole diuinity or of
Geometry or Astronomie, were pillaged in yt wicked
& pilfering age wherin H. 8. & Ed. 6. ruled, as
for ye reft yt remained, wch, with ye former had their
initiall & great letters limned with much Curiosity
& their Margins some of them painted with seuall
fancies & deeked with diuers sorts of flowers, (wch
was cheifly performed by yt Exquisite painter
Antonius Marius ye son one of ye cheif of his pro-
feffion in Italy while this noble Bishop was there)

haue bin by Idle childish & impertinent people
either cut out or shamefully abused, such hathe bin
ye negligence of those y^t were obliged by oath to
take care of them : w^t other Benefactours this library
hath had, haue bin many & those cheifly y^t were
fellowes or students of this house, but their gifts w^{ch}
were books, hauing bin inconsidable, I shall omitt
them, yet I must not escape ye Benefaction of
y^t learned Doctour Thom : Gascoigne somtimes
Chancellour of ye Vniŭsitie, who gaue seuerall MSS
(as in their fronts appeares ;) & moneys towards
its building time, a certaine historian saith was of
this Coll., & some therof y^t he was Fellow, as he
is by y^t title stiled in ye Regester of Benefactours to
this library wch was of late made & written ; but
hauing not yet seene any thing therof in y^e
M-S-S by him giuen or in ye glaffe-windowes of this
library wch were put up in & a few years after, his
time, or in any other writing (besides ye said regefter)
belonging to ye College or any other place I cannot
as yet consent to them knowing very well from
record y^t he had spent 20 years & aboue as a commoner in Oriell Colledge ; next after him, finding
none y^t haue scarce merited ye name of Benefactours
(except Dr Joh : Warner somtimes of this house &
afterwards of Allsoules Coll. who gaue 20^{li} 1564.)
notwithstanding seŭall there haue bin y^t haue giuen
bookes) I must descend to ye raigne of K. James

for then ye most reuerend Dr Georg Abbots Archb:
of Canterbury expended diũs sũms in repairing it &
enlarging ye number of Bookes A^o. 1619 after it had
laid in a carlesse manner from ye beginning of ye reformation of religion or rather before to y^t time.

'The next matters y^t I should take notice of
here are those inscriptions & uerses in ye windows
wch tell us of those y^t firſt put them up, ye builders
of ye library, & benefactours to ye house, neatly
written in old English letters in scrolls winding with
great variety about those armes in each light of
most of ye windows wch belong partly to ye putters
up of those windows but cheifly to ye speciall Benefactours of ye Coll: ; but because there is false metre
& gramer in diuers of ye said verses wch are in
Rithme according to ye humour of y^t age wherin
they were set up, viz in ye raigne of H. 6. u^n of[1]
lower part & in Ed: 4. u^n [1] ye upp part of ye library
was built I shall omitt ye inserting of them here as
also ye blazoning of most part of ye armes, & only
repeat y^e inscriptions ; for if I should take notice of
all, they would without doub proue tædious to y^e
reaď.

'In y^e Eaſt or upper window therfore w^{ch}
looketh into y^e chapple, is y^e picture of St Katherine
y^e Patronesse of this Colledge standing with her

---

[1] Probably meant for $w^n y$, and w^n.

wheele by her & before her yᵉ pictures of yᵉ afor-
said Dr. Tho: Chace & 9 fellowes kneeling, hauing
their Crownes shauen and formalities on them with
these verses ouer them :

> Hic tibi dans celis Thomam Chace concomitantes
> Hanc patrona uelis munire domum famulantes.

in wᶜʰ window at yᵉ top are yᵉ arēs of France &
England quartered. & at yᵉ bottome, yᵉ Colledges &
yᵉ sᵈ Tho: Chaces wᶜʰ are mentioned before in yᵉ hall.

' on yᵉ North side of yᵉ library.

' 1ˢᵗ window there, was giuen by mʳ Rob. Abdy as yᵉ
verse about his armes in yᵉ firſt light thereof ſheweth,
wᶜʰ are Ar: a cheuron betweene 3. Eagles displayed
sab. in yᵉ 2ᵈ light are bishop Greys armes (yᵉ same yᵗ
yᵉ Lords Grey of Wark are) with another verse
riming to yᵗ about R. Abdyes armes, telling us yᵗ he
gaue diũs books to this library & in yᵉ lower
diuision of yᵉ firſt light this inscription following

> Orate pro bono statu et anima
> Magistri Roħti Abdy Magistri
> huius Collegij qui istam partem
> Bibliothece construxit. anⁿ . . .

' 2ᵈ window giuen by Ralph Stanhop, fellow of
this house, in yᵉ 2ᵈ light of wᶜʰ are yᵉ armes of Erds-
wick & Stafford impaled set up later then yᵉ other
armes with this written under them.

> Thomas Erdswicke et Margar;
> Stafford Anⁿ Dni 1338,

' 5. window by John Spens where there is an Orate for him, besides ye verses wch tell us y^t Rob. Abdy & Bish: Grey pfected this library

' 6 window by 2. Bishops, but w^t their names were I know not.   ye armes therin are these.

Ar. 3 batunes in crosse sab. skirlaw B. of Durhā sab. a crosse ingrailed & a cressant in ye firſt quarter Erm:

' 7. Window by Hen: peircy E. of Northum-ƀland & Rich: Neuill Earl of Warwick

' 8. by Will: Ferbit

' 9. not expreſſed by whome giuen unleſſ y^o may collect it from ye verses therin wh^{ch} run thus

Has aliquando fores vitro Clausere priores
claustri Mertone . . . Mercede Corone.

' 10. Window by Gilb. Botilbery & John Maluerne somtiēs students in this house ye laſt of whome was D.D. & chapleyne therof about ye beginning of Ed. 4.

' Thus farre concerning ye library y^t now ſtands, w^t ye Coll: had before I find little or noe mention, they reposing their books in it, only soe farr y^t seuerall y^t had bin Oxford Scolars left in their wills books to ye Coll without any mention of a library viz among ye reſt was m^r Simon de Bredon ye worthieſt mathematician of his time who aᵒ 1372, left seuall books of Aftronomie & Mathematicks therto.   Will Rede Bishop of Chiceftre, 10 books, cˢ in money & one siluer cup 1382 & Roger whelpdale Bishop of Carlile Sᵗ Aufte de Ciuitate dei 1422.'

being confirmed at the same time by Thomas de
Ewe, son of the said John, did (after licence was
obtained from the King) give the same year, in the
month of May, the said tenement with three acres of
land on the east and north sides of it to Walter de
Foderyngey the Principal, and Scholars of the
House of Balliol, to settle themselves therein as a
perpetual mansion for them and their successors.
Which tenement the Lady Dervorgille afterwards
repairing, and joining to it necessary edifices, the
said Principal and Scholars removed from the tenement belonging to the University, (which from their
abode therein was afterwards called Old Balliol
Hall) to that which she purchased of John de Ewe,
soon after called New Balliol Hall.   So that nothing
now being wanting but a formal Foundation to settle
her Scholars, and this their House to them for ever,
and also allot them lands whereby they might be
sustained, did the same year, in the presence of
Anthony Bishop of Durham, Oliver, Bishop of
Lincoln, Mr. Roger Rowell Chancellor of this
University, and Simon de Gandavo, Archdeacon of
Oxford, and several knights and other persons, give
it with lands in Stamfordham, or Stanworthham, and
Howgh in the county of Northumberland, (purchased
by her husband's executors) to them and their
successors for ever.   And this she did, as in the
Charter itself is said, to the honour of the Holy

Trinity, Virgin Mary, and St. Catherine the martyr;
and that also the charity which her husband had
begun in Oxford ("ubi viget studium generale," as
'tis there said) might be settled and continued.

' Furthermore also that the said foundation might
stand firm against all opposition, it was, upon the
Foundress's desire, confirmed the said year by the
said Oliver, Bishop of Lincoln, and by her son Sir
John Balliol, afterwards King of the Scots, and
three years after, viz. 1287, (all which time her good
work ceased not, but trod on her heels even to
heaven gates) did with her husband's executors,
make a release to the said Principal and Scholars of
all debts between them from the beginning of the
world to that time.'[1]

The College being thus established by Dervorguilla, one of the first Benefactors to it was Hugh
de Vienne, who gave a soke of land, and several
houses, in the parish of St. Laurence, in the Jewry,
London, together with the advowson of the Church
of St. Laurence. The history of this soke of land,
and the advowson of the Church, is rather complicated. The College still preserves many interesting
and valuable documents, which relate to it; but only
the more important ones will be given here.

The earliest is a large parchment deed, which is
a model of beautiful and legible writing, in the old,

---

[1] *Antony à Wood*, ed. Gutch, vol. iii. pp. 73, 74.

abbreviated Latin.   It bears no date; but, judging from the dates on the other documents of the same period, and also relating to St. Laurence, Jewry, this deed must have been executed about the year 1180. The deed is in good preservation, and the two large seals attached to it are almost perfect.   It is a Grant from Robert, Abbot of St. Salvius, at Montreuil, to John of St. Laurence, in these words :—

'Sciant praesentes et futuri quod ego Robertus Abbas Sancti Salvii et Sancti Guingualoei de Monsteriolo et totus ejusdem Ecclesiae conventus concessimus et dedimus Johanni de Sancto Laurentio, clerico nostro, in perpetuam eleemosynam Ecclesiam beati Laurentii de Londoniis cum omni redditu quae habemus in civitate Londoniarum scilicet lx et xij solidos et vi denarios; de terra quam Guillelmus filius Isabel tenet de nobis viij solidos, et de terra quam Alulphus filius Fromundi tenet de nobis v solidos, et de terra quam Guillelmus Senex tenet de nobis viij solidos, et de terra quam haeredes Petri filii Galteri tenent de nobis vij solidos, de terra quam Gillebertus, cisor, tenet de nobis iiij solidos, de terra quam Philippus Sellarius tenet de nobis iiij solidos, de terra quam Radulphus de Winton tenet iiij solidos, de terra quam Aaron Judaeus tenet iiij solidos, de terra quam Rogerus Illefostre tenet iiij solidos, de terra quam Alwinus Finke tenet xviij denarios. Habendam et tenendam de nobis libere et honorifice

omnibus diebus vitae suae pro 4 marcis ad majus
pondus singulis annis ad Nativitatem Sancti Johannis Baptistae reddendis.   Et Johannes juravit quod
redditum praedictum non alienabit pro posse suo ab
Ecclesia nostra.   Et si forte Dominus Abbas vel ejus
nuntius in Angliam pro censu venerit, procurabit eum
praedictus Johannes per duos dies et quam diu ibidem pro defectu iiij praedictarum marcarum moram
fecerit ad sumptum praenominati Johannis erit.
Nisi vero Johannes praesens fuerit, procurator suus
de censu respondebit.   Ut autem haec concessio et
donatio nostra rata habeatur illam sigillorum nostrorum auctoritate confirmavimus et corroboravimus.
His testibus, Domino Baldvino priore, Remigio,
Nicholao, Hugone de Bernivule, Symone Petro,
Johanne, Alelmo, monachis, et toto capitulo ejusdem
Ecclesiae et Magistro Gilleberto, Giroldo, et Lau-
rentio et Fulcone presbyteris, Petro clerico, Guillelmo
nepote Domini Abbatis, Guillelmo filio Ysabel,
Alulfo filio Fromundi, Guillelmo Sene, Johanne filio
Roberti, Galfrido Blondo, Eustachio Mercerio,
Rogero clerico, et multis aliis.'

[*Abstract.*—Robert, Abbot of St. Salvius and
St. Winwaloe, of Montreuil, and the Convent, grants
to John of St. Laurence, ' our Clerk,' in perpetual
alms, the Church of St. Laurence, and the rents
which we have in London, held by his House, viz.
72*s.* and 6*d.*, from land which William, son of Isabel

holds of them, ..., he paying yearly 4 marks at the Nativity of St. John the Baptist. Witnesses : Baldwin, the Prior ; Remigius, Nicholas, Hugh de Bernivule, Symon Peter, John, Alelmus, Monks ; and the whole Chapter of the said Church. And Masters Gillebert, Girold, Laurence, and Fulke, Priests. Peter, the Clerk ; William, the Abbot's nephew ; William, son of Isabel ; Alulf, son of Fromund ; William Senex ; John, son of Robert ; Geoffrey ' Blondo ' ; Eustace, mercer ; Roger, the Clerk ; and many others.]

The next deed to this, in order of date, is a very small parchment document, very finely and carefully written, in angular and distinct letters, with clear abbreviations. It reads thus :—

' Omnibus ad quos praesentes litterae venerint Amalricus Dei Gratia Abbas totusque Conventus beati Salvii de Monsteriolo salutem et orationes devotas in Christo. Universitati vestrae notum facimus quod ad preces dilecti nostri viri venerabilis Johannis de Sancto Laurentio, canonici Sancti Pauli, Londoniis, de communi assensu, concessimus Willelmo Clerico suo redditus nostros et Ecclesiam nostram de Londoniis quiete quamdiu vixerit possidendos per sexaginta solidos legitimorum sterlingorum quos proinde nobis annuatim tenetur reddere in Nativitate beati Johannis Baptistae. Et post decessum ejusdem Willelmi Ecclesia ipsa et redditus praedicti ad manum nostram liberi revertentur. In cujus rei testimonium praesentes litteras sigillorum nostrorum appensione signamus. Actum anno gratiae M.CC. octavodecimo. Mense Februari.'

[*Abstract.*—Amalric, the Abbot, and the Convent of St. Salvius, of Montreuil, at the prayer of John of St. Laurence, Canon of St. Paul's, grants to William, his Clerk, their rents and Church, in London, for his life, for 60*s.*, to be paid yearly, at the Nativity of St. John the Baptist, with reversion at his decease to the said Abbot and Convent. Dated, February, 1218.]

To this beautiful little specimen of a Mediaeval letter, are appended, by parchment thongs, the Abbey seals, in white wax; but both have been broken, and only large fragments of them now remain.

There is also a small deed, equally finely written, probably by the same careful hand, whereby S., Abbot of St. Salvius, Montreuil, at the prayer of John of St. Laurence, Canon of St. Paul's, grants to William Facet, his Clerk, the Church of St. Laurence, and the rents belonging to it, for his life, he paying sixty shillings yearly for the same. It is dated, August 4, 1220. The two seals, attached by two cords, are much mutilated.

And 'a very small parchment document, in Latin, being a statement of the admission by Eustace,

Bishop of London, of William Facet, Clerk, to the
Church of St. Laurence Jewry; and setting forth
that he has personally installed him solemnly therein.   Witnesses, Philip Archdeacon of Huntingdon,
Master R. "our Official," Roger de Moris, "our
Seneschal," Richard de Berkinge, David de Tok,
and others.   Part of the Bishop's seal is left, attached
by a strip of parchment; representing the Bishop on
one side, and St. Paul, with a drawn sword, on the
other.'[1]

In October, 1247, 'on the morrow of the Octaves
of St. Michael,' we find Warnerius, Abbot of
St. Salvius, sending John, Prior of his Church, and
Adam, his Chaplain, with a Latin letter empowering
them to sell their soke in London, called 'the soke of
St. Winwaloeus.' Prior John and Brother Adam
appear to have sold the soke, and the houses, and
the advowson of the Church to William Facet. And
this William Facet, in earlier documents styled
'Clerk' to John of St. Laurence, is now called
'Canon of St. Paul's.'

Another document, of the date, probably, of 1247,
with one of the Abbey seals in fair condition, annexed by a silk cord, the other seal being lost, tells
us that Warner, Abbot of St. Salvius, Montreuil,
by reason of the 'urgent necessity' of the House, has
quit-claimed to Sir William Facet, Canon of St.

' *Hist. MSS. Com.*, Fourth Report, p. 449.

Paul's, 'all our Soke, lands, and rents, with the ap-
purtenances, and the advowson of the Church of
St. Laurence, Jewry,' to hold the same together;
the same Facet having paid forty pounds before-
hand, which had been 'converted to the use of the
Monastery.' This deed was witnessed by Michael
Tovy, then Mayor of London ; William Viel, and
Nicholas Bat, Sheriffs ; Adam de Basinge, Stephen
Bukerel, Roger Fitz-Roger, John Vyel, Laurence de
Frowie, Thomas Fitz-Thomas, John Horman, Ro-
bert de Cornhell, William Eswy, mercer, Thomas
Adrian, John le Meyner, James Buleys, Martin,
servant of the Abbot, John de Arkesdene, Clerk,
and others.

The soke, and other property, which William
Facet had from the Abbot of St. Salvius, he gave to
his foster-child, Henry Facet, together with various
sums of money. The deed of gift is on parchment,
and the names of several witnesses are inscribed on
it. The seal is lost ; and only the silk cord, which
attached it to the deed, remains. But there is
another, beautifully written, copy of this document,
which has an oblong seal, in good condition, representing a tonsured head. This seal is held by a
parchment thong.

The property next passed to Hugh de Wychenbrook. Both Antony à Wood and Henry Savage
state that Hugh de Wychenbrook and Hugh de

Vienne were the same person. They say that Hugh
de Wychenbrook was 'commonly called' Hugh de
Vienne. But a more careful study of the College
deeds would have led to the conclusion that the
property passed from Henry Facet to Hugh de
Wychenbrook, and from him to Hugh de Vienne.
There is a ' conveyance, in Latin, on parchment, by
Hugh de Wykhambroke, Canon of St. Martin's le
Grand, to Hugh de Vienne, of the property above-
mentioned ; dated in the 15th year of King Edward
the First. Witnesses, Ralph de Sandwich, then
Warden of the City of London and the same Ward,
William de Hereford and Thomas de Stanes, then
Sheriffs, Henry le Waleys, Gregory de Rokesle,
Philip le Tayllour, John de Banquelle, William de
Farndone, Joce Lachateour, Ralph le Blound, Peter
de Northwys, Thomas le Foundour, Roger le Bar-
bour, and others, with John le Barbour, "then
Serjeant of that Ward." The seal is oblong, and
nearly perfect, with good impression, of a priest
standing before the altar, with a chalice upon it.' [1]

The College also preserves ' a Latin deed, on
parchment, dated the Saturday after the Ascension,
A.D. 1294 ; whereby Hugh de Vyenne, Canon of
St. Martin's le Grand, grants to the Master and
Scholars of Balliol the Soke of St. Wynewall, in the
Parish of St. Laurence Jewry, with four houses, and

---

[1] *Hist. MSS. Com.*, Fourth Report, p. 449.

the advowson of the Church ; the which he had had
of the gift and grant of Master Hugh de Wykam-
broke : the houses being near the graveyard of the
said church, between the house of Stephen Aswy,
on the west, and the Court-yard of the Guildhall, on
the east.   Also, 20 shillings of yearly rent ; namely,
from the house of Martin the Arbalester, in Milk-
strete, 4 shillings ; from the tenement there of Master
Eadmund le Poter 8 shillings ; from the tenement
held by the said Martin, in Cattestrete, opposite the
Church of St. Laurence, 4 shillings ; and from that of
Adam de Horsham, opposite the Church, 4 shillings.
He acknowledges the receipt of 100 marks from
them " in gersummam," by way of fine.   Witnesses,
Sir John Breton, Knight, then Warden of the City of
London,   Martin   de   Aumbrisbire   and   Robert   de
Rokeslee, Sheriffs, Stephen Aswy, John de Bauk-
well, John de Byterle, Peter de Northwick, Adam de
Horsham, Walter Bloundel, Robert de   Colbroke,
John de Pessemeres, John at Church, and many
others.   The seal, originally a bad impression
(apparently of a thistle), is in good preservation, and
hangs by a silken cord.   There is a duplicate of this
deed, with a like seal, but a still worse impression.' [1]

And, also, a Licence in mortmain from King
Edward I. to Hugh de Vienne, sanctioning the
preceding conveyance.   The great seal, in white

---

[1] *Hist. MSS. Com.*, Fourth Report, p. 449,

wax, which hangs by two silken cords, has been much broken round the edge ; but the centre of the seal remains perfect, and is a fine impression. The Licence is written in a bold handwriting, on a large sheet of parchment.—

' Edwardus Dei Gratia Rex Angliae, Dominus Hiberniae, et Dux Aquitaniae, omnibus ad quos praesentes litterae pervenerint salutem. Licet de communi consilio regni nostri providerimus quod non liceat viris religiosis seu aliis ingredi feodum alicujus ita quod ad mortuam manum deveniat sine licentia nostra et capitalis Domini de quo res illa immediate tenetur. Volentes tamen Hugoni de Vienna gratiam facere specialem dedimus ei licentiam quantum in nobis est quod ipse advocationi Ecclesiae Sancti Laurentii in Judaismo Londoniensi dare possit et assignare Custodi Domus Scholarium de Balliolo in Oxonia et eisdem Scholaribus. Habenda et tenenda eisdem Custodi et Scholaribus et eorum successoribus Scholaribus in Domo praedicta commorantibus in perpetuum et eisdem Custodi et Scholaribus quod advocationem illam ab eodem Hugone sic recipere possint, tenore praesentium similiter licentiam concedimus specialem. Nolentes quod idem Hugo aut haeredes sui seu praedicti Custos et Scholares aut successores sui praedicti ratione statuti praedicti inde per nos vel haeredes nostros occasionentur in aliquo seu graventur,

Salvis tamen capitalibus dominis feodi illius servitiis inde debitis et consuetis.   In cujus rei testimonium has litteras nostras fieri fecimus patentes.   Teste me ipso apud Westmonasterium decimo octavo die Augusti, anno regno nostri vicesimo tertio.'

[*Translation.*—Edward, by the Grace of God, King of England, Lord of Ireland, and Duke of Aquitaine, to all to whom these presents shall come, Greeting.   Although, by the common counsel of our realm, we have provided that it shall not be lawful for Religious, or others, to enter upon possession of any fief, in such manner that it be held in mortmain, without permission from us, and from the principal Lord, of whom the fief is directly held. Wishing, nevertheless, to show special grace to Hugh de Vienne, we have granted him licence, so far as lies in us, to give and assign the advowson of the Church of St. Laurence, in Jewry, London, to the Warden of the House of the Scholars of Balliol, at Oxford, and to these same Scholars.   To have and to hold to these same, the Warden and Scholars dwelling in the House aforesaid, in perpetuity. And by the tenor of these presents we grant special licence to the said Warden and Scholars so to receive that advowson from the said Hugh.   And it is our will that the same Hugh, and his heirs, or the aforesaid Warden and Scholars, or their successors, should not in anything be harassed or burthened by

reason of the statute, by us, or our heirs.   Saving,
however, the services due and accustomed to the
chief Lords of that fief.   In witness whereof we
have caused these our letters patent to be executed.
Witnessed by myself, at Westminster, the 18th day
of August, in the 23rd year of our reign.]

Walter de Fodringeye was made Principal in
1282, when Dervorguilla gave formal Statutes to
the College ; and Brother Hugh de Hertilpoll and
William de Menyll were then Procurators.   In 1296,
Walter de Fodringeye resigned his Principalship,
and was made a Canon of Lincoln ; and Hugh de
Warkenby became Principal, or Warden, of Balliol
Hall.   But he could not have remained in office for
many years, for in 1303 ' Stephen Cornwall occurs
by the name of Custos domus de Balliolo 31 Ed. I.
He was succeeded by Richard de Chickwell, who is
mentioned as ' Custos ' in a writ of Edward II. to
the Mayor of Oxford, dated August 18, 1309.
Thomas de Waldeby appears to have been Principal
in the year 1321.   And, in another writ of Edward II.
the name of Henry de Seton occurs as Principal, in
1323.   Nicholas de Luceby was Custos in the first
year of Edward III. ; and, five years afterwards, we
find the name of John Poclynton.   Thus there
were, according to Antony à Wood, who is very
reliable in such matters, being more a careful
annalist than an historian, eight Principals, or

Wardens. The title afterwards was altered ; and the name of Hugh Corbrygge occurs as ' Master,' in 1343.[1]

Of these Principals two appear to have been Benefactors to the College ; one directly, and one indirectly. Hugh de Warkenby, together with William de Gotham, also a member of the College, gave four houses in School Street, with the area adjoining them, for the support of a Chaplain for the Chapel of St. Catherine, within the precincts of the College. These four houses were subsequently known as Balliol College Schools. They were ' situated sometime on the West side of Schoolstreet in the said Parish of St. Mary the Virgin. These having been Schools of old time, but by what name then known I know not, had this name given to them in the reign of K. Edw. II, because that then they belonged to the House of Balliol, who at that time and several ages after rented them to Clerks to perform their Exercise ; for as I have elsewhere told you, every Master and Bachelour were formerly bound to provide for themselves Schools. The said Schools being four in number were contained in one messuage, and were yearly let for very considerable rents. In the latter end of Hen. III, and beginning of Edw. I, they did, with the tenement itself

---

[1] These names, and dates, are given from Antony à Wood, without further verification.

belong to one Elias le Quitter, a Burgher of Oxford, who about the year 1291 did convey them with a court or yard adjoining, and certain revenews in the Parish of St. Peter in the East to Thomas de Sowy another Burgher, by the name of Beaufront Schools situated between a tenement of the Prior and Convent of St. Frideswyde, and another sometime belonging to Laurence Kepeharme. In the year 1295 the said Schools with three messuages at the North end of Schoolstreet on the West side, coming by sale from the said Sowy to Hugh de Warkeneby and Will. de Gotham, Clerks (the former then Master, and the other lately Fellow, of the House of Balliol) were in the year 1310 given by them to the said House, for the finding of a Chaplain to celebrate divine service daily in St. Catherine's Chapel there. Afterwards they let out the other messuages to Clerks, and they became also Schools and habitations for them.' [1]

Soon afterwards we find Richard de Hunsingoure giving property to the College. In 1316, he gave and 'confirmed to the Master and Scholars of the House of *Balliol* for ever, All that Tenement, with the Houses, Curtilage, and all other the Appurtenances in the Parish of St. *John de Merton*, lying between *Alban*-hall and *Lomb*-hall, which Tene-

---

[1] *Antony à Wood*, ed. Gutch, vol. ii. p. 731.

ment he had of the Legacy of *Walter de Fodringheye*, Canon of *Lincoln*.'[1]

Thus Walter de Fodringeye became, indirectly, a Benefactor to the College of which he had been the first Principal. The house, commonly known as Hert Hall, was afterwards leased to Merton College, and became a part of what was, until only a few years ago, St. Alban Hall. 'Hert Hall was given to Balliol College in the reign of Edward II by Mr. Richard Huntingore, but seems at the date of the Survey (1424) to have been pulled down or dilapidated, the site and ground being then converted into a garden.'[2] In a lease from the Prioress of Littlemore to Merton College, of a walled garden, 'late lying and longing to Albon Hall in Oxenford,' is a very exact description of the dimensions of this garden. It was $206\frac{1}{2}$ feet in length, and $38\frac{1}{2}$ feet in breadth. And its position is plainly stated in a 'Lease for ninety-nine years from Balliol to Merton College of a garden lying between Alban Hall and the " orchard " of Merton College, of which the south end projects to the wall of the said Scholars of Merton, and the north end to the King's highway close to Alban Hall, "containing in length $206\frac{1}{2}$ feet, and in breadth $38\frac{1}{2}$ feet," at a rent of two shillings. Merton College further

---

[1] *Balliofergus*, p. 34.
[2] *Memorials of Merton Coll.*, Brodrick, p. 314.

undertakes the liability, formerly devolving upon Balliol, of keeping in repair the northern and eastern walls of this garden, and is empowered to dig there and use it otherwise for its own purposes.'[1]

The Warden of Merton, in his *Memorials* of the College, calls our attention to an old doorway, which ' may still be seen, blocked up and built into the wall of Merton College Garden opposite the New Schools and the back entry to the old Angel Inn. This door may have been the one outlet from the gardens into what is now Merton Street, when St. Alban Hall and other adjoining Halls belonged to other owners.'[2]

The same Richard de Hunsingoure, who gave Hert Hall and garden, also gave to the College, in about the year 1320, twelve acres of meadow, called Bayly-mead, in the parish of Steeple Aston. Henry Savage tells us that, ' *Anno* 13 *Edw.* 2. which was about the Year, 1320. twelve Acres of Medow, commonly called *Bayly-mead*, were given by Mr. *Hunsingoure* to the Master and Scholars, to find a Chaplain for the celebration of Divine Offices in the Chappel of St. *Katerine*, within the Mansion of the said Master and Scholars, confirmed by Letters Patents of the said King, to be held of the Manor of *Wotton*, for the Service of 15d. *per annum*.'[3]

---

[1] *Memorials of Merton Coll.*, Brodrick, p. 315.   [2] *Ibid.*
[3] *Balliofergus*, p. 34.

Thus, by the charity of Benefactors, two permanent Chaplains were secured for the College, that Divine Office might be said daily in the Oratory within the precincts of the College. That Oratory was, as far as can be safely conjectured, the large hall which is now the Master's dining room. Tradition, in such a question, is of some worth; and the position of the hall, near to the new buildings, which Dervorguilla had erected, and also joining the tenements which she gave to her Scholars of Balliol, confirms the tradition. The structure of the hall tends to the same conclusion. It has evidently always depended for light on a large window looking east; it is entered by a wide double-door at the west; there was, originally, a raised dais at the east end;[1] the roof is high, and the walls are massive. The argument against its having been the Oratory is, that the great bay-window, looking eastward, was built by Bishop Grey. But, when he was building his new hall and Library, might he not, for the sake of uniformity in the appearance of the quadrangle, have built anew the east window of the Oratory, a work which possibly was much needed?

Dervorguilla's Oratory was built about the year 1293, out of money left by her to the College.

---

[1] When the Master's house was rebuilt, 1868—1870, the floor of this hall was raised to the level of the new rooms. It was raised to the height of the dais, which existed up to that time.

K

Before that time the Scholars of Balliol had, for their
Chapel, one of the aisles of St. Mary Magdalen's
Church.   It appears to have been a custom, if not a
rule, for Scholars to be present at Divine Office,
and to hear Mass, in the Church of the parish they
lived in ; but there is no record of their attendance
being compulsory.   The attendance of Graduates
was strictly required, by many different statutes,
'and the omission of any mention of the juniors
would seem to imply that it was taken for granted
they should accompany their masters.'[1]   And we
find in the Chancellors' and Proctors' Books, about
the year 1311, among the Ordinances issued for the
Scholars of Master William of Durham,—'*Item*,
ordinatum est quod dicti Scholares, qui pro tempore
fuerint, duas missas, singulis annis in parochia ubi
degunt, pro anima fundatoris faciant celebrare.'[2]

The Balliol Scholars had no great distance to go.
A few steps between the plots of ground at the back
of Old Balliol Hall, and then across the open space
at the east of the Church.   A minute's run, for Mass
in the early morning.   Not far to go from their books
or play, for the Divine Office.   And even in the
dusk of winter evenings, when the Oxford mist and
fog would, then as now, creep stealthily across
Canditch, and the fields of Beaumont, there would
have been some glimmering oil lamp near the City

[1] *Munimenta Academica.* Preface, p. lxxv.   [2] *Ibid.* vol. i. p. 89.

Gate, or the Sanctuary lamp showing faintly through the Church window, to guide them to their Vespers. They were poor-looking lads, who, in garments of various colours and shapes, left their scantily furnished rooms, or broke away from prolonged Disputations and tedious lectures, when the near bell called them to their prayers. In Agas' map of Oxford, 1578, can be seen the opening, between buildings, through which they probably must have passed before crossing the road to St. Mary Magdalen's Church. 'The north aisle, or a part of it, was repaired and fitted up about 1280 by Dervorgilla, the foundress of Balliol college, as an oratory for the use of her scholars. Hence it has been known by the name of Dervorgilla's aisle, or St. Catharine's chapel. The payment of 40s. per annum to St. Catharine's priest is mentioned so late as the time of Henry VIII., and the "mass book of St. Catharine" was "mended" in the 24th of his reign. . . . This aisle, or the part dedicated to St. Catharine, was used by the scholars of Balliol college from their first foundation until 1293; after which Oliver Sutton, and other bishops of Lincoln in succession, granted them permission to celebrate divine service in their own oratory within the walls of the college; except on particular solemnities, when they were bound to attend in the parish church.'[1]

---

[1] *Memorials of Oxford*, Ingram.

K 2

The frequency of Disputations seems to have been pleaded, by the Balliol Scholars, as a reason for their having the Divine Office in their own Chapel, within the College precincts. And Dervorguilla's last gift of money having built the Chapel, Oliver Sutton granted the Licence asked for. The words of the Licence are :—

' Oliverus permissione Divina Lincolniensis Episcopus dilectis in Christo filiis, Magistro et Scholaribus domus de Balliolo in Oxonia, salutem, gratiam, et benedictionem. Considerantes fructus multiplices qui ex vestro laudabili studio hactenus pervenerunt et in futurum sperantur Deo auspice proventuri, quietem quam possumus vobis cupimus providere ; cum igitur lectionum et disputationum occupationibus impediti parochialem Ecclesiam infra cujus parochiam domus vestra praedicta consistit pro Divinis audiendis adire ut praetenditis saepius nequeatis nos vestris supplicationibus favorabiliter inclinati, ut in oratorio vestro infra domum vestram praefatam constructo dum tamen decens fuerit et honestum, Divina vobis et familiae vestrae per sacerdotem sumptibus vestris propriis exhibendis faciatis licite celebrari licentiam vobis concedimus per praesentes. Ita tamen quod nullimoda Sacramenta Ecclesiastica in dicto oratorio ministrentur et, quoad oblationes in eo faciendas, obventiones, ac alia jura consimilia, nullum matrici Ecclesiae praedictae praejudicium generetur quodque ut honor debitus eidem Ecclesiae servetur ipsam in majoribus anni solemnitatibus, visitetis prout alii Scholares suas Ecclesias parochiales visitare tenentur et quilibet capellanus in dicto oratorio vobis ministraturus de indemnitate ejusdem Ecclesiae in praesentia Abbatis et Conventus Oseneyae ipsam in usus proprios possidentium seu ipsius Ecclesiae Vicarii praestet ad Sacra Dei Evangelia juramentum. Quae omnia et singula sub poena revocationis hujusmodi gratiae nostrae a vobis volumus observari. In cujus rei testimonium sigillum nostrum praesentibus est appensum. Data apud Eynesham III Idus Iulii, anno Domini MCC nonagesimo tertio.'

[*Translation.*—Oliver, by Divine permission, Bishop of Lincoln, to his beloved sons in Christ, the Master and Scholars of the House of Balliol, at Oxford, Health, Grace, and Benediction. We, considering the abundant fruit which has been derived from your praiseworthy zeal up to this time ; and, with the blessing of God, is expected in the future ; are anxious, so far as we can, to provide for your peace and tranquillity. Since, therefore, as you allege, you are often unable, owing to your time being engrossed by lessons and Disputations, to attend for the Divine Offices the parish Church, of the parish in which your House aforesaid is situate ; we, favourably inclining to your petition, by these presents grant you licence lawfully to have the Divine Offices celebrated for yourselves and your household, in your own Oratory (provided it be fair and becoming) constructed within your House aforesaid, by a Priest to be maintained at your own expense. Provided always that none of the Sacraments of the Church be administered in the said Oratory; and that with regard to offerings made therein, revenues, and other rights of like nature, no prejudice accrue to the aforesaid mother Church; and provided that on the more solemn Feasts of the year, in order to keep up the honour which is due to the said Church, you make a visit to it, in the same way that other Scholars are bound to visit their parish Church; and provided that every Chaplain, who is to serve the said Oratory, take an oath on the Holy Gospels of God concerning the indemnity of the same Church, in the presence of the Abbot and Community of Oseney, who hold it to their own use, or of the Vicar of the said Church. All which and singular, it is our will that you should observe, under penalty of the revocation of this our grace. In witness whereof our seal is to these presents appended. Given at Eynsham, 13 July, 1293.]

This letter is one of the most valued of the documents relating to the early history of the College, and it has been carefully preserved in the College Archives. It is a small slip of parchment; but the writing is distinct, and legible. Only a small portion of the seal remains ; but there is a duplicate copy of this letter, which has a nearl perfecty seal attached to it.

It is difficult to determine exactly what the Ecclesiastical Sacraments refer to. Bishop Oliver may have meant that the Holy Communion was not to be given, in the Chapel, on the more solemn Feasts ; but that the Scholars were to go to the parish Church. Or, Ecclesiastical Sacraments might simply refer to those of Ecclesiastical precept ; such as, Baptism, and the Easter Communion. Several succeeding Bishops of Lincoln granted the same Licence ; and in one of these documents the Oratory is called the Chapel of St. Catherine.

Finally, in 1364, Pope Urban V. gave a Licence, in the following words. As this document is now much injured by damp, it is here given, as it is written, in the abbreviated Latin.—

'Vrban⁹ ep̃s seru⁹ seruorᵱ dei / Dilectᵱ filijs Magr̃o & scolarib₃ Collegij clĩcorᵱ dom⁹ de Balliolo de Oxonia Lincolnieñ diocᵱ Salᵗ & apticam beñ . Pia deuotorᵱ deo & ecclĩe desideria que diuini cult⁹ augm̃etũ ac iporᵱ quietᵱ comodũ respicer'̃ dinoscunt̃. aptico fauore ᵱsequim̃ eisq₃ benignũ imptimᵉ assensũ. Exhibita siquidẽ nob̃ ᵱ pte vr̃a cõtinebat qᵈ vos in quadã Capella sita infra septa dom⁹ vr̃e de Balliolo de Oxonia Lincolnieñ dioᵓ iuxta statuta dicte dom⁹

p̄ nos [1] iuramēto vallata singuł diebȝ p̄ p̄p̄ios sacer-
dotes diuina officia faꝭe celebrari ac certꝭ diebȝ
eisdem misse & horis canonicis psonaliꝭ inꝑesse
tenemini.   Nos vr̃is in hac p̄te supplicacionibȝ inclinati . vt in Capella p̄dicta singuli vr̃m qui fuerint in
pbr̄atꝰ ordine constituti & alij pbr̃i dicte domꝰ missam
& alia diuina officia eciam ī festꝭ maioribȝ sūmissa
& alta voce iure parrochiał ecclī̃e & cuiuslibet alteriꝰ
ī oĩbȝ semp̄ saluo celebrar̃ valeatꝭ quibuscūqȝ Con-
stitucionibȝ apłicis contrarijs nequaquā obstantibȝ
deuocioni nr̃e auctoritate apłica tenor̃ p̄senciū̃ in-
dulgemꝰ Nulli ergo oĩo hominū̃ liceat hāc paginā
nr̃e consessionis infringere vel ei ausu temerario
contraire Si quis autē̃ hoc attē̃ptare p̄sumpserit in-
dignationẽ omnipotentꝭ dei & beator̃ꝭ Petⁱ & Pauli
apłor̃ꝭ eiꝰ se noūit incursurū̃ Dat̃ Auinioñ xvj kł
Maij Pontificatꝰ ñri anno Secundo.ˈ

[*Translation.*—Urban, Bishop, Servant of the
servants of God, to Our beloved sons, the Master
and Scholars of the College of Clerics of the House
of Balliol at Oxford, in the diocese of Lincoln,
Health and Apostolic Benediction.

It is Our wont graciously to extend Our Apostolic
favour and consent to the pious desires of men, who
are devoted to God and the Church, in those things
which regard the increase of Divine Worship, and
the advantage of Our peace.   Now it has been

---

[1] Written *nos* ; but probably a mistake for *vos*.

made known to Us in your behalf that, according to
the Statutes of your House of Balliol, at Oxford, in
the diocese of Lincoln, to which you are obliged
by oath, you are bound to cause the Divine Offices
to be celebrated daily in the Chapel situated within
the limits of the said House, by your own Priests,
and on certain days to be present personally at
the same Mass and Canonical Hours. We, inclining to your petitions in this regard, by the tenor
of these letters, by Our Apostolic authority, permit
to your devotions that you who are Priests, and the
other Priests of the said House, to celebrate in the
aforesaid Chapel, Mass and the Divine Offices, as
well aloud as in a low voice, even on the greater
Feasts, the right of the parish, and any other Church,
being in all things and always safeguarded, and
notwithstanding any Apostolic constitutions to the
contrary.

Therefore let no man, whoever he may be, infringe this Our document of concession, or dare
rashly to contradict it. But if any one should presume so to do, let him know that he will incur the
anger of God Almighty and of His blessed Apostles
Peter and Paul. Given at Avignon, on the 16th
day before the kalends of May, in the second year
of our Pontificate.]

There can be little doubt about Masses having
been celebrated in the College soon after its first

foundation. Dervorguilla's Statutes, given to the Scholars in 1282, asked for certain Masses to be offered on certain days; and although the Scholars' first Chapel was one of the aisles of St. Mary Magdalen's Church, yet in 1293 they had their own Oratory, within the precincts of the College. In 1310 Hugh de Warkenby and William de Gotham gave four houses in School Street, for the support of a Chaplain, for the Chapel of St. Catherine, in the College. And in 1320, Richard de Hunsingoure gave the twelve acres of meadow, at Steeple Aston, for the support of another Chaplain. In 1341, Sir Philip de Somervyle, when giving new Statutes to the College, ordained that a third Chaplain, presented by him, or by his heirs, should live in the College, and celebrate certain Masses, in perpetuity. The College evidently had its own Chapel, or Oratory, in which the Holy Sacrifice was frequently offered; but it was, probably, not licensed for Masses on Days of Obligation, nor for the public recitation of the Divine Office. Bishop Oliver's Licence was that the Divine Office might be said in it; but, it would appear, the Scholars were still bound to be present at Mass, and at the Office, in the parish Church, on all greater Feast Days, that is, on all Days of Obligation. Pope Urban's Licence, though it carefully guarded the interests of the parish Church, in all questions of rights and dues, gave the Scholars

what they needed, permission to have Mass celebrated in their own Chapel, ' as well aloud as in a
low voice, even on the greater Feasts.'

In 1327, the Abbot of Reading was a Benefactor
to the College. There is a letter in the College
Archives, which tells of the good Abbot's gifts. It
is a small piece of parchment; but the writing is
bold and regular. The pendent seal, in red wax,
vesica-shaped, is broken round the edge ; but is,
otherwise in good preservation, and is a fine specimen of an Abbey seal. The Abbot is represented,
standing : he has his crozier in his right hand, and
in his left he holds a book. His chasuble and alb
have been very carefully and delicately traced. The
letter reads :—

' Noverint universi per praesentes quod Dominus
Nicholaus de Quappelad, Dei gratia . . . . Abbas
Radyngiae liberavit Scholaribus Domus de Balliolo
in Oxonia, viginti libras sterlingorum pro anima
Adae le Poleter burgensis Radyngiae ad fabricam
capellae Sanctae Katerinae ejusdem Domus. Item
dedit praedictus . . . Abbas praefatis Scholaribus
decem marcas argenti ad fabricam Capellae praedictae
quas ab eodem . . . Abbate prae duo scripta obliga-
toria prius ex mutuo receperunt. Dedit etiam prae-·
dictus . . . Abbas praefatis Scholaribus unam fenestram vitream pretii decem librarum et amplius pro
capella supradicta, summa totius xxxvj li. xiij s. iiij d.

Item dedit eis meremium, lath et alia minuta cum
cariagio eorumdem quae hic in specie non numeran-
tur.   In cujus rei testimonium tam praedictus. . . .
Abbas quam praedicti Scholares praesenti indenturae
alternatim sigilla sua apposuerunt.   Hiis testibus:
Magistro Thoma Othom tunc Cancellario universi-
tatis Oxoniae ; Magistro Nicholao de Luceby, tunc
Custode praedictae Domus ; Magistro Nicholao de
Tyngewykes ; et custode sigilli communis praedictorum Scholarium ; et multis aliis.   Et remanebit
una pars hujus indenture penes praedictos Scholares
et alia pars penes custodem altaris Capellae Beatae
Mariae Virginis infra Abbathiam Radynges.   Dat.
apud Radyngiam die Veneris in festo Circumcisionis
Domini, anno Domini millesimo tricesimo vicesimo
septimo.'

[*Translation.*—Be it known to all by these presents, that Lord Nicholas de Quappelad, by the
Grace of God Abbot of Reading, has released to
the Scholars of the House of Balliol at Oxford,
twenty pounds sterling, for the soul of Adam le
Poleter, Burgess of Reading, for the construction of
the Chapel of St. Catherine of the same House.
Item : the aforesaid Abbot gave to the aforesaid
Scholars ten marks of silver, for the construction of
the aforesaid Chapel, which they had previously received as a loan under two written bonds.   Moreover, the aforesaid Abbot gave to the aforesaid

Scholars, one glass window, of the value of ten pounds and more, for the above-named Chapel. Sum total ; 36*l.* 13*s.* 4*d.* Also he gave them timber, lath, and other small items, which are not here specifically enumerated, with their carriage. In witness whereof the aforesaid Abbot, and the aforesaid Scholars, have in turn affixed their seals to the present indenture. Witnesses : Master Thomas Otham, present Chancellor of the University of Oxford ; Master Nicholas de Luceby, present Warden of the aforesaid House ; Master Nicholas de Tyngewykes ; and the keeper of the common seal of the aforesaid Scholars; and many others. And one part of this indenture shall remain with the aforesaid Scholars, and the other part with the warden of the Altar of the Chapel of the Blessed Virgin Mary, within the Abbey of Reading. Given at Reading, Friday, the Feast of the Circumcision of the Lord, A.D. 1327.]

CHAPTER VII.

THUS we have followed the foundation of the College, and have seen Dervorguilla endowing it with her gift of lands in Stamfordham and Howgh; and her gift of all the debts due to her husband at the time of his death. Then the College was enriched by the property in the Jewry, London; and the advowson of the Church of St. Laurence. Soon afterwards came the gift of four houses in School Street, with the area adjoining them, by Hugh de Warkenby and William de Gotham; and of Hert Hall, given by Richard de Hunsingoure. 'As for the *Area*, we must understand that into the Schools of Arts, no Undergraduates were permitted to enter, as to the doing of any Exercise therein, but were left to dispute in the *Area*, or Court-yard adjoyning: which in French being *Parvis*, our Answering of Generals, is thence call'd answering in *Parvisiis*, or in *Parviso*.'[1]

Mr. Maxwell Lyte explains, that 'in the third year of his residence at the University, the student of the liberal arts was allowed to become a "general

[1] *Balliofergus*, p. 33.

sophister." As such he was required to attend the logical " variations " that were held " in the parvise " for at least a year, " disputing, arguing, and respond- ing " on sophisms. The ecclesiastical origin of these disputations is shown by the phrase " in parviso," the parvise being a cloister, paved platform, or other open space, immediately adjoining a church. A curious instance of the survival of old names is to be found in the "*testamur*" or Latin certificate which is nowadays issued by the examiners at " Re- sponsions," to the effect that a successful candidate has answered to the questions of the masters of the schools " in parviso." [1] And he adds, in a foot- note, that ' in the eighteenth century, the variations in the parvise were held three times a week and known by the name of Generals.'

After Richard de Hunsingoure there ' followed other benefactors, who gave several messuages in Oxon.' In the meantime, however, there were liberal friends, whose generosity to the College de- serves notice. Richard Hunsington and Walter Horkstow ' gave two Messuages ; one call'd St. *Hughs-hall*, the other *Hert-hall*, *Anno* 18 *Edw.* I. confirmed by Letters Patents. It appears by a Court Roll of the Major of *Oxon*, held *Mercurii in Festo Sancti Edw. Regis*, *Anno Edw.* 3. 19. that we had a Tenement in St. *Mildreds* Parish [the Church

[1] *Hist. Univ. Oxford*, Maxwell Lyte, p. 205.

whereof stood where *Lincoln* Colledge Ball-Court now is] called St. *Hughes-hall*, which my Friend, who brought me a Transcript of the Record, would have to be understood of this St. *Hughs-hall*, which I contend to be part of our Colledge : he supposing it not to be so, but that it was the Site of the Divinity School [which the University pays us Rent for, to this day, whereof elsewhere]. But whatever the name of the said Site of the Divinity School was, it is as clear as may be that they are distinct things given us by distinct Benefactors : for this St. *Hughes-hall*, which I will have to be a part of our Colledge (together with that *Hert-hall*) was given, as you see, by *Richard Hunsington* and *Walter Horkstow*, *Anno* 18 *Edw.* 1. but the place of the site of the Divinity School was given by *Jeffrey Horkstow* and *Richard Staynton*, *Anno* 11 *Ed.* 2. He will likewise have *Hert-hall* here mentioned too, to be that slip of Ground annexed to *Alban-hall*, which is proved to be otherwise by the same observation. This *Hert-hall* being given by *Rich : Hunsington* and *Walter Horkstow*, but that piece of Land was given by *Richard Hunsingoure*, of the legacy of *Walter de Fodringheye*, whereof elsewhere. Many Halls bearing the same name heretofore, no Argument can be drawn from the Identity thereof to the sameness of the places.'[1]

[1] *Balliofergus*, p. 28.

The Grant to the College, by Geoffrey de Horkestow and Richard de Staynton, of 'the place of the site of the Divinity School,' is thus worded :—

'Sciant praesentes et futuri quod nos Galfridus de Horkestow et Ricardus de Stayntown, Clerici, dedimus concessimus et hac praesenti carta nostra confirmavimus Magistro et Scholaribus Domus de Balliolo Oxoniae et eorum successoribus in eadem Domo in perpetuum totum illud tenementum cum domibus et omnibus aliis pertinentiis in Oxonia quod fuit quondam Walteri de Sanford contra muros ejusdem villae in parochia Sanctae Mildredae situatum inter tenementum eorundem Magistri et Scholarium ex parte orientali et tenementum quondam Thomae de Hengseye ex parte occidentali in subventionem sustentationis praedictorum Magistri et Scholarium. Tenendum et habendum praedictum tenementum integre cum domibus, curtilagio, et omnibus aliis pertinentiis praefatis Magistro et Scholaribus praedictae Domus et eorum successoribus in eadem Domo libere, jure, integre, in perpetuum juxta formam, vim, et effectum cartae Domini Regis nobis et eis in hac parte licentiam specialem tribuentis, statuto de terris et tenementis ad manum mortuam non ponendis edito non obstante ; faciendo inde capitalibus dominis feodi illius servitia inde debita et de jure consueta. In

L

cujus rei testimonium sigilla nostra praesenti cartae
sunt appensa. Hiis testibus Magistro Johanne
Luterel tunc Cancellario Oxoniae. Willelmo de
Birmcestre tunc majore ejusdem ; Ricardo, Cari,
Gilberto de Grimstede tunc ballivis . Johanne de
Dokelyntone, Andrea de Pyri, Ricardo le Spicer,
Johanne de Bischoptone, Thoma de Pyri tunc
Clerico ejusdem villae et multis aliis. Scripta et
consignata V^{to} Kal. Dec^{br}. Anno regni Regis
Edwardi filii Regis Edwardi undecimo.'

[*Abstract.*—Geoffrey de Horkestow and Richard
de Staynton, Clerks, grant to the Master and
Scholars of the House of Balliol, the tenement with
houses and appurtenances, in Oxford, which belonged to Walter de Sandford, near the City Wall,
in St. Mildred's parish, towards the maintenance of
the said Master and Scholars. Witnesses. Master
John Luterel, then Chancellor of Oxford. William
de Birmcestre, then Mayor. Richard, Cary, and
Gilbert de Grimstede, bailiffs. John de Dokelynton,
Andrew de Pyri, Richard le Spicer, John de Bischoptone, Thomas de Pyri, then clerk of the town ;
and many others. Written on the 5th day before
the kalends of December, 11 Ed. II.]

But, in order of date, another benefaction should
have been mentioned before these gifts.

Henry Savage tells, in his rather rambling
fashion, how · K. *Ed.* I. taking occasion to banish

all Jews out of this Kingdom, with Licence to sell or carry away their moveables onely, all their Lands came into the Kings hands as Escheats. Now I find that of Jews Houses in *Oxford*, the King, in the nineteenth Year of his Reign, granted to *William Burnel* Provost of *Wells*, nine Messuages, with their Tenements and Appurtenances [whereof seven were in the Parish of St. *Aldates*, one in St. *Martyns*, and another was a School of the Jews] one of those nine Messuages was call'd *The Synagogue*, whereunto did belong the entrance in at the great Port or Gate, and the sollar over it; from which great or broad Port or Gate, as it is thought, the House of the Students [now *Pembrook* Colledge] was call'd *Aula Lateportensis*, or *Broadgateshall*. This Synagogue and Port was given to *Stephanus de Cornubia*,[1] Master of this House, and the Scholars, 35 *Ed.* I. The rest of the premises, together with ten Shops, did the same *William Burnel* bestow upon our said House: For the confirmation whereof, we have Licence of *Mortmain*, and other Letters Patents from the King, a confirmation of the Gift from *Queen Margaret*, 8 *Edw.* 2. [which King was her Son] the disclaim of *Edward Burnel*, Heir to the said *William*, with all other circumstances of Law contain'd in a multitude of Writings; which makes

---

[1] Stephen Cornwall?

me wonder how it comes to pass that we have scarce one of those Houses remaining to us in St. *Aldats* Parish, and none of the shops. [That House in Grandpont [vulgò Grampool] though in the same Parish now, yet then in St. *Michaels at the South Port* [which St. *Michaels* hath been since consolidated with St. *Aldats*, being of another Foundation] unless it were to make way for the Building of Christ Church, called the *Cardinals Colledge.* And indeed it was mostly to that end ; in recompense whereof, we were promised Lands, Houses, or Money, but never received any, as appears under the hand of a Publick Notary of the Bishop of *London, Anno* 1529.'[1]

In the College Archives there is 'a small parchment deed, in Latin, with two seals, one broken, the other nearly perfect ; being a lease by John de Aylesbury and Agnes, his wife, to Master Stephen de Cornwall, " Master of the Hall of Balliol, and the Scholars thereof," of a messuage in Oxford, " which is called the Synagogue," in the parish of St. Aldate's, with the entrance at the great Gate, and the sollar over the gate, between the new tenements, formerly of Master William Burnel, from the Purification in the 35th year of King Edward the Third, to the Feast of St. Michael in . . . Witnesses, John de Dokelintone, Mayor of Oxford,

---

[1] *Balliofergus*, p. 27.

Walter de Wycombe and William de Pennarth, Bailiffs, and others, therein named. Given on the Sunday after the Feast of the Purification, in the above-mentioned year.'[1]

And also ' a Latin deed, on parchment, with four small seals, three of which are perfect ; whereby the Master and Scholars of Balliol covenant to build, in the messuage last-mentioned, a chamber " of competent timber," with a sollar, and a cellar also ; John de Aylesbury thereby agreeing that they may have the stones and timber of an old chamber there removed. Dated on the same day as the above. By another deed, it appears that John de Aylesbury was also known as " John the Taverner," of Oxford.'[2]

By a deed, on a small piece of parchment, in fine and delicate writing, with one large capital letter at the beginning, Margaret, Queen Dowager of England, the second wife of Edward I. sanctioned the conveyance of these Tenements in St. Aldates, to the College. The large seal, in light brown wax, which is attached by a thick parchment thong, is a very beautiful, and nearly perfect, impression. The Queen is represented, standing, and holding in her hand a sceptre. The words of the deed are :—

' Universis Sanctae matris ecclesiae filiis ad quos praesentes litterae pervenerint Margareta Dei

---

[1] *Hist. MSS. Com.* Fourth Report, p. 450.   [2] *Ibid.*

Gratia Regina Angliae salutem in Domino sempiternam. Noverit universitas vestra quod nos habentes respectum ad profectum et commodum quae ex studio Scholarium aulae de Balliolo in Oxonia hactenus provenerunt et auxiliante Deo in posterum sunt uberius proventura, pro salute animae illustrissimi domini nostri domini Regis Edwardi dudum consortis nostri et pro salute nostra, inspectis cartis appropriationis et confirmationis Regis praedicti ac illustris domini et filii nostri domini Regis Edwardi filii Regis praedicti super tenementis omnibus, quae quondam fuerunt magistri Willelmi Burnel in Oxonia, Magistro et Scholaribus praedictae aulae concessis et appropriatis, eisdem cartis et appropriationi quantum in nobis est nostrum consensum adhibuimus et quicquid juris in dictis tenementis habuimus seu habere poterimus salvo nobis redditu consueto et antiquo de tenementis eisdem dictis Magistro et Scholaribus concessimus per praesentes. In cujus rei testimonium has litteras nostras patentes sibi fieri fecimus sigillo nostro signatas. Data apud Feckenham, vicesimo septimo die Augusti anno regni domini et filii nostri carissimi domini Regis Edwardi filii Regis Edwardi octavo.'

[*Translation.* —To all the sons of Holy Mother Church to whom these presents shall come, Margaret, by the Grace of God, Queen of England, everlasting Health in the Lord. Be it known to all you, that we, having respect to the advantage and convenience which have hitherto been derived from the zeal of the Scholars of Balliol Hall at Oxford, and which, with the help of God, will in the future be derived more abundantly, for the salvation of the soul of our most illustrious Lord, the Lord King Edward, our late consort, and for our own, having perused the Charters of appropriation and confirmation of the aforesaid King, and of the illustrious Lord our son, the Lord King Edward, son of the aforesaid King, concerning all the tenements which formerly belonged to Master William Burnel, at Oxford, and which have been granted and appropriated to the Master and Scholars of Balliol Hall aforesaid, have given our consent, as far as in us lies, to the Charters and appropriation, and by these presents we grant whatever right we have or shall have in the said tenements, to the said Master and Scholars, saving always the ancient and customary rent due to us on the same tenements. In witness whereof we have caused these our letters patent, sealed with our seal, to be executed. Given at Feckenham, on the 27th day of August, in the 8th year of the reign of the Lord and our most dear son, the Lord King Edward, son of King Edward.]

And now we have to speak of a tenement in Oxford, to the memory of which is attached a special interest. Most Histories of England give

us some account of 'the coming of the Friars,' and
of their work of reformation. The Dominicans
were the first to arrive in England, and the first to
come to Oxford. They settled in the midst of the
populous district near to St. Edward's Church.
There is still existing a very narrow, winding, foot-
way, from Boar Lane to the High Street, known
only to few people, and so narrow that the
entrance to it from the High Street is hardly
noticeable, which passes by some of the old walls
and windows of earlier Oxford. This narrow pas-
sage gives us some idea of St. Edward's parish of
Mediaeval days. In that parish the Friar Preachers
were first established. After the lapse of so many
years, and the almost entire destruction of buildings,
and the loss of records, it is impossible to speak
with certainty about any one definite house. We
know that the Friar Preachers had one or two tenements granted to them, for their habitation. Afterwards, they probably rented them; and, subsequently, bought them. Their Rule would have
obliged them to live together, in Community; and
so we may conjecture that the houses, very small
ones, were connected, and became one House.

The Friars Minor were not long in following
the Friar Preachers, who entertained them with
all hospitality in London, in 1225. 'Et statim ante
festum Omnium Sanctorum, et antequam Frater

Angnellus venisset Londoniam, profecti sunt Frater Ricardus de Ingewrth et Frater Ricardus Devoni-ensis Oxoniam, et ibi similiter a Fratribus Prædicato-ribus familiarissime suscepti sunt ; comederunt in suo refectorio, et jacuerunt in suo dormitorio, sicut con-ventuales, per dies octo.'[1] This must have been at the House of the Black Friars, in St. Edward's parish.

Among the numberless deeds in the College Archives, is a small document, which tells how some property in St. Edward's parish, in all probability these tenements, came to the Dominicans. It is a small, and carelessly cut, piece of parchment ; but in good preservation. The writing, on ruled lines, is clear, large, and very easy to read. The date is supposed to be about 1230. The seal is lost. The words of the Grant are :—

' Sciant praesentes et futuri quod ego Thomas filius Thomae filii Edwini de Oxonia concessi, dimisi et liberavi et hac praesenti carta mea confir-mavi Fratribus Praedicatoribus de Oxonia totam terram meam cum omnibus pertinentiis suis quae est in parochia beati Edwardi in Oxonia, illam videlicet quae jacet inter terram quae est Roberti With et terram quae fuit Johannis de Navare, habendam et tenendam de me et haeredibus meis sibi et suis assignatis in perpetuum libere et quiete et integre. Reddendo inde annuatim domui Hospitalis de Sancto

---

[1] *Monumenta Franciscana*, vol. i. p. 9.

Johanni extra portam orientalem de Oxonia tresde-
cem denarios ad duos anni terminos pro omni servitio
et exactione et demanda, videlicet ad festum Sancti
Michaelis vi denarios et obolum et in Annunciatione
Sanctae Mariae vi denarios et obolum.   Et ego
praedictus Thomas filius Thomae et haeredes mei
warantizabimus praedictis Fratribus Praedicatoribus
et suis assignatis totam praedictam terram cum
omnibus pertinentiis suis contra omnes homines
mares et feminas.   Pro hac autem concessione dimissione liberatione confirmatione warantizatione praedicti Fratres Praedicatores dederunt mihi centum
solidos argenti in gersummam.   Ut igitur haec
omnia praedicta firma et stabilia permaneant hoc
praesens scriptum sigilli mei impressione roboravi.
Hiis testibus Petro filio Toroldi tunc majore Oxoniae,
Roberto filio Oweni, Philippo Molendinario, Waltero
Aurifabro, Laurentio With, Henrico Ingo, Alewico,
Johanne Pille, Ricardo Molendino, Roberto Minnoth,
et aliis.'

[*Abstract.*—Thomas, son of Thomas, son of
Edwin, of Oxford, grants to the Friar Preachers of
Oxford, all his land in the parish of St. Edward, in
Oxford, viz. that lying between the land of Robert
With and that late of John de Navare, they paying
an annual rent of 13d. to the Hospital of St. John
without the East Gate of Oxford. For this conces-
sion, the said Friar Preachers have given him 100s.

of silver. Witnesses, Peter, son of Torold, then
Mayor of Oxford. Robert, son of Owen ; Philip, the
Miller ; Walter, the Goldsmith ; Laurence With ;
Henry Inge, Alewic ; John Pille ; Richard, the
Miller ; Robert Minnoth ; and others.]

And the next deed to this is a most beautifully
written document, on an evenly cut, but small, piece
of parchment. The writing reminds us of the fine
and careful penmanship of the letter from Amalric,
Abbot of St. Salvius ; and is a contrast to the round
schoolboy-like hand of the preceding deed. This
small strip of parchment shows writing, on very
faintly ruled lines, which is a marvel of evenness,
fineness, and delicate finish. The very diminutive
letters, and the abbreviations, are a work of art ;
while the upright strokes, all in beautiful parallels,
are finished by a fine lace-work running down
them, as if the pen had been loth to leave its task.
Perhaps the hand which guided it was trained for the
better work of illuminating Missals, and transcribing
manuscripts, and contributing to the ' rarities ' and the
' precious treasures ' that made the riches of Oxford
Libraries. The thin parchment of this deed is turn-
ing yellow. The seal is lost ; and only the parchment
thong remains. The words are :—

' Sciant praesentes et futuri quod ego Frater
Willelmus de Tyford et Conventus Fratrum Praedi-
catorum Oxoniae dedimus et concessimus, dimisimus,

et liberavimus et hac praesenti carta nostra confirmavimus Randulfo de Chiltune Capellano totam terram
nostram cum omnibus pertinentiis suis quae jacet
inter terram quae est Roberti With et terram quae
fuit Johannis de Navare in parochia Sancti Edwardi
Oxoniae ; illam videlicet terram quam emimus a
Thoma filio Thomae filii Edwini de Oxonia.
Habendam et tenendam sibi et haeredibus vel
assignatis suis in perpetuum libere, et quiete, integre,
et pacifice. Reddendo inde annuatim domui Hospitalis Sancti Johannis extra portam orientalem Oxoniae
tresdecim denarios ad duos anni terminos, videlicet
ad festum Sancti Michaelis sex denarios et obolum et
ad Annunciationem beatae Mariae sex denarios et
obolum, pro omni servitio et exactione et demanda.
Et nos pro nobis et successoribus nostris dicto R. et
haeredibus suis vel assignatis tanquam veris assignatis nostris cessimus et concessimus totum jus
nostrum quod habuimus vel habere potuimus in
praedicta terra cum omnibus pertinentiis suis. Ita
quidem quod dictus Thomas filius Thomae filii
Edwini et haeredes sui omni eodem modo teneantur
dicto R. et haeredibus suis vel assignatis warantizare
praedictam terram cum omnibus suis pertinentiis
contra omnes homines et feminas sicut nobis tene-
bantur warantizare pro ut in carta dicti Thomae
quam praedicto R. concessimus continetur. Pro hac
autem donatione, concessione, dimissione, liberatione,

et hac praesenti cartae nostrae confirmatione dedit nobis praedictus R. septem marcas argenti. Et ut haec omnia praedicta firma et stabilia in perpetuum permaneant hoc praesens scriptum sigilli nostri impressione roboravimus. Hiis testibus Petro filio Thoraldi tunc temporis Majore Oxoniae, Philippo Molendinario, Henrico filio Symonis, Galfrido de Stokwelle, Adam Feteplace, Waltero Aurifabro, Henrico Ynge, Johan Costard, Willelmo filio Alani, et aliis.'

[*Abstract*.—Brother William de Tyford, and the Convent of the Friar Preachers of Oxford, grant to Ralph de Chiltune, Chaplain, all their land lying between Robert With's, and that late of John de Navare, in the parish of St. Edward, in Oxford ; viz. that which they bought from Thomas, son of Thomas, son of Edwin, of Oxford ; paying an annual rent of 13d. to the Hospital of St. John, without the East Gate. For this donation, the said Ralph gave them 7 marks of silver. Witnesses. Peter, son of Thorold, then Mayor of Oxford. Philip, the Miller ; Henry, son of Simon ; Geoffrey de Stokwelle ; Adam Feteplace ; Walter, the Goldsmith ; Henry Ynge ; John Costard ; William, son of Alan ; and others.]

Various deeds, in the College Archives, show that this property passed from Ralph de Chiltune to Alice Haket of Lambourne, about 1270 ; from Alice de Lambourne to Robert de Grettone, about 1280 ;

from Robert de Grettone to William Burnel, in 1299 ; and from the executors of William Burnel to the College, in 1314, or at about that date.

At about the same time, Hugh de St. Ivo and Geoffrey de Horkestowe gave Chimers Hall to the College. Chimers Hall was in Sydyerd Street, near to King Street, in the parish of St. Edward the King. Sydyerd Street[1] reached from High Street to the entrance to Canterbury College.[2] It was the narrow, but busy, thoroughfare where the parchment sellers congregated, and where most of the parchment shops and stalls were to be found. In those days, when books were books, and manuscripts were worth copying, the selling of parchment was a great trade in Oxford. So, in 1304, Ralph le Wal, the Fisherman—' piscator '—sold to Richard Overhe, the Skinner—' pellipario '—a tenement, ' quod situm est in parochia Sancti Edwardi Regis in Oxonia, in vico qui vocatur Sydyerd inter tenementum Abbatis de Abyndone ex parte una, et tenementum Prioris Sanctae Frideswidae ex altera.'   And the next year, 1305, Richard Overhe granted to Masters Hugh de St. Ivo and Geoffrey de Horkestowe the same tenement, but described as ' quod vocatur Chimere Halle, quod situm est in parochia Sancti Edwardi Regis in Oxonia, in vico qui vocatur Sydyerd inter tenementum Abbatis de Abyndone ex parte una, et

---

[1] Now Oriel Street.   [2] Now Canterbury quadrangle, Ch. Ch.

tenementum Prioris Sanctae Frideswidae ex altera.'
In 1310, Hugh de St. Ivo and Geoffrey de Horkestowe gave this Chimers Hall, in Sydyerd Street,
to the Master and Scholars of Balliol College.   In
Balliofergus is a detailed account of what became of
Chimers Hall ; and also a description of the very
beautiful, and almost perfect, large seal, in red wax,
attached to the document granting the Hall to Canterbury College, now kept in the Balliol Archives.
There is another impression of this seal, on another
deed, that has also been carefully preserved.

  ' In the fourth Year of *R.* 2. the Master and
Scholars of our Colledge, called then *Balliol*-halle,
gave to *Canterbury* Colledge, now part of *Christ-
Church* Oxon : a messuage called *Chimer* hall,
formerly mentioned, lying towards *Kings-street*,
called there *Sydeard-street* East, and the Garden of
the said *Canterbury*-Colledge West, North and South
[which must be just opposite to *Oriel* Colledge] as
appears under the Seal of the said *Canterbury*
Colledge : In which Seal is represented [in regard of
that Colledges dependance on the Prior of *Christ-
Church* in *Canterbury*] *Austin the Monk*, in a Pulpit
with his Cross and Banner, Preaching to the barba-
rous Infidels [for such the *Saxons* then were] with
this Inscription in the Ring of the Seal, which is not
oval but orbicular ; *viz. Sigillum Collegii Aule Can-
tuarie in Oxonia*: upon which consideration, the

Prior and Convent of the said place granted, *Anno Dom:* 1393. and in 17 *R.* 2. to Mr *Tho: Tyrwhit* Master, and the Scholars of our said Colledge, and their Successors, an annual Rent of 26 s. 8 d. to be taken off their Mannor of *Newington* and its Appurtenances, in the County of *Oxon*, at the Feasts of *Easter* and *Michaelmas*, by equal portions for ever : which Grant was the same Year confirmed by the said King his Letters Patents, with Licence to distrain upon the foresaid Mannor in case of *non*-payment at either or any of the said Feasts.   But upon the dissolution of Religious Houses, and the return of the Lands into their Crown, the Rent was not paid, till Dr. Cotes, Master of our Colledge, and the Scholars thereof, had it decreed to them and their Successors, by the Chancellor and Court of Augmentations, in 34 *H.* 8. to be paid, together with the arrearages due from the dissolution, by the hands of the particular Receiver of the Court of Augmentations of the Revenues of the Crown, in the said County of *Oxon*, for the time being.   All which, may appear by the Exemplification of the said Decree under the Great Seal, and several other Writings in our Archives in *Oxford*, and *Canterbury* Box there.   This Rent was received down to the taking away of Cathedrals, by the late Rebellion, and that for many Years by the hands of Auditor *Squib* in *London*, who told us, That we were never

like to receive it more, unless we bought some of the
Lands belonging to the Church of *Canterbury*, and so
got it allowed in the Purchase. To this purpose a
Sollicitor was imploy'd at *Worcester*-house, for the
Purchase of a Quit-rent of about 38 s. *per annum*,
upon a Mannor in *Kent*, or some other such small
matter then left unsold. But since that time, I never
heard of the Sollicitor or Business : It may be that
the greediness of Purchasers went between him and
home ; for Men having devoured the whole dishes of
the Church, they were ready to fall together by the
Ears for the scraps. But how the dissolution of
Canterbury Church, either first or last aforesaid,
should extinguish our Rent setled in maner aforesaid, *restat inquirendum.*' [1]

The other Benefactions to the College, of about
this date, appear to have been, ' three Tofts and one
Garden, with the appurtenances contiguous to the
House of the Master and Scholars of *Balliol*-hall,
for the enlargement of their Mansion,' [2] given by
Hamond Haskman, and Thomas Cinlow. Also
Saucer Hall, which was given in 13 Edward III.
This Saucer Hall was sometimes called Sparrow
Hall ; and, at one time, Old Balliol Hall. It was
the tenement in Horsemonger Street rented for
John de Balliol's Scholars before the Lady Dervoi-
guilla established them in St. Mary's Hall. And we

---

[1] *Balliofergus*, p. 66.   [2] *Ibid.* p. 60.

read that, 'that Messuage of ours in St. *Giles's*
Parish, together with the Land in *Walton*-fields
thereunto belonging, was given 12 *Edward* 3. One
other Tenement in St. *Giles's* Parish was given
6 *Edw.* 3. A third Messuage and Garden in
St. *Giles's* Parish, was given 39 *Edw.* 3. The House
and the Appurtenances in St. *Peters* Parish in the
Bayly, given by *Jo: Burton* Bedel of the University,
49 *Edw.* 3. There are also six Writings tyed
together, of six Houses in St. *Ebbs* Parish : whereof
one was given in the Reign of *Edw.* 3. another by
George Nevil B. of *Exon*. The corner Tenement,
over-against *Candych*, was given 1 *R.* 2. but when
or how the Tenement adjoyning to it, which is now
the South-part of the *Katherine-wheel*, came to be
the Colledges, I doe not find ; the said Tenement
seemed to have belonged to St. *Fridesweds*, as being
formerly described to be on the west-part of *Old
Balliol*-hall. . . . That which now is the *Katherine-
wheel*, was given us 3 *Ric.* 2. as being described in
the Deed to be directly opposite to the East-end of
Magdalen Church. In the same Year also, *John
Duke* and *Julian* his Wife, gave a Messuage and
Shop in St. *Giles's* Parish : so that four Messuages
were given in St. *Giles's* Parish, but three of them
only remain to us : whereof, unless two united and
made one since, I cannot shew a reason. And last
of all, a shop under a room belonging to *Oriel*

Colledge in St. *Marys* Parish, was given 8 H. 4. which is part of Mr. Cryps's shop, late Book-seller in the High-street.   There is mention made in a Deed without date (and therefore very ancient) of a Messuage situate between a Tenement of the Universities, called *Old Balliol*-hall on the West, and a Tenement of the Master and Scholars of *Balliol*-hall, call'd *New Balliol*-hall ; which Tenement stood next to, or upon part of that ground where now *Hammonds* Lodgings do stand, which have been formerly call'd the *New buildings.*'[1]

There is no record of what the Catherine Wheel, here mentioned, was.   But it may be assumed that it was a small Hostel, or Inn, opposite to the east end of St. Mary Magdalen's Church ; and that it took its name from the fact of its near proximity to the College, of which St. Catherine was the Patroness.

The College Archives are rich in Royal Charters. Among them is the Grant of the Jews' land in Oxford, to William Burnel, from Edward I. in 1291. It is a small deed, fairly well written ; but the large seal, in green wax, attached by two silk cords, is much broken.   There is, also, a Licence from Edward I. for the land of William Burnel to be given to Balliol College.   This is a more elaborate document, and is better written.   It commences with a

---

[1] *Balliofergus*, p. 60.

fancy capital letter, and is ornamented with sprays of oak leaves and acorns.   The seal is quite perfect. There is another Licence from Edward I. for William Burnel's land to be given to the College ; but the seal is broken.   And an Inspeximus of Charters of Burnel's lands, from Edward II.   The large seal, partly broken, is in a thin linen wrapper, which was probably its original cover.   The date is 1314.

CHAPTER VIII.

' HITHERTO as it now appeares, ye scolars of this house had each but 8^d a weeke allowed them and y^t noe longer than till they were Masters of Arts, wch degree being taken by them, they were put out from y^t allowance and noe gratuity at all giuen to them to set them forth in ye world ; soe y^t diũs of them being poore & nothing to subsist on, were either exposed to beggery, or forced to relinquish their studyes and seek maintenance mechanically ; wch great inconuenience being beheld by many & pittied, it pleased one Sr Will: Felton K^t in ye 14 Ed. 3. or therabouts to giue to ye Coll: ye Rectory of Abboldesley with ye Mannour therof in Huntingdonshire to augment their number, & increase their commons to 12^d a weeke and supply them with bookes clothes & other neceffaryes, wch Rectory pope Clement 6 did not only apppriate to ye Colledge (a competency being reserved for ye support of ye Vicare there) but confirmed y^t wch Sr Will: Felton had began viz y^t ye fellowes of this house might keepe their places, notwithftanding they were Masters or Doctours till they had got an ecclefiaftial benefice ; as for ye increase of ye diet and number ye next Benefactour as it seemeth pformed.' [1]

So wrote Antony à Wood.

Sir William de Felton's gift was considerable ; and it greatly augmented the growing riches of the College. The House of Balliol was rapidly becoming an important centre of learning in the University. But a difficulty had arisen in the internal organization of the House, a difficulty which was likely to fall heavily upon the Scholars, and which might prove detrimental to the further development of the foundation. Sir William de Felton's gift helped to meet the exigency. The Lady Dervorguilla had provided well, and with all solicitude, for the needs of her Scholars ; but she had thought of them only as Scholars, the boys whom her husband had wished to maintain while they were studying at Oxford. And Dervorguilla did not live long enough, after the promulgation of her beautiful Statutes, to see the new need arise, the necessity to give further aid to her Scholars after they became Masters in Arts. This was a growth in the design of the House of Balliol, which could only come with the practical experience of the working of the Collegiate system, and which could only be met by the generosity of additional Benefactors.

[1] *Antony à Wood. MS. in Bodleian Library.*

In the Archives are very many documents relating to Abboldesley.   The first which comes under
our notice is a rather large, very yellow, piece of
parchment, with writing on it, still quite legible, in
faded brown ink.   It is a Grant, from Ralph Ridel
to the Abbot of Jeddeworth, of the advowson of
Abboldesley ; and a short paragraph at the end is the
confirmation by Malcolm, King of Scotland.   There
does not appear to have been any seal.   The date
is about 1256.   The next is a long, narrow, equally
yellow, and now very stiff, slip of parchment.   The
Latin writing on it is in round letters, much abbreviated, and complicated by many flourishes.   This
document tells us that ' John, the Abbot of Jeddeworth Monastery, and the Convent thereof, grant to
Sir William de Felton, Knight, for his life, and that
of his heir, an annual pension of 3 marks, which
they have from the parish Church of Abboldesley,
with the right of patronage to the same.   Dated at
the Monastery of Jeddeworth, on Monday after the
Feast of St. Andrew the Apostle . 1340.'   The large
Abbey seal, in white wax, is in fairly good condition ;
but was never a good impression.   It is attached to
the deed by a strong parchment thong.

There is also ' A Latin grant, on parchment, to
William de Felton, Knight, by King Edward the
Third, of the advowson of the Church of Albol-
desleye, which had come into his hands by the

forfeiture of the Abbot of Jeddeworth [Jedburgh];
with permission to the said William to give the same
to the Master and Scholars of Balliol, the Statute of
Mortmain notwithstanding. Dated the 12th of April,
in the 14th year of his reign. The impression of
the great seal of England, still covered with what
was probably its original linen wrapper, is in fair
condition.' [1]

There are, besides these, several different Grants,
or copies of Grants, from Sir William de Felton to
Balliol College. They are, mostly, small slips of
parchment : but each with Sir William de Felton's
seal, in brown wax, securely affixed by a broad
thong.

The appropriation of the Rectory of Abboldesley
to the College was confirmed by a letter from Pope
Clement VI. This document is, in one place, very
difficult to read ; for across it is a broad brown stain,
as if, at some time, chemicals had been used. Some
words are almost obliterated ; but the transcript
given here, though obviously faulty, is as correct as
the dark stain, and the varied contractions of the
original, will permit. The words are,—

'Clemens, Episcopus, Servus servorum Dei, ad
perpetuam rei memoriam. Scientiarum fructus, per
quos non solum animarum salus sed etiam tempor-
alis quietis et pacis commoda provenire noscuntur,

Hist MSS. Com. Fourth Report, p. 448.

augeri ubilibet affectantes, ad illa Nos promptos libenter et favorabiles exhibemus ex quibus fructus ipsi exuberare ac continuum, actore Domino, suscipere valeant incrementum. Exhibita siquidem Nobis dilectorum filiorum universorum Clericorum et Scholarium domus seu aulae Ballioli vulgariter nuncupatae, de Oxonia, Lincolniensis diocesis, ubi viget studium generale, petitio continebat quod in dicta aula, pia largitione et elemosina ipsius Fundatoris, quamplures Studentes Clerici, singuli videlicet eorundem octo denarios sterlingorum tantum singulis septimanis ab antiquo perceperunt et percipere dinoscuntur, et cum Magistri in Artibus facti fuerunt extunc ab aula expelluntur eadem, ita quod in aliis scientiis liberalibus propter ipsorum paupertatem proficere nequeunt sed interdum, studium dimittentes, victum mechanice querere compelluntur. Quibus dilectus filius nobilis vir Willelmus Felton, miles, dictae diocesis, comparens[1] numerum dictorum Scholarium affectat in aula hujusmodi augmentari[2] ac ordinare quod Scholares ipsi libros diversarum Facultatum habeant in communi, et quod singuli eorum vestes sufficientes et duodecim denarios monetae praedictae percipiant singulis septimanis, et quod possint in dicta aula libere remanere, ac praedicta intege[3] percipere ad quemcunque statum Magistratus seu Doctoratus diveniant donec fuerint

Probably.—   [1] *compatiens.*   [2] *augmentare.*   [3] *integre.*

competens beneficium ecclesiasticum assecuti et
extunc aulam ipsam dimittere tenebuntur quibus alii
idonei debeant surrogari, et quod idem miles jus
patronatus Ecclesiae parochialis de Aboldesleye,
dictae diocesis, elemosinariae dictae aulae ac Clericis
et Scholaribus ejusdem procuravit et etiam acquisivit,
sperans quod sedes Apostolica Ecclesiam ipsam
onnes [1] sic sunt patroni eidem elemosinariae et aulae
praedictae concedere in usus proprios dignaretur.
Quare praefati Clerici, Scholares, et miles Nobis
humiliter supplicarunt ut Ecclesiam ipsam, onnes [1]
fructus, redditus, et proventus quadraginta Marcha-
rum sterlingorum secundum taxationem decimae
valorem annuum ut asserunt non excedunt, Scholaribus aulae et elemosinariae praedictis in usus
praedictos concedere, ipsamque ipsis unire perpetuo
dignaremur. Nos itaque, hujusmodi supplicationibus
inclinati, praedictam parochialem Ecclesiam cum
omnibus juribus et pertinentiis suis exnunc praefatis
Scholaribus et elemosinariis pro complendis praemissis in proprios usus Apostolica auctoritate concedimus, illamque ipsis auctoritate praedicta connecti-
mus et unimus, ita quod, cedente vel decedente
Rectore ipsius Ecclesiae qui nunc est, vel alias
Ecclesia ipsa quovismodo vacare [2] liceat Scholaribus
aulae supradictae possessionem ipsius Ecclesiae
auctoritate propria apprehendere, ipsamque in usus

Probably.—   [1] *omnes*, or *cujus*, written *cuius*.   [2] *vacante*.

dictorum Scholarium aulae perpetuo retinere. Reservata tamen et assignata perpetuo Vicario in ipsa Ecclesia, per loci Ordinarium in ea ad praesentationem dictorum Scholarium instituendo, de ipsius Ecclesiae fructibus, redditibus, proventibus congrua portione ex qua dictus Vicarius congrue sustentari, jura Episcopalia solvere, et omnia alia sibi incumbentia onera valeat supportare. Non obstantibus si aliqui super provisionibus sibi faciendis de hujusmodi Ecclesiis vel aliis beneficiis ecclesiasticis in illis partibus speciales vel generales Nostras vel praedecessorum Nostrorum Romanorum Pontificum aut Legatorum sedis Apostolicae litteras impetrarunt, etiam si per eas ad inhibitionem, reservationem, et decretum, vel alias quomodolibet sit processum ; quas quidem litteras et processus habitos per easdem ad dictam parochialem Ecclesiam volumus non extendi sed nullum per hoc eis quo ad assecutionem Ecclesiarum et beneficiorum aliorum praejudicium generari. Et quibuslibet privilegiis et litteris Apo stolicis generalibus vel specialibus quorumcunque tenorum existant per quae praesentibus non expressa vel totaliter non inserta effectus praesentium impediri valeat quomodolibet et . . . . . ferri[1] et de quibus quorumcunque totis tenoribus de verbo in verbum habenda sit in Nostris litteris mentio specialis. Nos enim exnunc . . . . .[2] decernimus et inane si secus

Probably.—   [1] *vel differri.*   [2] *irritum.*

super hiis a quoquam quavis auctoritate scienter vel
ignoranter contigerit attemptari.   Nulli ergo . . . .
hominum liceat hanc paginam Nostrae concessionis,
connexionis, unionis, voluntatis et constitutionis infringere vel ei a . . .[1] temere [2] . . . contraire.   Si
quis autem hoc attemptare praesumpserit indigna-
tionem Omnipotentis Dei, et Beatorum Petri et
Pauli, Apostolorum Ejus, se noverit incursurum.
Datum apud Pontem Sorgiae, Avinionensis diocesis,
iiij kalend. Maii, Pontificatus Nostri anno primo.'

[*Translation.*—Clement, Bishop, Servant of the
servants of God, for everlasting remembrance.
Knowing well that the fruits of Science promote,
not only the salvation of souls, but the advantages
of temporal peace and quiet, it is Our desire that
they should everywhere multiply ; and, therefore,
We gladly show Ourselves ready and favourable in
arrangements by which such fruits are likely to become abundant, and to receive at the Hand of the
Lord continuous development.   A petition presented
to Us by Our beloved sons, all the Clerks and
Scholars of the House or Hall commonly called
Balliol, in Oxford, of the diocese of Lincoln, which
is the seat of an University, contained that in the
said Hall, by the pious bounty and alms of the
Founder, many clerical Students receive, and have
from ancient time received, to wit, each of them,

Probably.—   ¹ *ausu.*   ² *temerario.*

eight pence sterling a week, and no more ; and that when they have been made Masters in Arts, they are immediately compelled to leave the same Hall ; and, in consequence, through poverty, they are unable to pursue the study of the other liberal Sciences, and are sometimes forced to quit the University, and to seek their living in some mechanical trade. To whom cometh Our beloved son, the noble William Felton, of the same diocese, Knight, desiring to raise the number of the said Scholars, and to order that they should have books pertaining to the various Faculties in common, and that each should have sufficient clothing, and receive twelve pence a week of the said money ; and that they should have liberty to remain in the said Hall, and to receive the aforesaid in full, to whatever degree of Master or Doctor they may reach, until they have obtained a competent Ecclesiastical benefice ; and then they shall be bound to withdraw from the Hall, and other fit persons are to be substituted in their place ; and that this same Knight has secured and acquired for the Almshouse of the said Hall, and its Clerks and Scholars, the right of patronage of the parish Church of Aboldesleye of the said diocese, in the hope that the Apostolic See would deign to grant this Church (for by this arrangement all are joint Patrons) to the aforesaid Almshouse or Hall for their own use. Wherefore, the aforesaid Clerks, Scholars, and Knight, have

made Us humble supplication that We should deign
to grant and unite in perpetuity, for the uses aforesaid, this same Church (now all the fruits, rents, and
revenues do not, they say, exceed the annual value
of forty marks sterling, according to the tithe rate)
to the Scholars, Hall, and Almshouse aforesaid.
We, therefore, favourably inclining to this supplication, by Our Apostolic authority, do grant to the
aforesaid Scholars, and Almshouse, the parochial
Church aforesaid, to hold henceforward with all its
rights and appurtenances to their own use, for the
recited ends ; and by the authority aforesaid, We
connect and unite it to them, in such wise, that, on
the retirement or decease of the present Rector of
the Church, or on its vacancy from any other cause,
it shall be lawful for the Scholars of the aforesaid
Hall to take possession of the Church by their own
authority, and to retain it in perpetuity, for the uses
of the said Scholars. With the reservation, however, and assignation to a perpetual Vicar, who is
to be instituted in the said Church by the Ordinary
of the diocese, on the presentation of the said
Scholars, of a suitable pension from the fruits, rents,
and revenues of the Church, by which the said Vicar
may be suitably maintained, and placed in a position
to pay the Bishop's dues, and to bear all the other
burthens incumbent on him. Notwithstanding any
Letters, whether special or general, which may have

been obtained by any persons, either from Us or Our predecessors, the Roman Pontiffs, or from Legates of the Apostolic See, with regard to provisions to be made for them from Churches of this kind, or other Ecclesiastical benefices in those regions, even if by their means they have come to inhibition, reservation, judgment, or any other process whatsoever. It is Our will that such Letters, or the processes taken in virtue of them, shall not extend to the said parish Church, yet so that hereby no prejudice accrue to them as regards obtaining other Churches and benefices. And notwithstanding any privileges or Letters Apostolic, general or special, whatever may be their tenor, by which, through their not being expressed or recited at length in these presents, the effect of these presents might be anywise impeded . . . . and of which, and of whose entire tenors, word for word, special mention should by rights be made in Our Letters. For We decree that henceforth . . . . whatever contrary may be attempted in these matters by any one, on whatever authority, whether with knowledge or ignorantly. Let it not, therefore, be lawful for any man to infringe or rashly oppose this page of Our concession, connection, union, will, and constitution. Should any one have the presumption to attempt it, let him be sure he will incur the indignation of Almighty God, and of blessed Peter and Paul, His Apostles. Given

at Pont de Sorgues, in the diocese of Avignon. April
28.   In the first year of Our Pontificate.]

It would be interesting if we could find, in the
Vatican Archives, the petition which was sent from
Dervorguilla's ' poor Scholars' to the Holy Father,
asking him, in his universal care for his children, to
make secure to them and to their House the increase
of income, which was being given to them.[1]   That
petition must have explained the need of the Scholars
to remain for longer time in the House ; and their
want of money, for their support, while studying the
other Sciences.   It spoke, doubtless, as did most of
the early letters about the College, of ' the alms given
by the devoutness of the Founder, Sir John de
Balliol.'   And then it pleaded that the Scholars'
share in those alms did not admit of their getting
some necessary books, nor did it enable them to meet
some of the expenses, which would fall upon them
when they became Masters in Arts.   The worn and
shabby Scholars' coats would not last for ever ; and
Scholars found it hard to relinquish studies, and take
up trades.   To-day we can smile at the thought of
such poverty.   To-day, the story of the struggling

---

[1] Mr. Bass Mullinger states that this Licence was obtained from
the Pope by John Wyclif, in 1361 ; and quotes it as an instance of
Wyclif's efforts on behalf of the Secular Clergy at Oxford. (*University
of Cambridge*, vol. i. p. 264.) But Pope Clement VI. sent the letter
to the College in 1342 ; and John Wyclif was not Master of Balliol
until nearly twenty years after that date.

life of the poor Oxford Scholar is like a strange tale
told to the incredulous. At Pont de Sorgues, near to
Avignon, the petition was read, and thought over ;
and there the wise and kind answer, from the 'Servant of the servants of God,' was dictated. The
Pope's reply seems to tell us almost the words of the
Scholars' petition. He speaks to his ' beloved sons '
about the advantages of the studies they wish to
pursue ; and he decides that they must have books
pertaining to the various Faculties, and that they
should have sufficient clothing ; and he speaks of
their House by the homely and honourable name
of Almshouse. Nor does the Letter forget other
questions, about a just and fair arrangement for the
Priest, who was to have charge of the Church at
Abboldesley.

Fatherly care met with filial obedience. There
are, in one of the documents relating to Abboldesley,
minute details of a composition made for the Vicar,
by John Synwell, Bishop of Lincoln, in 1361. From
it we learn, among other things,—

' In primis, videlicet, quod idem Vicarius habeat
sexaginta acras terrarum dominicarum ipsius ecclesiae, ac omnes et omnimodas decimas, minores oblationes quascunque et cujuscunque generis fuerint,
necnon mortuaria viva et mortua, decimas molendin-
orum et quicquid ad alteragium dictae ecclesiae de
jure vel consuetudine noscitur pertinere. Percipiat

N

insuper idem Vicarius et habeat de Clericis seu Scholaribus praedictis annuatim pensionem sexaginta soli-
dorum sterlingorum in supplementum portionis suae
in festo Sancti Michaelis Archangeli apud Abbotesley
annis singulis persolvendorum. Exhibeant insuper et
tradant iidem Clerici seu Scholares praefato Vicario
infra annum a tempore confectionis praesentium continue munerandum unum mansum competentem in
eadem villa cum una aula, una camera, una coquina,
uno stabulo et una grangia sumptibus dictorum
Scholarium nostro arbitrio aedificandum, decimis
blandorum et feni et residua parte terrarum dominicarum illius ecclesiae dictis Clericis reservatis. Iidem
vero Clerici cancellum illius ecclesiae et fenestras
ejusdem quotiens indiguerint cooperiant, construant
et reficiant ac reparent seu suis sumptibus faciant
congrue reparari ac solvant procurationes Archidiaconi dicti loci. Praefatus quoque Vicarius vestimenta
ornamenta ac libros ejusdem ecclesiae ipsius sumptibus propriis reparet reficiat seu faciat reparari, Syno-
dalia persolvat panem, vinum pro sacramento altaris,
thus, ciramen et cirpos pro ecclesia et lumen in
cancello, et solvat decimam et procurationem Car-
dinalium et aliorum nunciorum Apostolicorum pro
rata taxa portionis suae, et ministret.'

[*Translation.* — Firstly, to wit, that the said
Vicar shall have sixty acres of Church lands, apper-
taining to the said Church ; and all and every kind

of tithes, lesser offerings whatsoever, and of whatever kind they may be; as well as burial fees, in kind or in specie, tithes of grist, and whatsoever by right, or by custom, is known to belong to the revenue of the said Church. Moreover, the said Vicar shall receive and have, from the said Scholars, an annual pension of sixty pence sterling, to make up his dues at the Feast of St. Michael the Archangel, at Abboldesley; to be paid each year. Moreover, the said Clerics or Scholars shall present and give to the aforesaid Vicar, within a year from the drawing up of these presents, one suitable dwelling, always to be kept furnished, in the said Village, with one reception room, one sleeping chamber, one kitchen, one stable, and one granary, to be built at the expense of the said Scholars, to our satisfaction: tithes of corn and hay, and the remaining portion of the Church lands of the said Church, being reserved unto the said Clerics. And the said Clerics shall roof, construct, renew and repair the chancel of the said Church, and the windows as often as need shall be; or at their own expense shall cause them to be suitably repaired. And they shall pay the fees of the Archdeacon of the said place. The aforesaid Vicar, at his own expense, shall renew and repair, or cause to be repaired, the vestments, ornaments, and books of the said Church; he shall pay the dues decreed by

Synods, and shall provide bread, wine, for the
Sacrament of the Altar, incense, wax, and rushes,
for the Church, and a light in the Sanctuary ; and
shall pay tithes, and processes of Cardinals, and of
other Nuncios, according to the rate fixed for his
income, and shall do service.]

' About ye same time y^t S^r W: Feltons gift was
one Sr Philippe Someruile Lord of ye mannour of
Wichnor in staffordshire became a considerable
Benefactour by giuing ye church of Mikell Benton
with lands in y^t parish in ye Dioceff of Durham &
ye County of Northumberland for ye maintenance of
6 Scolars aboue ye antient number of 16 fellowes y^t
had bin before in ye house . and because they should
be all under one gouornment, & not be altogeather
confined to Deruorgills statutes he was pleased to
proceede soe farre as to giue them a new body of
Statutes, (much croffing those of ye said Deruorgille).' [1]

Sir Philip de Somervyle distinctly states that it
was not his ' intention to destroy the ancient foundation, or the laws or Statutes of the earlier Founders,
but rather to confirm them.' And he further adds,
that the Scholars shall not be bound to observe
anything in his Ordinance, which might be contrary
to the existing Statutes. Therefore, Antony à
Wood's statement about the ' new body of Statutes,

---

[1] *Antony à Wood. MS. in Bodleian Library.*

(much croſſing those of yᵉ said Deruorgille),' is questionable ; unless we take the brackets, which separate the words from the context, to imply a doubt, in his mind, on the subject. Sir Philip de Somervyle, like Sir William de Felton, wished, not to put aside the Lady Dervorguilla's Statutes and Ordinances ; but only to add to them the new regulations, which the growing wealth, and the requirements of the House of Balliol, and the increase of the number of the Scholars, made necessary.

The Statutes of Sir Philip de Somervyle have, like many other documents in the College Archives, their own special and great points of interest. They bear witness to the importance of Dervorguilla's ' House of the Scholars of Balliol.' The House must have earned some reputation in the University. It was taking its place, and doing its work, in the intellectual world. It was fulfilling its purpose ; helping poor Scholars ; uniting, under a common name, those who were eager to devote themselves to study, and who recognized, even in those early days, the peculiar advantages of the Collegiate system. Such an House attracted the attention of the rich and the generous, who wished to contribute to the good work begun, and who were proud to associate their names with such a foundation. Sir William de Felton, and Sir Philip de Somervyle,

were liberal Benefactors. And their gifts, freely
and charitably bestowed, strengthened and for-
tified Dervorguilla's work; and were like seals of
approbation, affixed by time, to her foundation
deeds.

Dervorguilla's Statutes are instinct with tender
solicitude for her Scholars, and that spirit of self-
reliance which she wished her House to maintain.
In Sir Philip de Somervyle's Statutes we trace the
same thoughtfulness, and firmness. Edward, King
of Scotland, gave his name to the new Statutes.
Edward had experienced strange and sad vicissitudes. He had seen his father a King; and then,
without cause, disgraced. He remembered his own
early imprisonment, with his father; and his banished
life, when a boy, in France. Still fresh in his
memory was his recall to England, and to Scotland.
Around him, he saw the sad dying of all his family;
the miserable state of his kingdom, the instability of
his subjects, the uncertainty of his throne; perplexi-
ties and troubles everywhere. But one good work
was growing steadily; and he was asked to add his
name to the House, which was to be a lasting
memorial to his family. Many dim memories grew
vivid again, as he thought of the House at Oxford;
recollections of his childhood, household names, and
home traditions. In the midst of all that was sad
and drear, one proud day came; when, in his name,

and with his sanction, Sir Philip helped to perpe-
tuate Dervorguilla's work.

Sir Philip de Somervyle's Statutes preserve to
us the name of Edward, King of the Scots; and
also the name, so honoured by all lovers of books
and Libraries, of Richard de Bury, Bishop of
Durham. When a certain number of Monks, from
the Benedictine Monastery at Durham, came to
Oxford, and established themselves near to Balliol
College, Bishop Richard greatly helped them, gave
them books, and, to some extent, endowed their
House. And when he died, in 1345, he left to the
Benedictine Monks of Durham, at Oxford, all his
books. It was a munificent gift. We discern, in
Sir Philip's new Statutes, the influence of Bishop
Richard. As Dervorguilla had wished Brother
Richard de Slikeburne, and, after him, other
Franciscans, to have some control, and a certain
discretionary power over the affairs of her House;
so, in the new Statutes, the Prior of the Benedictines was to have, and to exercise, much the same
kind of authority and influence. We have read how
the Balliol Scholars pleaded to the Pope their need
of more books; and the thought comes, that they
must have seen the beautiful volumes which were
already in the Library of the Durham Monks,
perhaps often used them, and so the desire for more
books originated, and grew. Bishop Richard's

influence was at work in Oxford, and had a part in the Scholars' petition.

Sir Philip de Somervyle's Statutes are written in very contracted Latin, on one large sheet of parchment. The writing is diminutive; and the ink has much faded. The parchment has been kept folded to a small size, and the many folds have added to the difficulty of reading some words. To this document is attached, by a long parchment thong, the seal of Sir Philip. It is in dark green wax; a rather large seal, in fairly good preservation. These Statutes are given at length in *Balliofergus*; but have been badly copied from the original. There are many obvious mistakes in the Latin of the transcript; and very many printer's errors. The following is a full translation.—

'Edward, by the Grace of God, King of Scotland, Founder of the original foundation of the Master and Scholars of the Hall or House of Balliol, in Oxford, to all and each to whom these presents shall come, Salvation in the Arms of the Saviour. We have seen the Charter of Sir Philip de Somervyle, Lord of Wichnore, Knight, and the Statutes contained in the said Charter, concerning the Master and Scholars of the Hall or House of Balliol, in Oxford, bearing the seals of the Lord Richard, late Bishop of Durham, of blessed memory, and of the Venerable Religious, the Lords, the

Prior and Chapter of Durham, and of the Reverend and discreet Lord Chancellor of the University of Oxford, and of the Master and Scholars of the Hall or House of Balliol, in Oxford, likewise the seal of the said Sir Philip de Somervyle; and have caused them to be read aloud in our presence, in the following form of words.—

' In the Name of the Most Holy and Undivided Trinity, the Father, the Son, and the Holy Ghost, and of the Glorious Virgin Mary, and of the Blessed Virgin and Martyr, Catherine, and of all the Saints, I, Philip de Somervyle, trusting to the goodness of the Supreme Author of all goods and possessions, and confidently relying upon the Grace of the Same, Who disposes and directs the wishes of men to a good end, according to His Will ; and being often exercised in mind, pondering whether I could do aught for the Honour of His Name, in return for the abundance which He has granted me in this life ; I have granted, as a free gift, the advowson of the Church of Mickle-Benton, in the county of Northumberland, and in the diocese of Durham, together with two plough-lands[1] of arable land, and twenty acres of meadow, in the fields of the same City, to the Master and Scholars of the House of Balliol, in Oxford, and their successors, for the

---

[1] ' As much as two ploughs will till in a year.' *Note in Balliofergus*, p. 37.

augmentation of the number of Scholars, and the sustenance of the same in perpetuity, and for the salvation of my soul, and the soul of my beloved wife, Margaret, and for the Honour and Glory of our Lord, Jesus Christ, and Saint Catherine, Virgin and Martyr. And this Grant I approve, ratify, and confirm, of my own free will, and after due deliberation, and I ordain that it shall remain in the hands of the same Master and Scholars in perpetuity, subject to the forms and conditions hereinafter written, which are strictly to be observed, if God be willing, in the matter both of persons and of rules. Therefore do I ordain as follows, with the full consent of the aforesaid Master and Scholars.—

' That, in addition to the sixteen Fellows elected according to the ancient usages of the Fellows of the said House, supported by the means at present in its possession, six Scholars be chosen henceforth by the Fellows of the said House, who shall study Arts. And in their election or admission to board and lodging, those shall have the preference who come from places nearest to the place where the aforesaid property, granted by me to the said House, is situate ; provided that in them, or some of them, be found the conditions mentioned in former Ordinances ; namely, that they excel in poverty, ability, and manners.

' And there shall be a Superior, dwelling in the

said House, who shall always be called by the name
of Master, a man circumspect in matters spiritual
and temporal, who shall be set over the Scholars
that dwell in the House itself, and the Ministers of
the Altar, and all other officers or servants, whatever place or title they hold, appointed for the ex-
ternal or internal administration or management ;
and all Scholars, as well as Ministers of the Altar,
officers and other servants whatsoever, shall obey
him and give heed to him as their Superior, in those
things which concern their duties.　Concerning the
conditions of his entering on office, his election or
his deposition, and all other things regarding him, I
desire that those rules be strictly observed, which
are hereafter laid down on this head.　And I desire
and order that, from the number of the Scholars of
the aforesaid House, there be chosen, after the
manner below laid down, six Fellows who shall have
been Regents in the Faculty of Arts, who shall
attend the Schools in the Faculty of Theology ; they
shall be permitted also to study other Faculties, in
the Vacations ; and they shall, for the space of at
least two years, be instructed in decrees and
decretals.

'I also order that the election of a permanent
Master take place after the following manner.　All
the Fellows in residence, and those absent from just
and necessary cause, provided that they can come

without very great difficulty, shall be assembled. The Principal, or he who supplies his place, shall enjoin on each and all most faithfully to do what may be best for the House; they shall choose two Masters in Arts, who shall sit in scrutiny with the Principal, or him who fills his place. And they, being elected by common consent, shall take a Corporal oath before him who is senior in the House according to standing; and the Principal shall, in his own person, take the same oath before the same senior, that he has not induced, and will not induce, any one by any means whatsoever against his own free will to speak for any man in the election of a Master. And every Fellow of the House shall, on the strength of his own oath, be strictly charged by the same senior to observe this oath. Also, they shall each and all swear, touching the Holy Gospels, in the presence of all the Fellows, that they will faithfully, and without any respect of persons, and with no consideration of past or future reward, speak for him whom they know to have most knowledge, most ability, and most zeal for advancing the affairs of the House. Hereafter the Principal, and the two elected by common consent, shall sit in secret and faithfully receive the votes of each, and write them down; they shall faithfully declare him elected Master, for whom a majority of the votes are given. And if it happen that some receive an equal number of votes, he who is chosen by the senior part of the Community shall be elected Master. And I ordain that one part shall be called senior, according to pre-eminence in learning, and longer standing in the House, and the like matters, according to which one man is counted senior to another in a College, or one part of it to another. After the election, the Principal, or the senior according to standing in the House, shall cause the Master to swear before all that he will observe faithfully the Statutes and Ordinances laid down by me. Also I desire and order that the Master so elected shall be sent to my Manor of Wichnore, with a letter certifying his election, before entering upon his office, and shall call upon the Lord of the said Manor for the time being, if at that time there be a Lord of the said Manor, of my blood, and explain to him the reason of his coming : and the said Lord of that Manor shall take no exception to the form of election, or the person elected, nor make any kind of objection ; but shall receive him as Master of the said House. But if the Lord of the Manor be not there present, it shall suffice if he present himself to him who is in charge of the said Manor, and explain to him the reason of his coming. And if it chance that my inheritance be divided among my sisters, he shall present himself to the elder sister, or her heirs (provided that they be of

my blood), at the said Manor of Wichnore, under
the form already prescribed.   And the said Master,
when he returns from the said Manor to Oxford,
shall be presented by the Principal and one senior,
or by two seniors, to the Chancellor of the University for the time being, or to his representative ; and
to the Prior, or Warden, of the Monks of Durham,
studying at Oxford, who is the deputy there
appointed by the Lord Prior of the Monks of
Durham ; and to two Masters belonging to other
Colleges, who shall be present at the presentation.
They shall make no objection, but confirm everything done ; and he shall take a Corporal oath
before them, faithfully to observe the Ordinances
and Constitutions laid down by the said Sir Philip,
with the consent of the said Scholars ; and he shall
take the same oath at the Manor of Wichnore,
before the Lord of the said Manor, if at the time of
his presentation the said Lord be present ; and if the
Chancellor, or his representative, or the said Prior,
or Warden, of the Monks, or the said two Masters,
fail to attend to this matter, or in any other way
refuse to carry out the said confirmation, he shall be
considered to have been confirmed by the mere fact
of being thus elected, and afterwards presented to
the said persons.   And the same form shall be
accurately observed concerning the admission of any
member of the said House elected to study

Theology, and his reception by the said Chancellor or his representative, and the aforesaid Prior or Guardian of the Monks, and the said two Masters.

' And let this be specially observed in the said House, that concerning them who are to be elected to study Theology, great caution be exercised lest any be elected save those who are upright, pure, peaceful, humble, having ability for the pursuit of learning, and a desire to make progress. And I ordain that they be elected by the Community of the Fellows, after the following manner, provided that they have been Regent in Arts. The Master shall assemble the Community of the said House, and after administering to them the Sacrament of the Lord, shall strictly enjoin upon them faithfully and without respect of persons, and putting aside all favour and affection, to elect some one or more to study the said Faculty, whom from experience they know to be likely to make progress therein, and to be most able, and of good manners. And that one, or those who receive the votes of the majority, shall be elected to attend the Schools in Theology. And if it chance that some of those to be elected receive an equal number of votes, the senior according to standing in the House, shall be preferred. And that one, or those elected to study Theology, shall in the sixth year of their attendance of the Schools, bring forward theses, and for one year, or two if it seem that his doing so is of profit to the Community, and in the ninth or tenth year he shall lecture on a book of Sentences, and in the twelfth or thirteenth year he shall begin to teach in the said Faculty, unless he be hindered by legitimate or honourable cause. And the Master shall attend the Schools in any Faculty that he will.

' So also the number of the Scholars to be elected to the said House, as aforesaid, and supported by the income given by me. And of these each shall receive eleven pence from the hands of his Master, or of those who are deputed to receive and expend the revenues of the said House, provided that the allowance of each of the Fellows in the said House, supported by other revenue, be raised to eleven pence by the aforesaid revenues granted by me. And in time of scarcity, the share of each Fellow of the said House, shall, according to the decision of the Master and the Community, be raised to fifteen pence inclusive, weekly. And I desire that each of the said Scholars shall receive in the weeks of the great Feasts, such as the week of the Nativity of our Lord, and Easter week, and the like, four pence in addition to what he was accustomed to receive in that week formerly. The Master shall have a chamber assigned to him alone, and a boy to serve him, who according to the Ordinance of the said Community shall receive his sustenance from the common revenues. And since it will often be necessary that strangers coming to the said House on business be received by the Master, I order that, in the case of such strangers, for the honour of the Community, he shall have for himself and his guests, (if it seem expedient to him), a table, in no way luxurious, in his own chamber, at the common expense, and for such time only ; unless he be compelled by sickness, or some other reasonable cause. The said Master shall receive forty shillings yearly for his necessary expenses, when the revenues granted by me shall suffice for this, or until better provision be made for him by me, or by others, or by the Community. And I order that the said Master shall take a Corporal oath, that every year on St. Margaret's day, or at some time to be assigned by the Community, he will give a faithful account of his administration, and of all goods belonging to the said House, before the whole Community, or some few deputed by it to hear his rendering of account. And he shall with all care attend to his office, externally and internally, as the nature of the case, or the necessity of time or place, demand ; and in every year diligently visit all the property belonging to the said House, either in person, or through some discreet Fellow chosen by the Community for this purpose, if so it seem well to the Community. And he shall estimate and value the property in each place, and faithfully enter this estimate and valuation in the books, and being so entered shall give it into the hands of the Scholars, that thereafter when his accounts are to be heard, the faithfulness of these accounts may be the better attested by a comparison of these books.   And when the account of the Master has been rendered in full, if there be any residue from the goods of the said House over and above the expenses incurred by the Community, he shall be bound within a month from the rendering of his account to hand over the residue to the Treasurer, or publicly make acknowledgment of the debt, or in some other way satisfy the Community.   And if there be any such residue, I order that a part be converted to the use of the Fellows, and a part for the support of charges falling on the House.

‘ And if it chance that the Master be incapacitated by a short illness, a full share in proportion to the time, or some further support, sufficient and in no way excessive, shall be granted him from the common funds.   And if any of the other Scholars of the said House be sick, a similar allowance shall be made them at the common expense, from that time forward, if they be deemed of service or necessity to the House.   And if the sickness of the said Master be incurable, and there be no hope of his recovery ; and if by reason of his sickness, the Community decide

that the Master is unable to do the business of the
House, and properly to exercise the office of Master;
then, by that fact, he shall be bound to give up his
office, and according to the prescribed form of election, another Master shall be elected in his place;
and he shall receive some sufficient support, as the
Community shall decide, for the rest of his life, at the
common expense. And if one of the said Scholars
shall suffer from an incurable disease, by reason of
which he is unable otherwise to gain his living, he
shall receive as charity nine pence weekly outside the
House, from the revenues granted by me, if he
obtains no better support elsewhere, provided always
that the means of the said House suffice for this.
Also I order and determine that every Fellow at his
admission shall take a Corporal oath, that he will not,
through himself or others, procure and knowingly
cause himself to be elected to some other College,
where the stipend is higher, in the said University.
And if it happen that he be elected to some College
of this kind, by that very fact, he shall cease to receive
a stipend from the aforesaid House. But let the
Master know that he is not bound to observe this
article. And every Fellow, on his admission to the
aforesaid House, shall swear that he will with all his
strength preserve and defend the rights and possessions of the said House in all parts of the world, and
will faithfully labour to improve them; and when, by

the Favour of God, they attain to better fortune, he will advance them in every lawful and honourable way, and especially by always giving help and counsel for the defence and preservation of the rights of the said House, and for their improvement; and that whenever need be, he will constantly give faithful advice to the said House, if it be asked of him. And if the said Master, from patrimony, or spirituality, or in any other way, advance to an income of the value of forty pounds, he shall from that time no longer perform the duties of his office, and shall be excluded from all advantage accruing from the said House. And I order that the same form be observed for any other Fellow, if in any way aforesaid his income be raised to one hundred shillings. Also since the industry, uprightness, and diligence of the said Master are above all things necessary, and advantageous, lest by his neglect (which God forbid), or misconduct, loss or more serious danger result to the said House, I order in addition to what has gone before, that when the Master of the said House for the time being, be found by reason of waste of the goods of the said House to be useless, or negligent in fulfilling his office, or luxurious, or notoriously vicious—as is below mentioned concerning the Fellows—he shall thrice be duly warned by the Principal, at the consent of the Community, to refrain himself entirely from such negligence and miscon-

duct.   And if, after three warnings, he appear
incorrigible, or neglect to refrain himself from the
aforesaid offences, he shall be denounced to the
Chancellor or his representative, and to the Prior or
Warden, and to the Masters belonging to other
Colleges, aforesaid ; and they being informed of his
wrong doings, and of the proceedings taken against
him, shall without the least delay remove him from
the office of Master.   And if they refuse to come for
the purpose of doing as aforesaid, or if any of them
refuse, within three days after he has been duly denounced to them, it shall be lawful for the Principal
and the Community of the said House to depose a
Master of this kind from the office of Master, and
after his deposition to elect another in his place,
according to the form aforesaid.   And if any of the
aforesaid Fellows commit murder, adultery, theft,
robbery, perjury, sacrilege, or simony, or any grave
offence, or be disgraced by some grave sin of the
flesh (which God forbid), and be likely to raise some
very grave scandal in the said House ; or if any of
them be quarrelsome, or a frequent exciter of discord
among the Fellows ; or one who grievously strikes
the said Fellows, or, what is more, be intolerable to
the Master, or Fellows, or others in the said Society,
as being convicted of complicity with any of the
aforesaid offenders, either by public notoriety, or in
any other way ; a transgressor of this kind shall be

entirely excluded from the House and its advantages. Moreover, the Master of the said House, with the help of two of the older and more discreet Scholars of the said Society, shall hear, pacify, and decide, according as it shall seem well to them, all discord arising among the said Scholars, and all quarrels or less serious offences, without commotion or delay, within their own House. And if any one attend not the Disputations of his Faculty, or the Schools, on lawful days, or Divine Office, as he ought ; or if he wander idly in the City, or outside the City, at unlawful times ; or if he behave himself at all amiss at the Disputations, at table, or on other occasions towards the Master or a Fellow, by reason whereof a scandal or evil may evidently arise to the said House or Fellows, I desire that the aforesaid Master, with those two associates, shall chastise and correct any one whom they find offending in any way aforesaid, and shall impose some penalty, as the nature of the case in their estimation reasonably demands. And if any of them refuse to obey the Ordinance, he shall be punished by the loss of his Commons for a fortnight. But if such a transgressor, having thus been for the third time corrected for his misdoings, by the Master and those assisting him, and having been thrice punished by the loss of his Commons, yet refuse to refrain himself from such misdeeds, he shall be finally expelled from the aforesaid Society, as incorrigible

and rebellious. And those expelled from the aforesaid House shall be denied all benefit accruing from
it, and all share in its advantages. Nor, being thus
ejected or removed, shall they take proceedings
against the Masters or Scholars, or any others whom
such proceedings could affect, either by bringing an
action, or by making an appeal or complaint, or by
demanding complete restitution, or obtaining Letters
of any Court, secular or Ecclesiastical, or using
Letters obtained from any one, or through any one,
against their aforesaid ejection. Likewise in the removal of the Master, when he has been removed for
any of the causes above mentioned, I determine that
the same should be observed ; and let an oath be
taken to this effect by each one on his admission.
Yet that all humanity be not denied to those who
have been ejected, as above laid down, owing to
smaller offences, and who desire to study ; if thereafter they show worthy fruits of penitence, and have
in no way caused the Master and Scholars of the
aforementioned House to be molested, by bringing
an action or making an appeal, or in any of the ways
aforesaid, on the occasion of their ejection, and if
they make an humble request, let them be admitted
afresh to the premises and to the advantages of the
House ; if in other ways the merits of an upright
life give assurance that the goods of the House will
not be expended on vain or on worthless persons :

and this may be granted as a special grace, all the aforesaid notwithstanding, if it so seem good to the Master and Scholars.

'I order also that no man shall be admitted a Fellow at the request or owing to the Letters of any Lord, and that no stipend be given to any one at the request or owing to the Letters of any man of great power, chargeable to the revenues granted by me. But I decree that there be a Chaplain in the aforesaid House, and shall remain there in perpetuity, who shall be presented by me and my heirs to the said House ; and the Master and Scholars shall make no objection to him, but receive him, provided that he be a fit and upright person. And he shall celebrate Mass in perpetuity for me, and for my wife, and for the soul of Sir Roger de Somervyle, and for the Venerable Father Richard, Lord Bishop of Durham, and for my heirs, and parents, and the Benefactors of the said House. And if he demean himself with tolerable uprightness and moderation among the Scholars of the said House, and diligently perform his office, he shall dwell in the said House for life, and receive in full every benefit of the House in respect of board and lodging which one of the said Scholars shall receive, as is above decreed. And if he shall publicly disgrace himself, the Statutes prescribed for the ejection of Fellows shall be most strictly observed, as in the case of any of the Fellows, concerning his reproof, correction, and final ejection from the said House, as well as concerning any action on his part upon the occasion of his expulsion ; and neither I myself, nor any of my family, nor any other, shall make the slightest objection. And after his ejection, or quitting of office, if my heirs do not present another Chaplain in his place within a month of being assured of his departure, I order that the election of a Chaplain shall be in the hands of the said Master and Scholars, in all such cases and in such only ; and he being so elected shall celebrate Masses as aforesaid. And if any Chaplain presented by me, or hereafter to be presented by me or my heirs, or to be elected by the said Master and Scholars, be unfit to fulfil the said duties devolving upon him, from any cause whatsoever, I order him to be removed from the said House and its advantages, and another to be put in his place, according to the form before laid down. But let the Chaplain on every day of three Lessons, excepting between Easter and Trinity Sunday, say Mass for me and my wife as long as we live, using the Mass "Salus populi," with the proper Collect, Secret, and Postcommunion, that belong to it. But on other Feasts, of nine Lessons or Doubles, and also on the Feasts above excepted, he can say Masses of other Saints according as shall seem to him right. Yet in these, unless the Feast be a greater Double, after the first Collect, he shall say a special Collect for us, and in his private "Memento" shall earnestly and devoutly pray for us. But if I chance to go the way of all flesh during the lifetime of my wife, let him, on every day of three Lessons, say a Mass of Requiem with the proper Collects and Placebo and Dirige, with a commendation, for the health of my soul (in the form aforesaid), and of all the faithful departed, always devoutly adding some Collect for the health of my wife as long as she lives. But when both of us have gone the way of all flesh, et the Mass of Requiem be very devoutly celebrated by the aforesaid Chaplain, for us and the aforesaid persons, and for all the Benefactors of the hereinbefore named House, in the form aforesaid. Moreover, every year on the anniversary of my death, let a sung Mass of Requiem, preceded by Placebo and Dirige, be celebrated for the health of my soul, and of all the faithful departed. Which Mass and obsequies let all the Fellows for the time being be bound to attend personally. And as to the anniversary of my beloved wife, Margaret, let absolutely the same form be observed. And every Chaplain presented, or to be presented, by me or my heirs, to the said House, or elected, or to be elected, by the Community to celebrate the said Offices according to the form aforesaid, shall take a Corporal oath, touching the Holy Gospels, to observe faithfully each and all of these regulations. Likewise shall the Chaplain swear on

his admission to the House, not to reveal to any man
the secrets of the House, from which scandal or
injury might arise to the said House, or to any
Fellow, or Fellows.   Likewise, on his admission to
the House, shall he renounce in express words any
future action or legal remedy, either of Canon law, or
of customary rights, or of Common law, if owing to
his fault he be at any future time expelled from the
said House.   Also he shall swear to observe, as far
as in him lies, all the Ordinances made by me for the
advantage and honour of the said House; and any
other privileges of the said House.   And let the said
Scholars have a sung Mass of the Blessed Virgin
on every Saturday when they have no obligation
of celebrating another sung Mass, either in the
Parish Church, or elsewhere at one of the University
Masses.

  ' And at this Mass in honour of the Glorious
Virgin, all the Chaplains of the College, unless they
be hindered by some lawful cause, and the other
Fellows of the said House, who are not hindered by
their Scholastic duties, or some other lawful cause
approved by the Master or his representative, shall
be bound to be present.   And my Chaplain, or any
other Chaplain of the said House, before celebrating
this Mass in the Chapel, shall be bound specially to
pray for me.   And on every Friday when the aforesaid Antiphon is sung in the said Chapel, in the

Graces said at table, my name and the name of my wife shall be mentioned by the Chaplain or one of the Fellows of the said House, among the names of its principal Benefactors, and special prayer shall be made for us.

· Moreover be it noted that if the place of habitation, or the Society of the aforesaid Scholars devoting themselves to study, be transferred owing to any causes arising, which cannot easily be enumerated, they shall lose no advantage, right, or possession in the aforesaid revenues, or other things granted to them, or hereafter to be granted to them by the pious gift of good men ; but all shall remain to them in full. And these Ordinances, and any others hereafter to be made, and privileges granted to the said House, or to be granted in future times, shall hold good, on condition that they observe this ordinance, in word and deed : yet shall not the College lose its ancient name ; but, as aforetime, be called the House of Balliol. Nor is it my intention to destroy the ancient foundation, or the laws, or Statutes of the earlier Founders, but rather to confirm them by these presents. And if anything be contained in this my Ordinance contrary to the laws, Statutes, or customs of the said Scholars, to which the said Scholars have sworn, I do not desire the said Scholars to be bound to observe any such rule, but rather that the ancient rule be observed notwithstanding,

And while I have above ordered that six Scholars be elected at the charge of the revenues granted by me to the said House, and that every Fellow and Chaplain receive eleven pence weekly, and the Master forty shillings in addition to his share for his necessary expenses, at the charge of the aforesaid revenue, and have also ordered an increase of these allowances, as aforesaid, yet I desire that each and all of the aforesaid Ordinances be observed in so far only as the means granted as a free gift by me to the House suffice for this. And in addition to what has gone before, I decree that if the revenues here assigned to the said House, or hereafter to be assigned to the said House by the pious gift of good men, shall increase, the number of Scholars devoting themselves to the study of Theology shall be raised as far as possible, unless other regulations be made in regard to grants to be made in the future, by the Donors themselves.

'And lest by any chance any of the aforesaid Scholars hereafter pretend ignorance of these Statutes, I order that every year, on the Feast of St. Margaret, this writing be publicly read before all. Also I order, in addition to what has gone before, that the Prior or Warden of the Durham Monks studying at Oxford, appointed by the Prior of Durham, shall be a Colleague of the said Chancellor, or his representative, in all things, both in the admis-

sion and in the confirmation of the Master elect of
the House of Balliol, and in the taking of the oath
concerning the removal of the same Master, in the
case in which he is to be removed, of which matters
mention is above made, and also in the admission of
those who are elected to study the Faculty of Theology.   Also the said Prior or Warden shall, with
the said Chancellor or his representative, exercise all
the powers which are to be exercised in regard to the
said Scholars, or Master elect. So also the said Prior
shall have full power with the Extraneous Masters
to whom the six Scholars (or more, if the property
has increased), must be presented, to examine, admit,
or reject the said Scholars, and to exercise all other
powers in regard to them, which have commonly
been exercised in past time by the said Extraneous
Masters concerning other Scholars of the same
Hall.   I also desire, determine, and order, that the
Bishop of Durham for the time being shall have
power by all ways and means Canonical, as it
seems most expedient to him, to compel the said
Master and Scholars, upon information from the
said Prior or Warden of the Monks of Durham,
to observe the Statutes above laid down concerning the election of six Scholars and a Chaplain
at the charge of the revenues granted by me at
present, and concerning the raising of the number
of Scholars in case of the increase of the same

revenues, as aforesaid, and concerning all things above declared.

' And to testify to all these things, and that they may stand firm to all time, three instruments of like tenor have been prepared. To each of these I have caused to be affixed the seals of the Reverend Father, Lord Richard, by the Grace of God, Bishop of Durham, and of the Religious, the Lord Prior and the Chapter of Durham, and of the Venerable Lord Chancellor of the University of Oxford, and of the aforesaid Master and Scholars of the Hall or Balliol, together with my own seal. And of these instruments, I desire, order, and decree, that one remain with the said Prior and Convent, another with the said Master and Scholars, and a third with my heirs and assigns in perpetuity.

' And we, Richard, by the Grace of God, Bishop of Durham, at the request of Sir Philip, and the afore-said Master and Scholars, for the corroboration of the aforesaid Statutes or Ordinances, in so far as they are duly and Canonically framed, and so far as they concern us, have thought fit to affix our seal to these presents, on the eighteenth day of October, in the year of our Lord MCCCXL, in our Manor of Dukeland, without any prejudice to any of the rights, customs, and dignity of ourselves, and of our Church of Durham.

' And we, the Prior of the Church of Durham,

and of the Convent of the same City, at the instance of the aforesaid Sir Philip, and the aforesaid Master and Scholars, in so far as in us lies, by unanimous consent, and by the affixing of the common seal of the Chapter of Durham, do ratify, approve, and confirm, the aforesaid writing reasonably laid down, ordered, and decreed, by the said Sir Philip, and supported by the Pontifical authority of the said Reverend Father. Given in our Chapter house at Durham, on the twenty-fourth day of the month of October, in the year of our Lord aforesaid.

'And we, the Chancellor of the aforesaid University, at the request of the said Sir Philip, and the Master and Scholars of the House aforesaid, to testify to the above Ordinances, in so far as they are lawfully and duly made, have set the seal of our office to these presents on the morrow of the Purification of the Blessed Virgin Mary, in the year of the Lord aforesaid.

'Therefore, we, Edward, King of Scotland, aforesaid, Founder of the original foundation of the Master and Scholars of the Hall or House of Balliol in Oxford, do approve and ratify the said Charter, and the Statutes therein contained, one and all, as agreeable to law, and consonant with reason, and in so far as in us lies, do confirm them on our own behalf, and on behalf of our successors, notwithstanding any Statutes, privileges, or customs to the contrary, previously declared, granted, approved, or confirmed, by our predecessors. And to testify to all the aforesaid we have caused our seal to be affixed to these presents. Given '

The document ends thus, abruptly. It seems, from internal evidence, that this is not the original copy of Sir Philip de Somervyle's Statutes ; but only a transcript written for the sake of adding the name and sanction of Edward, King of Scotland. The original document was given to the College in the lifetime of Bishop Richard ; and had his seal, and the other seals, affixed to it. This transcript, while giving the date of the original, bears no other date, and has only one seal. It must have been written after the year 1345, as it speaks of ' the Lord Richard, late Bishop of Durham, of blessed memory.'

CHAPTER IX

' Now the Beneficies of *Fillingham*, *Risom* and *Bratleby*, in the County of *Lincoln*, did once belong to the Abbot and Convent of the Monastery of the Holy Trinity at *Aurenches* [so *Exaquium* is called in a French Deed] in the Diocess of *Constance* in *Normandy*, of the Order of the *Benedictines*. But in regard of the Troubles at Sea, occasioned chiefly by the Wars between the two Kingdoms, the Bishop of *Constance* aforesaid, at their *Instance*, gave License to sell the said Livings, as appears under his Seal in Writing, dated *Mar:* 3. 1343. And *Thomas Cave* Rector of *Welwick*, for the good affection he bare to the Master and Scholars of the House of *Balliol* in *Oxon*, had left in the hands of *William Brocklesby* Clerk, 100 l. sterling, to buy these three Benefices ; that out of the Profits thereof, in case they might be transferred to the proper use of the said Master and Scholars, the number of the Scholars might be increased.' [1]

In one drawer, in the College Archives, is the

---

[1] *Balliofergus*, p. 52.

small bundle of parchment deeds which refer to
this gift   Each bit of parchment is folded to a small
size, and they are all tied together with the inevitable
pink tape ; but the bunch of the different seals hangs
in luxurious carelessness.   Some of these seals are
extremely good.   The two seals of the Benedictine
Abbey at Avranches have been very fine ; but it is
difficult to decide who the seated figure, holding what
appears to be a large Crucifix, is meant to represent,
as on each of the Abbey documents this seal is much
broken.   The figure is well drawn.   The head is
fine, and the features are distinct, in spite of the
beard.   It might be St. Benedict.   The other seal is
far more perfect.   It represents an Abbot, standing ;
in one hand a book, and in the other a crozier.   The
vestments are beautifully traced, even to the lace
upon the alb.   Another seal represents the Bishop
of Coutances.   He also has his crozier ; but in his
left hand, while the right is raised in blessing.   The
Bishop's cope is elaborate ; but the seal is not so
finely cut as the Abbey seal, and has not such delicate work about it.   The three Broclesby documents
have each a small thick seal, in white wax, with very
indistinct impression : while the Licence from
Edward III. to William de Broclesby, for Balliol
College to receive the advowsons of the Churches,
has a magnificent royal seal, nearly perfect, preserved
in a rusty tin case.   One diminutive piece of yellow

parchment, folded to a very small size, and with a broken red seal attached to it, is of high value. It concerns the gift of 100*l*., from Thomas de Cave, and the purchase of the advowsons for the benefit of the College. The three different letters from Abbot John of Avranches are on slips of parchment, clearly written; but the writing is not like the beautiful writing of some other Monastery documents. Two of these bear the same date, and were probably written, or at least ' signed and delivered ' on the same day.—

' Omnibus Christi fidelibus praesens scriptum visuris vel audituris . . . Frater Johannes Dei patientia . . . Abbas Monasterii Sancte Trinitatis de Exaquio ordinis Sancti Benedicti Constantiae diocesis in Normannia et ejusdem loci Conventus salutem in Domino. Sciatis nos unanimi consensu nostro concessisse, dedisse et hoc scripto confirmasse dilecto nobis Willelmo de Broclesby, clerico, advocationes ecclesiarum de Filyngham, Brotelby, et Risom, in comitatu Lincolniensi cum omnibus juribus et pertinentiis ad easdem advocationes spectantibus, habendas et tenendas eidem Willelmo haeredibus ac assignatis suis cum eisdem juribus et pertinentiis suis quibuscunque de dominis feodi illius in perpetuum. Et nos praedicti . . . Abbas et Conventus et successores nostri warantizabimus praedicto Willelmo haeredibus ac assignatis suis advocationes praedictas cum omnibus juribus et pertinentiis suis contra omnes homines in perpetuum. In cujus rei testimonium huic scripto sigilla nostra duximus opponenda. Datum in Capitulo nostro et hora ejusdem secunda die mensis Augusti anno Domini millesimo trescentesimo quadragesimo tertio.

' Et ego Petrus Asce, clericus, qui de Constantiae diocesi extiti oriundus, publicus auctoritate imperiali notarius, omnibus et singulis dum agerentur ut praemittitur, loco et hora, anno, die et mense praedictis, indictione undecima, Pontificatus sanctissimi in Christo patris ac domini nostri . . . Domini Clementis divina providentia . . . Papae sexti anno secundo praesens interfui et praesens instrumentum manu mea propria scripsi. Et signo meo solito signavi requisitus et rogatus in testimonium praemissorum. Praesentibus : Venerabilibus et discretis viris Domino Radulpho le Monton, presbytero ; Magistro Willelmo de Kirnessale et Petro Walteri, clericis, testibus ad hoc vocatis specialiter et rogatis.'

[*Abstract.*—John, Abbot of the Monastery of the Holy Trinity, at Avranches, of the Order of St. Benedict, in the diocese of Coutances, Normandy, and the Convent thereof, grant to William de Broclesby, Clerk, the advowsons of the Churches of Filyngham, Brotelby, and Risom, in the county of Lincoln, with all rights and appurtenances. Dated in their Chapter, 2nd of August, 1343.

Peter Asce, Clerk, of the diocese of Coutances, Notary public. Witnesses, Ralph de Monton, Priest, Master William de Kirnessale, and Peter Walteri, Clerks.]

The second is the Power of Attorney.—

· Littera attornatoria ad liberandum seisinam de advocationibus ecclesiarum B. et F. et Rysum.

· Pateat universis per praesentes quod nos Johannes Dei patientia . . . Abbas Monasterii Sanctae Trinitatis de Exaquio Ordinis Sancti Benedicti Constantiae diocesis in Normannia et ejusdem loci Conventus ordinavimus et constituimus dilectos nobis Johannem de Litheare, Canonicum de Blancalanda, Johannem Orger de Keleby, Robertum Gosson de Keleby et Ricardum de Karleton de Lincolnia conjunctim et divisim procuratores et attornatos nostros ad liberandam plenam seisinam dilecto nobis Willelmo de Broclesby, Clerico, de advocationibus ecclesiarum de Filyngham, Brotelby et Risom in comitatu Lincolniensi habendis et tenendis eidem Willelmo haeredibus ac assignatis suis juxta formam cujusdam scripti eidem Willelmo inde per nos confecti, ratum et gratum habituri id quod iidem Johannes, Johannes, Robertus et Ricardus, vel eorum alter nomine nostro fecerint vel fecerit in praemissis. In cujus rei testimonium hiis litteris sigilla nostra duximus apponenda. Datum secunda die mensis

Augusti anno Domini millesimo trescentesimo quadragesimo tertio.'

[*Abstract.*—Power of Attorney from John, Abbot of the Monastery of the Holy Trinity, at Avranches, in the diocese of Normandy, and the Convent thereof, appointing John de Litheare, Canon of ' Blanca Landa,' John Orger of Keleby, Robert Gosson of Keleby and Richard de Karleton, of Lincoln, their proctors and attornies, to deliver seisin to William de Broclesby, Clerk, of the advowsons of the Churches of Filyngham, Brotelby, and Risom, in the county of Lincoln. Dated 2nd of August, 1343.]

There were one or two other benefactions, of early date, which may be here briefly mentioned. About the property at Woodstock, belonging to the College, Henry Savage says,—

' Although our Land at *Tackley*, and some of our Lands at *Old Woodstock* and *Wotton*, are anciently belonging to our Colledge, and confirmed by the Letters Patents mentioned in the former Section [but of whose gift I do not find] yet because other of our Lands there [and those the greater part of all] were bought in K. *James's* his Reign, I shall mention them together in this place. The Land at *Tackley* appears upon our Register, to be confirmed to us by K. H. 8. who took us Tenants for it. The ancient Lands in *Woodstock* and *Wotton*, I find confirmed unto us by the same K. H. 8. by the name of

one Messuage and one Yard Land in *Old Woodstock*,
called *Heynes* ; one other Messuage and half Yard
Land in *Old Woodstock*, called *Jewels* ; and one more
Messuage and half Yard Land in *Wotton* ; and this
done by receiving our Homage for them : but it
appears by a Survey, that *Balliol* Colledge hath two
Yard Land and a half in *Wotton* and *Woodstock*,
which is half a Yard Land more then in the Homage
is mentioned : All which, and many more, seem to
have been the Lands of *Thomas Harrow* [1] Clerk,
and passed over by him to divers persons joyntly,
9 H. 8. as it's recorded in our Register, by a full
recital of the Deed it self.   The other Lands of ours
in *Old Woodstock*, are the third part of the *Certes*
(now written *Sartes*) bought of *Thomas Ely* and
Nicolas Lucie, for 6 l. 6 s. 8 d. in 11 *Jac :* reputed
worth 1 l. 13 s. 4 d. *per annum*, as amongst other things
by the Deed is expressed. *Seacoales*, with other
Lands, and the rest of the *Sartes* bought of *Hierome
Nash* for 700 l. being part of moneys given by
Peter Blundel, Founder of *Tiverton* School in *Devon*,
in the last Year of Queen *Eliz :* upon which consideration, 13 *Jac :* our Colledge did agree with his
Feoffees to maintain one Fellow and one Scholar for
ever, to be chosen and sent from *Tiverton* School as
aforesaid, as amongst other things may by the Composition appear. Before the purchase of these Lands

---

[1] Thomas Harropp.

of *Hierome Nash* aforesaid, he the said *Nash* was Tenant to our other Lands, which lying intermingled with his, a Controversie arose, which were ours ? and which were his ? whereupon, by mutual accord of the Colledge and him, ours were set out precisely, as appears by a Deed to that purpose, bearing date *Octob.* 16. *Anno* 13 *Jacobi.* The particulars of the Land, afterwards purchased by the Colledge of him the said *Nash*, are expressed and bounded in a Schedule annexed to our Deed of purchase, bearing date, *Novemb:* 24. following; which Lands, toge-ther with others of the said *Nash* in *Old* and *New Woodstock* and *Wotton*, were the Lands of *William Seacoal* of *Stanton-Wyard* in the County of *Oxon*, who convey'd them to *Michael Nash*, by a Deed bearing date, *Octob.* 9. *Anno* 6 *Eliz.* Now these Lands thus bought of him are so small, and the charge is so great, that the said lands were set almost at a Rack-rent to defray it; and falling into the hands of beggarly Tenants, the Colledge hath of late Years, lost at least 200l. by them.'[1]

And Henry Savage tells us about ' another Farm of an ancienter Donation, *viz.* at *Morton* near *Tame*, conveyed by *George Nevil* Archbishop of *York*, to several Trustees, 14 *Ed.* 4. conveyed to *Nevil* by *Botelet*, conveyed by *Botelet* to *Jacket*,[2] conveyed to *Jacket* by *Pyron*, and to *Pyron* by *Wolundun*,

---

[1] *Balliofergus*, pp. 82, 83.   [2] Probably, *to* Botelet *by Jacket*.

14 *Ed.* 3. and so up, till we come to Writings without date.'[1]

Also, in *Balliofergus*, we find a careful description of the site of some houses in London, belonging to the College; and some interesting details about the history of the Farm at Otyndon.—

'I do not find any conveyance to the Colledge of the Houses now leased out, one to *Miller*, and the rest to the *Bradshawes*, in St. *Margarets Patens*, and *Rood-lane* in *London* : but I find several Letters of Attorney made, for giving of possession from person to person, from the time of *Edw.* 3. to 1 *Edw.* 4. when *Robert Kirkam, Custos Rotul: Cancellarie, Richard Friston* Clerk, *William Morland*, Parson of St. *Mary Bow London*, gave power to *Robert Abdy* Clerk, to give Livery and Seisin of them to *George Nevil*, Bishop of *Exeter*, and Lord Chancellor of *England, William* Bishop of *Ely, William Lambton, Robert Lowson*, and *William Appilby*, Clerks, who, 'tis like, were Trustees for the Colledge (*William Lambton* being then, or the same Year, Master) which was the way they took, it seems, during the Wars between the Houses of *Lancaster* and *York*, without mention made of the trust, for fear of Forfeitures, I suppose, and may be collected from the Pardons which the Colledge sued forth under the Great Seal of K. H. 6. and K. *Ed.*

---

[1] *Balliofergus*, p. 85.

4. yet in our Colledge, we have another Pardon from K. *Ed.* 6. too, which must be upon some other account. But now for the situation of the aforesaid Houses ; it was thus described, *viz.* between a Tenement of the Colledge of the B. Virgin *Mary* by *Guild*-hall *London* on the West part, and a little venue called St. *Margarets Patyns*-lane on the East part, and a little venue called *Smiths*-lane, *alias*, St. *Andrews Hoberds*-lane on the South, and a Tenement called *Patesden* Rent on the North part. I find also, that after the end of the said Wars, *John Segden* Clerk, and Master, or (*Gardianus*) Warden of our Colledge, and (*confratres*) Fellows, did set a Lease of the said Houses to three Citizens of *London* for 20 Years, at the Rent of four Marks sterling, dated *Anno* 1473. and 12 *Ed.* 4. As for our Farm at *Odyngton* in *Oxfordshire*, anciently called *Otyndon*, in a Deed without date : I find it by the said Deed to have been the Land of *William le Poure*, Son and Heir of *John le Poure*, who by that Deed convey'd it to *William*, the Son of *John Urlewyne* of *Otyndon*. After this, *viz.* in the time of *Ed.* 3. I find it to be *Brahall's* Land of *Otyndon*, passed over to him by *Stryvin* of *Otyndon*. Afterwards, it came to be the Land of one *Saunders*, 1 H. 5. in which name it seems to have continued till 5. *Edw.* 4. when it was conveyed by a Daughter and Heir of Thomas Saunders, and her Husband

William Wellis of *Otyndon*, to *Nich : Blunt* and *Agnes* his Wife, who made a Release thereof to *William Kyrby* of *Otyndon* and *Alice* his Wife, *Apr :* 20. in 3 H 7. which said *Kyrby* and his Wife, upon the same, conveyed it to *John Russel* Bishop of *Lincoln, James Stanley* Dean of St. *Martins London, William Bell, William Stephyns, John Smith, Richard Barningham, John Southwood,* Clerks. But by another Deed of *April* 27. in the same Year, did the said *Blunt* and his Wife grant it to the said *Kyrby* and his Wife, who, upon the 29 day of the same Moneth, convey'd it to *William Bell, John Smith, Richard Barningham, John Southwood,* Clerks, in trust, 'tis like, for the Colledge, *William Bell* being then, or soon after, Master of the House, whom *Richard Barningham* succeeded. The Conveyance is general, of all the Messuages, Lands and Tenements, Meadows of Pasture and Pastures, with the Appurtenances, which were the aforesaid *Blunts.* This said Farm is now held by a Lease of Lives, granted to *Abraham Watson,* and hath been so held by him and others time out of minde.'[1]

One of the later gifts to the College was the site, and some of the buildings, of a Convent in Clerkenwell. About this benefaction Henry Savage says,—

[1] *Balliofergus*, pp. 72, 73.

'In the 31 Year of *Hen.* 8.   The site of the
Monastery of *Clerkenwell,* was setled by Act of
Parliament upon the Duke of *Norfolk*; and in the
35 Year of the same K. H. 8. it was setled, by the
consent of the Duke of *Norfolk,* upon the King
again by Act of Parliament; then in the 37 Year of
his Reign, he granted it to *Walter Henley* and
John Williams, Knights, to be held in *Capite.*
After the death of Sir *Walter Henley,* his Widow
Dame *Margaret Henley,* conveyed one Messuage,
two Gardens, and one Cottage or little House, to
John Bell, 7 *Edw.* 6. (wherein *Bell* afterwards lived)
after this the said Lady *Henley* marryed *Thomas
Roberts* Esq: The same *Roberts* sold the Sisters
House and Garden to *John Bell,* Nov. 19. 2 and 3
Year of *Phil*: and *Mary,* and he the said *Roberts*
and his Lady acknowledged a Fine.   This Sisters
House, and the before-mentioned Messuage, with
the Appurtenances aforesaid, the said *John Bell* did
give to our Colledge, *March* 9. 2 and 3 of *Phil*:
and *Mary.*   After the death of *John Bell,* our
Colledge was questioned in the Exchequer for the
House, Gardens and Cottage, sold by my Lady
Henley, and given by *John Bell* without Licence
(the whole Case is recited in a Copy of a Rowl out
of the Exchequer) thereupon the transgression was
pardoned by Letters Patents, *Febr.* 1. 3 and 4 of
Phil: and *Mary*; and the Houses by the same

Letters Patents confirmed to the Colledge. But *Elizabeth Sackville* the Prioress being living (3 *Eliz.*) was thought to have a right to the Sisters House, which she did the same Year, *Septemb.* 8. release to the Colledge ; The bounds whereof, are the Church on the West, *John Bells* own House, bought as aforesaid, on the East of it, and the Church Yard on the South, as appears by the Deed, and several Leases since set by the Colledge of all the Houses, which are also noted as being within the Precinct of the said Monastery, not only by the said Leases, but also by the Original Deeds.'[1]

That short paragraph reads like one of the many sad chapters in the history of the Reformation. Here is not the place to discuss how the Convent at Clerkenwell, which belonged to the Benedictine Nuns, came into the hands of Henry VIII. The site of the Convent, and the buildings, passed from one person to another, until the 'Sisters House,' together with the garden and cottage, was given to Balliol. But there were some who held that the Prioress had still a claim to the Convent and the grounds. This claim she released to the College. The release is written on a small slip of parchment, which had originally two seals attached to it, but only one now remains. In the document the name is Isabella Sackfeld ; not, as Henry Savage writes,

[1] *Balliofergus*, pp. 78, 79.

Elizabeth Sackville. Among the Nuns expelled from their Convents, by Henry's Commissioners, we read of some, who so loved their religious life, that they could not be induced to go far from their former homes ; but chose to live, often in great poverty and privation, within sight of their Convent buildings. Dame Isabella Sackfeld was one of them. She is reported to have kept one or two of her Nuns near her for a long time.[1] Perhaps even after giving up all claim to their Convent property, the aged Prioress and her few remaining Nuns lived together, a small remnant of Religious, clinging still to Community life, and striving to keep their Rule, in spite of the desolation of those days of persecution.

The Charter of Pardon, from Philip and Mary, is a large document ; and it has been carefully pre-served. It is one large sheet of parchment : the writing on it is clear ; and the royal seal of Philip and Mary, attached to it, is very perfect, though not a very good impression.

Lastly, Henry Savage tells us about the Chapel, called 'the new Chapel,' when he wrote of it.—

'The Chappel, called the new Chappel, that now is, was built in the Reign of K. H. 8. (at the charge of the House, assisted probably by the contribution of Friends) for I find, that in the 13th year of the

---

[1] *H. 8. and English Monasteries*, F. A. Gasquet, vol. ii. p. 476.

raign of H. 8. [which was about *Anno* 1521.) an Agreement was made with a Mason of *Burford*, for the finishing of the 3 Windows thereof on the Quadrangle side, and one Window of the Treasury on the same side ; the rest may be presumed to have been finished before, *viz.* 9 H. 8. which by a mistake in our Register is written 19 H. 8. which if true, it were after the glazing of the Windows : But how long it was, before it received its perfection [both for Stone-work and Lead, with the Frame that bears it up] I cannot shew precisely : But that it was before *Anno* 1529. is evident by the date of the glazing of the Windows, it being then, that *Lawrence Stubbys* gave the East Window, which is so fair, that the Founder of *Wadham* Colledge is said to have offered the Society 200 l. for it, to glaze the East Window of his Chappel, as representing in lively Colours and exquisite Postures, the Passion, Resurrection, and Ascension of Christ : but the Chappel being fair, they thought not that Window too gawdy for it ; and I would they had not thought the Leads too heavy, I am sure others did not, for weaker Frames at the *Schools* upon which they were laid. The South Window was at the same time glazed by *Richard Stubbys*, containing the whole Story of the Martyrdom of St. *Katerine* : The next to that, was of the Gift of Dr. *Wentworth*, Fellow of this House, containing the story of

Hezekiah's sickness and recovery: that opposite thereunto, containing the story of *Philip* and the Eunuch, was the same year given by *Richard Atkins* Esq; of *Gloucestershire,* and Fellow-Commoner of this Colledge ; about which time, the whole Chappel was lined and adorned with Joyners work, at the cost of the Colledge and of many Benefactors, one of the greatest whereof was Mr. *Popham* of *Littlecot,* who had been of the House, and gave One hundred pound ; in memory whereof, his Arms engraven in Wood, are placed over the Screen doors of the Choir. The second best, was Mr. *Boughton,* Sub-dean of his Majesties Chappel Royol, who gave 50*l.* so that now it gives way to none of those of the lesser Colledges for beauty and proportion. One of the Chappel Windows appears, to be given by one of the *Comptons* (a Knight) Sir *William Compton,* of the Ancestors of the now Earl of *Northampton,* both by his Name and Coat of Arms, and probably he gave towards the structure it self : for his Charity was great, if it were answerable to his Piety, which his posture (with his Ladies) wherein he is represented in the same Window, shews to be devout. 1530.'[1]

It would not be well to turn from the subject of documents, deeds, and seals, without giving some description of the old College seal. We cannot, as

[1] *Balliofergus,* p. 77.

it were, close the door of the Balliol Muniment
Room, and leave unmentioned the seal which the
College must most prize. It has not been found
attached to any of the writings quoted in this book ;
and, again, Henry Savage must be our authority.
He says,—

'And upon this alteration of the Stile of the
Colledge,[1] a new Seal was Fabricated, with the
Image of St. *Catherine* in it, having her Sword in
one hand, her Wheel in the other, and her Crown
upon her head, with the several Coats of Arms . . . :
the Seal in use immediately before, being the Image
of the B. Virgin *Mary*, . . . sitting with a Crown
upon her head, with the Babe in her hands . . .
environed with St. *Kat*: and all the Saints, with
this engraveur in the Ring ; viz. *Sigillum commune
Domus Ball : servata, sancta, pia virgo . domui tuae
da te propitiam.'[2]

---

[1] 'Anno 30 Eliz.'　　　　　　　　　[2] *Ibid.* p. 81.

CHAPTER X.

ALTHOUGH Sir Philip de Somervyle wished that his Statutes should in no way cross those given by the Lady Dervorguilla, yet it would seem that, in some particulars, they at least gave rise to scruples in conscientious minds. Or, it may be, they formed a point of contention between the Scholars who had to leave, and the Scholars who were enabled to remain in the College, after they became Masters in Arts. In 1364, Simon Sudbury, Bishop of London, was deputed by Pope Urban V. to enquire into these difficulties, and to examine the Statutes ; and, if necessary, to frame new ones, in order that the peace and quiet of the House might be secured.

The Pope's letter to the Bishop of London, authorizing him to act in the matter, was forwarded by the Bishop to the College, with the request that it might be returned to him together with copies of the first and second Statutes, and any information which might enable him to better understand the points in question. As Henry Savage writes, ' The Letters Apostolick by him with all reverence

received, did he send to be perused, and to be ordered by *Mr. John Hethingham* Chancellour of the
University of *Oxon*, and *Hen. de Whitfield* Provost of
Queens Hall in *Oxon*, both Professours of Divinity,
and Mr. *Ralph Orgum* Inceptor in the Civil Law,
to be transcribed ; with Command by Apostolick
Authority to send him those Letters back again
with true Copies of the first and second Statutes,
and such further faithfull information as might enable him the said Bishop of *London* to proceed in
the premises accordingly.'[1]

In the old Latin Register of the College is preserved a copy of Pope Urban's letter to Bishop
Simon. The pages of the Register which contain
this copy are scored with many pen-marks across
them. These pen-marks, together with a short
entry, in English, at the top of page 25 of the
Register, point to all Papal documents in the College Archives, and the Latin Register, having been
demanded by the Commissioners of Henry VIII.,
when they visited the College. The original deeds,
or transcripts of the originals, were probably then
taken away ; and this may account for the copies in
the Register being the only copies which now exist
in the College of the letter of Pope Urban to Bishop
Simon, the letter of Pope Julius to the Bishops of
Winchester and Carlisle, and the letter from Pope
Eugenius.

[1] *Balliofergus*, p. 63.

In 1534, the College acknowledged the Royal Supremacy.

'Balliol College [Oxford], Linc. dioc., 1 Aug. 1534. *Signed* (with protest that they do not mean to do anything against divine law or the orthodox faith) by Will. Whytt, master, and five fellows. Rym. 498.'[1]

Some three years afterwards, the King, as Supreme Head of the Church of England, demanded the surrender of all Papal documents. That delivering up of documents may also account for the torn and stained condition of the Licence from Pope Urban for Masses to be said in the College Chapel. There was, perhaps, a tight holding of these parchment deeds by some members of the College, who prized the authority of Rome, and wanted to preserve the records of the rights and privileges of the College ; and a rough handing them about by the Commissioners, who were bent on obliterating a Pope's name, wherever they might find one. The large brown stain across the letter from Clement VI. is as likely to have been caused through the spilling of ink by eager Commissioners, as by the application of gall for the sake of more easily deciphering the writing,—which, by the way, is clear and distinct enough where the stain has not touched it. How those two documents came to be preserved, when

[1] *Calendar, Letters and Papers, Hen. VIII.* vol. vii., p. 439.

others were taken away, we shall never learn. Pope
Urban's letter is interesting, as it throws light on
what the particular difficulties in the College were at
that time.

At the top of page 25 of the Latin Register,
nearly at the edge of the paper, is written,—

· The copye and presydent off bullye off the
bishoppe off rome delyveride out off the Cheste the
11th daye off July in the 29th yere off kynge henry
the VIIIth hereafter folowith.'

This short entry is followed by the copy of Pope
Urban's Latin letter.—

[*Translation.*] · Urban, Bishop, Servant of the
servants of God, to his Venerable Brother, the
Bishop of London ; Greeting, and Apostolic Benediction. A petition presented to Us on behalf of Our
beloved sons, the Master and Scholars and College of
the Hall or House of Balliol, in Oxford, in the diocese of Lincoln, stated that Dervorguilla de Balliol
founded the said College for the good of her soul,
endowed it with her goods, gave certain Statutes for
the same ; and willed that the Master, and each of
the Scholars of the same College, at the time of his
reception into the same, should take a Corporal oath
to observe the said Statutes. And the said petition further stated, that, among other things, these
Statutes contain a provision that none should remain
in the said College unless they be Students in Arts ;

and that no one should reside in the said College
after he has taken the degree of Master in Arts, or of
any Faculty in Arts, except for the space of three
years only ; but should be compelled to depart from
it. And that a long time afterwards, Philip de
Somervyle, Knight, Lord of Wichnore, considering
with pious intention that Clerks or Fellows of the
said House were compelled to leave the House after
taking the degree of Master in Arts, although they
could nowhere else obtain sustenance, with authority
from the Ordinary, procured and gave to the same
College the Church of Mickle-Benton in the diocese
of Durham, which was in his patronage ; and willed
and ordained that, from the revenues of this Church,
a fixed number of Students of Theology should
always be kept in the said House or College ; and
gave certain Statutes, to the observing of which he
willed that all these same Scholars and Clerks should
be bound by their own oath. And that these enact-
ments, though they are reasonable and useful to the
College aforesaid, and made, as is believed, with a
pious intention, are yet very contrary to the earlier
Statutes ; and that such contrariety, in many ways,
troubles and disquiets the consciences of the Scholars
or Clerks of the said College, causes dissensions, and
acts as an incentive to quarrels. Wherefore, on
behalf of the said Master and Scholars, it was humbly sought that We would deign to provide them

with a timely remedy for these troubles. We, therefore, inclining Our ear to their supplications, by the tenor of these presents, grant to thee, Our Brother, —of whose circumspection both in these and in other matters We have, in the Lord, the fullest confidence —full power to cause these Statutes, both the first and the second, to be laid before you, to interpret, explain, reconcile, modify, correct, and change, to add to or take away from them, and to make new ones, as shall seem to you (according to the Lord, and in equity) to be useful, and for the peace of the College ; and by Our authority to absolve the Master and Scholars or Clerks of the said College from observing those of the Statutes which you have thought fit to modify, correct, withdraw, or change ; and, setting aside all appeal, to restrain by the Church's censure those who oppose or rebel. Notwithstanding any oaths whatsoever which the said Master, Scholars, and Clerks have taken ; or that an indult has been granted to any, together or singly, by the Apostolic See, that they may not be interdicted, suspended, or excommunicated, by Letters Apostolic, unless these make full, and express, and word for word mention of such indult. Given at Avignon, on the 13th day of February, in the second year of Our Pontificate.'

The Statutes issued by Simon Sudbury are not now in the Balliol Archives. They could not be found in Henry Savage's time ; and have not been discovered since. They may have been lost ; or, it may be, they shared the fate of other documents demanded by the Commissioners of Henry VIII. But we know that those Statutes were twice corrected by subsequent Bishops of London. The College preserves the large, closely-written, parchment document, which contains the corrections made by Robert, Bishop of London, in 1433 ; and, also, the alterations made by Thomas, Bishop of London, in 1477. But, in spite of these corrections and alterations, causes of dissatisfaction seem to have grown in the College ; and, it would seem, another petition was sent to Rome some twenty years after the issue of the third code by Bishop Thomas. These petitions are the documents we most need, to tell us what the grievances in the College were ; but they are exactly the documents we cannot quote. We can only learn what each petition asked, by the reply sent. So, it appears, a petition was sent to Rome at the end of the 15th, or at the beginning of the 16th, century ; for in the College Archives is a rough paper copy of a letter from Pope Alexander, addressed to the Bishops of Winchester and Norwich, asking them to examine the different Statutes, and to enquire into the College grievances. The writing of this paper copy is very much, and very badly, abbreviated ; some words are denoted only by prominent letters

and have to be read by the help of the context;
while other words, here and there, are quite illegible.
The Blue Book of Historical Manuscripts describes
this document as ' written about the time probably
of Henry VIII., and so abbreviated, as to be with
difficulty deciphered.'[1]

Mr. Riley's opinion about the handwriting settles
the question of the date of this copy, and points to
the letter being from Pope Alexander VI., who
reigned from 1492 to 1503.

[*Translation.*] ' Alexander, Bishop, Servant of
the servants of God, to Our Venerable Brothers, the
Lords Bishops of Winchester and Norwich, Health,
and Apostolic Benediction.   The petition presented
to Us, on behalf of Our beloved sons, the Master
and Scholars of the Hall, College, or House of
Balliol, Oxford, of the diocese of Lincoln, contained
that Simon, of happy memory, sometime Bishop of
London, having, by virtue of Letters Apostolic to
him directed, faculty to enact Statutes in the said
House, as equity might advise, and he himself judge
most expedient, ordained, among other things, that
as soon as a Master was elected in the said House,
the same Master should enjoin on all the Fellows
faithfully to elect two Rectors ; to wit, one Friar
Minor, and another secular Master of the University
of Oxford, that is, one not belonging to the Society.

' *Hist. MSS. Com., Fourth Report*, p. 443.

And that these Rectors, so elected, should have full authority to overlook the Scholars of the said House ; to admit to their Society Scholars presented to them by election of the Fellows ; to make a visitation of the aforesaid House and Scholars, ordinarily at least once a year, at a fitting time, or oftener if necessity or the common good demand ; to punish offenders against the form of the Statutes, as well for light as for grave offences, if the Master be found negligent or remiss in correcting lighter matters ; and totally to expel those whom, on suit of the Fellows, they shall find to be notably vicious. Now though this Statute was enacted, as is believed, with a pious intention ; nevertheless the Rectors elected under it, having no care for the said House or College, but being absolute strangers to it, often inflict grave injuries on the Scholars of the same College or House. They harass and disquiet them, and try to compel them to the observance of certain ancient Statutes, which from time immemorial have fallen into disuse ; and of others which are quite contrary to newer Statutes. And, in fact, they have actually and unjustly expelled from the said College some of the Scholars, on the ground that meanwhile they did not observe the aforesaid alleged Statutes, totally, as is maintained, abrogated by desuetude, and others contrary to newer Statutes. And thus they distract and disquiet the study, which, by the wholesome ordinance of the Founders, the said Scholars are obliged to pursue in Philosophy and Sacred Theology; and they minister a kindling spark for dissension and strife, to the damage of the said House or College. Wherefore, on behalf of the said Master and Fellows, humble supplication was made to Us, that We would deign to provide for an opportune remedy for them in this matter. We, therefore, favourably inclining to these petitions, lest that which was intended as a remedy should verge to destruction, by the tenor of these presents, do grant in the Lord to you, in whose circumspection in these and other matters We repose in the Lord entire confidence, to both jointly, and to each of you severally, full faculty to establish the aforesaid College anew, and to cause each and all the Statutes of the said House to be exhibited to you, or to one of you; faculty also to interpret, declare, harmonize, moderate, correct, and change them, and to add to them and to take away from them, and to enact others *de novo* according as, in God and in equity, you, or one of you, shall judge expedient for the good and quiet of the said College. Likewise faculty to absolve, by Our authority, the Master and Scholars or persons of the said College from the observance of such Statutes, as you, or one of you, shall think fit to moderate, correct, declare, or change; and also faculty to coerce, by Ecclesiastical censure, setting aside all appeal, those who may contradict and rebel.   Notwithstanding any oaths taken by the said Masters and Scholars. Notwithstanding also if to any, either in common or individually, an indult of the Apostolic See has been granted, that they may not be interdicted, suspended, or excommunicated, by Apostolic Letters, which do not make full, express, and word for word rehearsal of such indult.

‘ Given at Rome.'

There is no duplicate copy of this letter in the Latin Register.   The Pope's death, in 1503, may have been the reason why no steps were taken in the matter by the two Bishops.   But the question did not rest there.   The Balliol Scholars were not left uncared for ; nor were the College grievances allowed to remain unsettled.   In 1504, we find Pope Julius writing, on the same subject, to the Bishops of Winchester and Carlisle ; and a copy of his letter is in the Latin Register, scored through, like the copies of other Papal documents, with many pen-marks.   The tone and purport of it so closely resembles the last-quoted letter, that it leaves no doubt about the troubles, which it alludes to, in the College being those about which the Master and Scholars had written to Alexander VI.   The fact that the Bishop of Winchester is again one of the Bishops to whom this letter is addressed, makes it probable that this letter followed very soon after the other, and that the

Bishop of Winchester mentioned in the first letter
was the same Bishop, Richard Fox, who was removed from the See of Durham to Winchester, in
1501.   This gives a further clue to the time of Pope
Alexander's letter.

[*Translation.*] 'Julius, Bishop, Servant of the
servants of God, to his Venerable Brothers, the
Bishops of Winchester and Carlisle, Greeting, and
Apostolic Benediction.   The care of the Pastoral
Office, which, notwithstanding the insufficiency of
merits, We have received from on high, and undertaken, induces Us to listen to the supplications of
those, for whose indemnity and good We are able to
provide ; and if We see that what they ask is expedient, to respond to them with timely favours.

' A petition lately presented to Us, on behalf of
Our beloved sons, the Master and Scholars of the
College, of the Hall, or House of Balliol, in the
University of Oxford, and the diocese of Lincoln,
stated that Simon, Bishop of London, of blessed
memory, by virtue of a certain Apostolic Letter,
which he asserted had been granted to him from
above, at one time decreed and ordained, among
other things, that whenever a new Master of the
Scholars of the said College was elected, he should
immediately after his election, enjoin upon all the
Scholars or Fellows of the same College the election
of two Rectors ; viz., one of the Order of Friars

Minor, and another secular Master of the said University, not being a member of the College aforesaid. And that these said Rectors, thus elected, should have full authority over Scholars, thrusting themselves into the said House or College ; and power to admit into the Society the Scholars elected and presented to them by the Fellows or Scholars aforesaid ; and once at least in each year, or more often if necessity and the good of the Society so demand, to make a visitation of the House or College and Scholars aforesaid, to punish transgressors of the form of the Statutes, as well for small as for grave offences, and because the Master aforesaid might be negligent or remiss in correcting the faults of the said Scholars, and totally expelling those whom, on the accusation of the Fellows, he should find to be of notoriously bad character : all which is said to be contained more fully in the same Statutes. And that, though this Statute and Ordinance was made and put forth, as is believed, with a pious intention, yet the said Rectors, thus elected, interfere in many matters which do not pertain to them, and often grievously wrong the Scholars of this College, molest, and disquiet them, and even endeavour to compel them to observe certain Statutes which are so old that no man remembers when they were first made, and have already passed into disuse ; and also others which are altogether contrary to the new

Statutes of the said College ; and they have, on that
account, unjustly expelled *de facto* from the said
College certain Scholars, who, though they were
received and admitted into the said College in order
that they might apply themselves to the study of
Philosophy and Theology, are withdrawn from the
study of the same.   And that, on account of the
contrariety, and disuse, or non-observance of the said
Statutes put forth both by the said Simon, Bishop,
and, it may be, earlier or even later, it is necessary
for the peace and tranquillity of the Scholars aforesaid, that the said Statutes should one and all be
revised, reformed, corrected, and amended.   Wherefore, on behalf of the present Master and Scholars
aforesaid, it was humbly sought that, of Our Apostolic Beneficence, We would deign to command the
aforesaid Statutes, both the old and the new, to be
inspected, and examined, modified, corrected, and
emended ; and otherwise make timely provision for
removing the aforesaid evils.   We, therefore, after
a diligent consideration of the quality of each, by
reason of the Pastoral Office entrusted to Us, desire
that burdens be imposed upon each one according to
his power and strength, and be not made heavier
than he can bear ; and, further, that all who wish to
become proficients in Science, should be freed from
the hindrances which prevent them from attaining
their desire ; inclining Our ear to these supplications,

commit and entrust to you, Our Brothers, that conjointly, by Our own commission, you may on your
own authority, diligently examine, and enquire into.
all and single Statutes and Ordinances of the said
College, both the old and the new, as well by Simon,
the Bishop aforesaid, as by any others whatsoever,
put forth and made, and even confirmed by Apostolic
authority ; and may interpret, explain, reconcile,
reform, correct, modify, change, add to or take from,
or, if necessary, altogether cancel and annul them,
and may give new ones, as you shall find to be for
the peace and tranquillity of the Master and Scholars
aforesaid, now and for the time being, and for the sta-
bility of the said College ; and may cause these Statutes, thus by you reformed, corrected, or changed,
or interpreted and explained, and others newly promulgated, after their promulgation, to be observed
by the Master and Scholars aforesaid, restrain-
ing by Ecclesiastical censure, and other remedies
of the law, appeal being postponed, any whatsoever
who oppose. For which We grant to you, and to
each one of you, conjointly and separately, licence
and power by these presents. Notwithstanding the
Bull of My predecessor, Pope Boniface VIII. of
happy memory, by which it is provided, among other
things, that no one be summoned outside his City
or diocese, unless in certain excepted cases, and in
these not more than one day's journey from the

R

boundary of his diocese ; or that Judges deputed by
the Apostolic See may not presume to proceed
against any whatsoever, or to entrust their powers to
another, or others, beyond the City and diocese to
which they have been delegated ; or the Bull made in
General Council concerning two days' journey, provided that no one by the authority of these presents
be called to judgment at a place distant more than
three days' journey ; and notwithstanding the Constitutions and Ordinances of Octo, and Octoboni, of
blessed memory, formerly Legates of the said See in
the Kingdom of England, or any other Apostolic,
general or special, Constitutions and Ordinances
made in Provincial or Synodal Councils ; and notwithstanding the Statutes and Customs confirmed
to the aforesaid, and others, of the said College
by oath, Apostolic, or any other confirmation, even
though the said Master and Scholars have taken
oath to observe these things, and not to procure
Letters Apostolic contrary to them, from which
oath We, by the same Apostolic authority, release
them as far as concerns this same, whatever there be
to the contrary, by the tenor of these presents ; or
that the same Master and Scholars, or any others
whatsoever, conjointly or separately, have received
an indult from the same See that they may not be
interdicted, suspended, excommunicated, or called to
judgment outside of or beyond certain places, by

Letters Apostolic, unless these make full, and express, and word for word mention of such indult.
Given at St. Peter's, in Rome, on the 13th day of
August, in the year of the Incarnation of our Lord
1504, and the 1st of Our Pontificate.'

The name of Bishop Richard Fox is conspicuous
in the history of the Church, in the history of the
Nation, and in the histories of the Universities of
both Oxford and Cambridge.   He was the ' large-
minded ecclesiastic who perceived more clearly than
many of his brethren that the Church ought to
encourage and direct the movement that had arisen
in favour of the New Learning.' [1]   As ' Prelate,
statesman, architect, soldier, herald, and diplomatist,
he appears to have combined extraordinary powers
and capacities.' [2]   His Biographer tells us that ' to
the resolute and munificent Fox, beyond all other
men, was it due, that the mendicant Muse of Greek
literature found, on her exile from Constantinople, a
local habitation in the University of Oxford : he it
was who gave her the earliest welcome to a new
home, and wished to give her station and dignity in
Corpus Christi College.' [3]   And it was Bishop Fox
who was commissioned, by two successive Popes, to
revise the Statutes of Balliol College.   The new
Statutes, which he formulated for the College, are

---

[1] *Hist. Univ. Oxford*, Maxwell Lyte, p. 405.
[2] *Memorials of Oxford*, Ingram.   [3] *Life of Fox*, G. M. Ward.

too long to be given here in full ; but some extracts
from them will be of interest. They are published in
the *Statutes of the Colleges* ; but the Latin of that
printed copy, when compared with the manuscript
copy of Bishop Fox's Statutes, in the Balliol College
Statute Book, is found to have some errors.   There
is faulty spelling, and there are mistaken words, in
the Latin of the printed copy.   The following extracts are translated from the Balliol Statute Book.—

At the beginning of the new Statutes, Bishop
Fox described the College as an human body.   The
Master was the head, having the five senses : seeing,
hearing, smelling, tasting, and touching.   The senior
Fellow was the neck ; and the Deans were the
shoulders.   And so he continued the metaphor
throughout the Statutes.

[*Translation.*]   .   .   .   .

.   .   .   .

' Having now determined the place and position
of the Head, that is, the Warden, we have deemed
it right to pass on to the arrangement and disposition of the remainder of the body, that pleasure
may be afforded by the beautiful harmony resulting
from the well-ordering of the whole, and of its
several members.   Firstly, we will treat of the more
important members ; that is, the Fellows.   And
though, in the division of the whole body at the
beginning of these Statutes, we have spoken of

these as ten in number, we here interpret that in this wise ; viz., that though now content with this number, we decree that it shall be increased if, and when, more can be conveniently maintained out of the income, revenues, and proceeds of the College. If, on the other hand, there shall be any very great decrease in the revenues, we will that their number should also decrease, in proportion. Each of these cases, however, we leave to the judgment and consciences of the Visitor, the Master, and the three senior among them.

*   .   .   .   .   .*

· All the grace and loveliness of a visible body is begotten of the beauty of its members. We, therefore, desiring that the parts of the body shall be beautiful, decree that those who shall in future be elected Fellows of this College, shall be born in lawful wedlock, of good morals, modest, sober, not implicated in any notable crime, or of ill repute ; devoted to study, and learning, and Students of no Faculty other than those of Logic, Philosophy, and Theology, according to their degree and status in the University. (We permit, however, Students of Theology to attend lectures on, and to study, the Canon law during the long Vacations.) That they shall observe the Statutes and customs of the College ; or if they violate the same, shall with all modesty, without dispute, or complaint, submit to the

punishment and correction enjoined by the same;
shall dwell together in unity, and bring those who
are at variance to agreement; shall give and attend
lectures, dispute, and respond, according to their
degree, in the Schools of the University; shall be
present at the Disputations, and lectures, in the
University, which pertain to their status, and from
which they can derive profit; shall prepare to take
degrees, according to the Statutes and customs of the
University, and of the College; and shall, in all that
they can, act for the good of the College.

　　·　　·　　·　　·

· That neither the electors, nor the candidate for
election, may urge any idle plea of ignorance, we lay
down the conditions to be observed, and determine
that, setting aside any preference of country, or
person, hatred, carnal affection, corruption, or favour,
they shall nominate and elect as Fellow one who
has taken the degree of Bachelor in Arts only; and
whom they know to be the more fitting and suitable,
according to the three conditions; viz., that he is the
poorer, the better conducted, and the more profi-
cient, or whom they at least believe to possess these
qualities in the greater degree: rejecting, as ineligible, any one who has a living; or who, from a
fixed and perpetual exhibition, provision, patrimony,
Chapel, Chaplaincy, or Prebend, is able, after a fair
deduction for expenses, to spend more than forty

shillings a year. Moreover, we add that no candidate may corrupt any one with a bribe, or make use of any one's entreaties or letters ; and we decree that any candidate procuring such letters, or knowingly making use of any such letter procured by another, shall be, *ipso facto*, ineligible. This, too, we add, that if any Scholar of the College be equal to a " Stranger," in morals and learning, he shall have preference in the election, even though he has not taken the degree of Bachelor in Arts.

   .   .   .   .   .

' Moreover, we add that every Saturday, immediately after the singing of the Antiphon " Beata es Regina coelorum," by the junior Fellow, the names of all our original Founders and Benefactors, living and dead, shall be recited, nor shall the name of the then Visitor be omitted. And for the living shall be said the Psalm " Deus misereatur nostri," with the usual Versicle and Collect ; and for the dead, the Psalm " De profundis," with the accustomed prayers, and the Collect "Inclina, Domine, aurem Tuam ad preces nostras, quibus misericordiam Tuam supplices deprecamur, ut animas fundatorum, benefactorum, visitatorum, et cujusvis fidelium defunctorum," etc. ; nor shall they omit the Offices of the Dead, and Masses which they are under obligation to celebrate on certain days, for Founders, and other Benefactors.

'That the Mistress, Theology, grow not idle while her handmaidens, Logic and Philosophy, are toiling, we decree that if there are in the College three or more Fellows, who have spent a whole year in the study of Theology, they shall once a week, during full Term, or at least once a fortnight, on Friday, have Disputations; the senior being the opponent, the junior the respondent. Those who have taken the degree of Bachelor, in that Faculty, we desire to compel to be opponents, and not respondents. We will that all Students of Theology shall be present thereat: but entrust the management, as far as concerns the beginning, end, manner, order, and time, to the senior Student of Theology.

.   .   .   .   .   .

'As is the harmony of a lyre's well attuned strings, so ought the life and behaviour of our Clerks to be. Wherefore, we decree that the Fellows shall conduct themselves in a seemly manner, both within and without the College; shall not voluntarily, or of set purpose, by word or deed provoke the Master, or any of the Fellows, to anger; shall, either of themselves, or by means of others, bring those who are at variance to agreement; shall avoid factions, dissensions, and contentions, which sow the seeds of discord; shall apply themselves to virtue, and to books; and shall incite, and, in any way they can, assist others in the same. In Hall, and at table, they shall behave themselves in a seemly manner, without clamour, or immoderate laughter, listening attentively to the reading of the Holy Scripture, avoiding tales and idle talk ; and discussing such things as nourish virtue and learning ; using Latin only, except when they speak to one ignorant of that language, (we allow however the Master, or his Vicar, to give permission for the use of the vernacular on Festivals) : any one transgressing this order shall be fined one farthing on each conviction before the Master, and his Dean. That propriety be also preserved without the College, the Fellows shall attend the Disputations, ordinary lectures, and the Festival sermons, which are preached in the Church of the Blessed Virgin Mary, and also during Lent the Church of St. Peter in the East, wearing their proper habits : and we decree that any one who refuses or neglects to do so, unless for a good reason approved, or to be approved, before the Master, or his Vicar, his Dean, and one Treasurer, and is in their presence convicted of the same, shall be fined one week's Commons : that they shall not bring into the College friends or guests who are an hindrance to study, or an inconvenience to the College ; any one so doing, to be punished by deprivation of Commons, according to the judgment of the Master, or his Vicar, his

Dean, and one Treasurer, as to the gravity of the offence.

.   .   .   .   .   .

' Our predecessors have rightly determined that some portion of Holy Scripture, or of the works of a Doctor of the Church, be read aloud at table during dinner, that the ears be feasted at the same time ; and that there be something to give rise to conversation, that it turn not to tales and idle talk. Wherefore, we decree that each Scholar in turn shall, on one day in every week, read one chapter of the Bible.'

CHAPTER XI.

TRANSLATION OF THE EARLY PORTION OF THE LATIN REGISTER.

OF those who are permitted to proceed to the degree of Master in Arts.

[1524] *Firstly*, on the 29th day of the month of November, in the 15th year of Henry VIII., Mr. Henry Scott, and Mr. Edmund Burton, were permitted to proceed to the degree of Master in Arts, so that they might give public lectures in School Street, before becoming Regent Masters.[1]

[*On the reverse of page* 1.]

Know all men, by these presents, that . . .[2] in the University of Oxford, have by these presents, appointed . . . our beloved Mr. . . . Babington, our true and lawful attorneys for the re-entering, . . . in our stead and name, into our houses in Clerkenwell, in the County of Middlesex, and for taking full and peaceable possession of and into our estate, on behalf of us and of our name, and for expelling and

---

[1] This entry occurs on one of a few unnumbered pages at the beginning of the book.

[2] A few words are wanting in the first three lines.

removing thence all persons whatsoever, tenants or
occupiers of the same, or of any part of the same.
We giving, and by these presents granting, to our
attorney aforesaid, full and complete power, our authority, and special mandate, to make and cause the
said persons, or any one of them, to be attached and
arrested, and to produce and cause them to appear
before Judges and Justices, for any unjust detention,
retention, or occupation of the aforesaid houses, or
of any part or parcel thereof; and, further, in the
case aforesaid, in our stead and name, to raise,
affirm, and take all and single actions, suits, decrees,
and processes lawfully sought, and necessary for the
aforesaid wrongs, against those persons, and each
one of them, wherever it shall appear necessary, to
sue and prosecute them, or him, as the law permits,
in any circumstances thence arising, and to declare,
expound, and notify our aforesaid right and title
before the Judges and Justices aforesaid, and to
cause the said persons, or any one of them, to be
arrested with all the rigour of the law, to be impri-
soned and condemned, to release them from prison,
and to recover and receive from the persons themselves, and from each one of them, the expenses
incurred, or to be incurred, in each case, and to give
acquittances for what they have received and re-
covered, and for fine and agreement, and in our name
to make and seal other exonerations ; and, further,

to carry out both all and single mentioned in the aforesaid, and such as are necessary and proper ; and in our name to do, execute, exercise, conclude, and complete everything as fully and completely as we should be able, or ought to do, if we were ourselves acting in the aforesaid ; we, by these presents, holding, and to hold settled and agreeable, all and whatsoever the said attorney shall do or cause to be done in our name. In witness whereof we have affixed our seal to these presents. Given, the 24th day of October, in the 1st year of the reign of Queen Elizabeth.

[*Page* 1.] . . . expulsions of Masters and . . .[1]

On the 20th day of the month of April, in the year of our Lord 1521, Mr. John Peyrson voluntarily resigned, and left the College.

On the 12th day of the month of October, in the same year, Mr. Thomas Appylbe left the College.

On the 10th day of February, in the same year, Mr. Thomas Kendal resigned.

On the 4th day of the month of July, in the year of our Lord 1522, Mr. Peter Hoghton, Treasurer[2] of the same College, died.

On the 14th day of the month of May, in the year of our Lord 1528, in the presence of the Master and

---

[1] A few words are wanting.

[2] Or Bursar. The words ‘ Thesaurarius’ and ‘ Bursarius ’ are both used in the early part of this Register.

all the Fellows in residence, Mr. William Bradley resigned, having been appointed Vicar of the parish of Saint Martin, Leicester.

[*Page* 2.] On the 11th day of May,[1] Mr. Blunston produced Gerard Plughe before Mr. Doctor Coyolde, Mr. Brodley, Mr. Burton, and Mr. Walter Brown, as his surety for the repayment to the Society of the money which he has received, or will receive, as is thought, wrongly, if it be proved that our Master has rightly declared that he has ceased to be a Fellow.

On the same day, Mr. Scot produced George Hecsaum and Thomas Morras before the above-mentioned four, as sureties for the repayment to the Society of the money which he has, as we maintain, wrongly received, or will in future receive, if it be proved that the same Mr. Scot has been justly and rightly expelled from the Society.

In the year of our Lord 1568, and 11th of the reign of Elizabeth, on 6th day of the month of February.

On the year and day above-written, for a lawful impediment, approved by the Master and three senior Fellows, in the Chapel dedicated to Saint Catherine, Mr. Atkinson was excused from taking Orders (in obedience to the Statute [2] ' On promotion

---

[1] Date not given.

[2] The references in the Register to the Statutes are to the Statutes of Bishop Fox, given to the College in 1507.

to Livings') before the 19th day of the month of February, 1570.[1]

[*Pages* 4. 5.   No entries.]

[*Pages* 5. 6.]   A copye off a proxye made the 28th yere off king henry the viiith.

Know, all men, by these presents, that we, William White, S.T.B., Master of Balliol College in Oxford, and the Fellows of the same place, for the under-named purpose capitularly assembled, ordain, nominate, make, and constitute, by these presents, our beloved in Christ, Mr. William White aforesaid, and, further, Mr. William Wright, M.A. and the Rev. David Mungumbre, Curate of our Church of St. Lawrence, in Old Jewry, London, to us and our aforesaid House annexed and appropriated, and Roger Barker, Layman, together, and either of them singly and conjointly, so that there be no better way of discharging the office but that what one of them has begun, each one of them may be equally competent to take up, carry on, and conclude, our true and lawful proctors, agents, and representatives in business, and our special delegates; and we give and grant to these, our same proctors together, and to each one of them, as aforesaid, for himself separately, general power and special mandate to appear on behalf of us and our

---

[1] This entry has been crossed out, and put in its proper place in the Register.

names, and of the name of our aforesaid Church of
Saint Lawrence, in the presence of our most illustrious in Christ, Prince and Lord, Lord Henry VIII.,
by the Grace of God, King of England and France,
Defender of the Faith, Lord of Ireland, and under
Christ Supreme Head of the Church of England on
earth ; or before the illustrious and most potent
Thomas Crumwell, Knight, Lord Crumwell, Keeper
of the Privy Seal of our aforesaid Lord the King,
Secretary, and in Ecclesiastical cases Vicegerent,
Vicar-General, and Chief Officer, or before a deputy commissioner, surrogate, or any one having
authority for the under-named from the renowned
Lord Crumwell aforesaid ; and, further, to appear and attend before Archbishops, Bishops, and
other Judges and Ordinaries whatsoever, at all and
single visitations, congregations, and convocations
whatsoever, both of our most illustrious Prince
aforesaid, and of all other Judges aforesaid ; to
make excuses for our not attending in person, and
explain and, if need be, prove the cause and causes
of this our absence ; and with their hands laid
on the Holy Scriptures to offer, take, and swear,
on our souls, the oath of loyalty and obedience to
the said Most Serene Royal Majesty, his heirs, and
successors, and of renunciation of the present authority or jurisdiction of the Bishop of Rome, and
whatsoever other oaths can in that case lawfully be

required to be taken, according to the force, tenor, and effect of the Statutes of this realm of England lately promulgated in the Parliament of our said Lord the King, held in the 28th year of his reign. And, further, to state, and in our names promise, that they will produce these things in writing, with our seal and, if need be, with the subscription of our own hands ; to present and exhibit these writings thus (as aforesaid) certified, at a suitable and opportune time and place, before the Kings most sacred Majesty, or before Judges for that purpose deputed ; to show, or seek a suitable time for showing, letters of the appropriation of our aforesaid Church, and of dispensations, and privileges granted to our House ; to hear what things are first proposed in the visitations, and humbly to receive any canonical injunctions, and to promise, on our part, faithful observance of the same ; to carry out the business of the aforesaid visitations to the final conclusion of the same ; further, to do what such visitations, or their nature, quality, and office, lawfully demand and require ; to beg that we may be dismissed from the same visitations, at a fitting and proper place and time ; duly to pay the procuration, and accounts of the aforesaid visitations, and acknowledge other ordinary and extraordinary expenses ; and generally to do, exercise, and conclude, all and single other which, in the aforesaid, and about these, are neces-

sary or at all expedient, even though they demand
a more special mandate than is expressed by these
presents. Moreover, we promise to hold for settled,
acceptable, and established for ever, everything and
whatsoever these our said proctors or any one of
them shall do, perform, effect, or transact in the
aforesaid matters, or in any one of them, under
pledge and obligation of all and single of our goods,
and thereto we by these presents pledge our faith.
In witness whereof we have attached our common
seal to these presents. Given in our aforesaid College, on the 28th day of the month of September,
in the year of our Lord 1536.

[*Page* 7. No entries.]

[*Page* 8.]   1514.

It is ordained, with the common consent and
assent of the Master and Fellows of Balliol College,
on the 8th day of the month of February, in the
year of the Incarnation of our Lord 1514, that if a
Fellow vacate his Fellowship, or leave the aforesaid College, whether by death, by promotion, or
from any other cause, having retained his Fellowship from the Feast of St. Luke to the middle of
the year immediately following, that is, to the day of
St. Alphege, the Martyr, inclusive, he shall receive
half the usual payment. If, however, he resign his
Fellowship before the said Day of St. Alphege, the
Martyr, he shall not be entitled to any payment

whatever. Moreover, if any Fellow retain his Fellowship after the said day, and resign the same before the Feast of St. Luke, the Evangelist, he shall be content with half the usual payment.

Moreover, seeing that the smallest uncertainty is sometimes the occasion of grave discord, we, the said Master and Fellows, on the aforesaid day and year, with common consent and assent, have established for ever, that if any Scholar of any Fellow be rendered destitute by the departure of his Master from the aforesaid College, it shall be lawful for any one of the Fellows to take him, without any re-admission, as his Scholar for the time determined by the Statutes, permission having been first obtained from the Master, together with the consent of the two senior Fellows, or of one of them. And if none of the Fellows shall see fit to place him among his company of Scholars, so that he be left destitute, and wander like a fugitive over the earth, we permit him, from the hope of help from afar, to provide for himself assistance from all the goods and revenues of our Scholars, for the space of not more than two months.

[*Pages* 9. 10. 11. No entries.]

[*Page* 12.] Elections of Masters and Probationer-Fellows.

On the 29th day of the month of November, in the year of our Lord 1520, Mr. Henry Skott, and

Mr. Edmund Burton were elected Probationer-Fellows ; and on the same day of the following year they were elected and admitted perpetual Fellows.

On the 17th day of the month of October, in the year of our Lord 1521, Mr. Thomas Kendall was elected Probationer-Fellow, as Priest of John Balliol.

On the 29th day of the month of November, in the year of our Lord 1522, Walter Browne, George Coot, and Thomas Austlyne, Bachelors in Arts, were elected Probationer-Fellows. The same day of the following year, they were elected perpetual Fellows.

On the 29th day of the month of November, in the year of our Lord 1523,[1] Mr. Thomas Alan was elected Probationer-Fellow of this College.

On the 23rd day of the month of May, 1528, during the year, on the Vigil of Ascension Day (Sunday Letter, D.) Mr. Thomas Brodley was elected Priest and Probationer-Fellow of this College.

On the last day of the month of July, in the year of our Lord 1538, Mr. John Nowell was elected Chaplain, in place of Mr. John Foster, promoted to the Rectory of Standlake on the 21st day of the month of July, in the year of our Lord 1537.

[*Pages* 13. 14. No entries.]

---

[1] Written in the Register 1503 ; but evidently a mistake for 1523.

[*Page* 15.]   Admissions of Masters and Fellows who have passed their year of Probation.

On the 29th day of the month of November, in the year of our Lord 1521, Mr. Henry Scot, and Mr. Edmund Burton were admitted perpetual Fellows of Balliol College.[1]

Mr. W. Whytte Master of this College.

{ On the 29th day of November, 1528, Mr. William Wryght, Mr. William Bayker, and Mr. John Kytson, were elected perpetual Fellows of Balliol College.

In the year of our Lord 1531, a controversy arose on the admission of the Probationer-Fellows, in that, in counting the votes, that of the Master was counted as two, as is provided for in the Statute concerning the election of a Probationer-Fellow : which admission was, however, approved at the visitation made by the Rev. Doctor Stubbs, the Visitor, on the 3rd day of July, in the above-named year, as also that this provision shall hold good both in the election of a Probationer-Fellow, and in the admission of the same.   And those who were named as admitted at the same time were Mr. Robynson, Mr. Mychell, Mr. Park, and Mr. Clygworthe ; and, on the same day, their admission was approved and ratified.

[*Page* 16. is headed 'Leases' ; but contains only

---

[1] Repetition, in a later hand, of an entry on page 12.

the beginning of one. The five following pages, 17–21, have no entries.]

[*Page* 22.] On the 11th day of the month of July, in the 29th year of the reign of King Henry VIII, before, and in the presence of, the Master and all the Fellows, five Episcopal Bulls were taken from the Chest, to be handed over to the King, with the intention that certain things might be reformed by the same, according to the Act of Parliament. Of these, the first was that of Urban V, Bishop of Rome, to the Bishop of London, for the correction and reformation of the Statutes of the College, at that time not altogether perfect. The second, also of the Bishop aforesaid, by which the Master and Fellows were permitted to celebrate within their own College. The third, that of Eugenius IV, for the appropriation of the Church of St. Laurence, in Old Jewry, London. The fourth, that of Clement VI, for the appropriation of the Church of St. Margaret, at Abboldesley, in the county of Huntingdon, and the diocese of Lincoln. The fifth, that of Julius II, given for the latest reformation of our Statutes.[1]

---

[1] The above entry, as well as the copies of the five Papal Bulls which follow, have all been crossed out. *Pages* 23. 24. are blank pages. *Pages* 25. 26. contain the copy of the Bull of Pope Urban, which has been already given, p. 230. *Page* 27. the copy of the second Bull of Pope Urban, given on p. 135. *Page* 28. given above. *Pages* 29. 30. contain the copy of the Bull of Pope Clement, given on p. 168. *Page* 32. is blank. *Pages* 31. 34. 35. contain the copy of the Bull of Pope Julius, given on p. 238.

[*Page 28.*] Eugenius, Bishop, Servant of the servants of God, to Our beloved sons, the Priors of the Priories of St. Bartholomew, near Smithefelde, and of Chrichirche,[1] London, and to Thomas Warde, Canon of London, Greeting, and Apostolic Benediction. The just and honourable requests of suppliants We willingly grant, and respond to with timely favours. A petition lately presented to Us, on behalf of Our beloved sons, the Master and Fellows or Scholars, of Balliol College (as it is called), in the University of Oxford, and the diocese of Lincoln, and Robert Rok, perpetual Vicar of the parish Church of St. Laurence, in Jewry, in the City of London, stated that formerly the Master and Fellows or Scholars aforesaid, and Richard Collinger, perpetual Vicar of the same Church, proceeded against Our beloved son, John Hertwell [2] . . . of the parish of the said Church, which, canonically united and joined to the same College, the Master and Fellows or Scholars held, and now hold, for the use of their Society, by reason of his delay, he being lawfully bound to make certain oblations then named on certain days also then named, to the said Master and Fellows or Scholars, on account of the said Church ; they petitioning that he be pronounced and declared bound to make these same oblations ; and, further, be condemned and compelled to give them in the

---

[1] *Sic.* [2] A few words are wanting here.

presence of Our beloved son, the Officer of London, without any Apostolic delegation. And the said Officer, proceeding in that matter legitimately, and in accordance with the ordinances of law, pronounced a definitive sentence in favour of the Master and Fellows or Scholars aforesaid, and against the said John, and condemned him in the legitimate costs of the said suit, reserving to himself the future taxation of the same. In the interim the aforesaid Richard died, and Robert obtained and now holds the perpetual Vicarship of the said Church. Wherefore, on behalf of the Master and Fellows or Scholars, and of Robert aforesaid, who asserted that, as no appeal was pending, the sentence became one of an adjudicated case, it was humbly sought that We would pronounce the same sentence to be valid. We, therefore, inclining Our ear to these supplications, entrust to your discretion, by Our Apostolic Writings, that you, or two, or one of you, may by your authority cause the said sentence to be enforced, as it was justly pronounced, setting aside all appeal. Notwithstanding any indult which the said John or any others, together or singly, have received from the Apostolic See, that they may not be interdicted, suspended, or excommunicated by Letters Apostolic, unless these make full, express, and word for word mention of such indult.

Given at St. Peter's, in Rome, on the 15th day

of July, in the year of the Incarnation of our Lord 1446, and the 16th of Our Pontificate.

[*Page* 33.] To all believers in Christ, to whom the present writing may come, Richard Stubbs, Master or Warden of Balliol College, in the University of Oxford, and the Fellows of the same, Eternal Health in the Lord. Though the law of Divine Charity binds us, and makes us debtors to all believers in Christ in general, yet more especially are we bound to those who show that they have a feeling of greater devotion to us, and to our College. Wherefore, on account of the merits of the pious devotion, which the Venerable Mr. Robert Aschum has, by his most munificent gifts, shown that he bears towards our College, though he asked nothing of us, but rather kept before his eyes the thing which was itself to plead for him ; we, the said Master and Scholars, not unmindful of the benefits he has bestowed upon us, on behalf of ourselves, and of our successors, as far as in us lies, grant to him, both in life and in death, full participation in all Divine Offices which in our College aforesaid are now celebrated, or which by the Grace of God will be celebrated for ever ; to wit, in Masses, Prayers, Meditations, Services, and all other Divine Offices whatsoever. And, further, that his name be inscribed on our Roll, and be recited every Saturday among our Benefactors, for all the living among whom we

say the Psalm ' Deus miseratur,'[1] with the Suffrages,
and the Collect ' Deus qui caritatis,' etc. ; and for
the dead, the Psalm ' De profundis,' with the Suffrages, and three Collects ; viz. ' Inclina, Domine,'
etc. ; ' Quaesumus, Domine, pro Tua pietate,' etc. ;
and ' Absolve.'   Over and above which, we grant
to the aforesaid Robert Ascham, for the term of his
life, free use of a tower situated over the College
gates, containing two rooms, an upper and a lower ;
in such manner that he shall not in his absence
assign the use of this same tower to any one, or any
others, except with the consent of the aforesaid
Master, and the majority of the Fellows of the said
College.   In testimony and witness of all and single
of the aforesaid, we have caused our common seal
to be affixed to this our writing.   Given in our
Chapel of St. Catherine, on the 21st day of July, in
the 15th year of the reign of Henry VIII.

[*Pages* 36–43.   No entries.]

[*Page* 44.]   A.D. 1538.

Here begin the decrees of the Master and Fellows
of Balliol College, in the University of Oxford, on
the 21st day of the month of October, in the year of
our Salvation 1538.

Firstly.   It was ordained and decreed by the
votes of all, that one of the aforesaid Fellows be
each year appointed Secretary to the said Master

---

[1] *Sic.*

and Fellows for the year following, in all business concerning the state of the College, or the decrees of the same ; and that the Fellow who shall hold this office, be nominated each several year within three days after the Feast of St. Luke, in the same manner as other officers, and receive a salary of 6s. 8d. for the year during which he holds such office.

Item. It was ordained and decreed on the above-written day of the month, with the consent of all, that Mr. Cosinn hold the office above-named for the year next following the date of these presents.

Item. On the same day of the same year, Mr. Thomas Parke, and Mr. John Smythe, were appointed Deans ; Mr. Christopher Worseley, and Mr. Robert Cosyn, Treasurers of the said College.

Item. At the same time, with unanimous consent and assent, it was granted, under our common seal, to the Venerable widow, Lady Anne Danvers, that the Office of the Dead be said every year (according to the regulation concerning the same, written in the Statute Book) for the good of her soul ; and for her benefactions, on account of her gift of £30. to the Master and Fellows aforesaid, for the repair of the buildings and tenements situated in the parish of St. Margaret Patens, in London, given us by Robert Beamond, which had at that time unfortunately been almost entirely destroyed by fire.

Item. It was granted that if £20. can be expended by the aforesaid Lady Anne Danvers, in addition to the above-named sum, through Mr. John Foster, her Chaplain, and formerly a brother Fellow, that then the Master shall receive 12d., each Fellow 8d., and each Scholar 2d., when this Office is said. For, indeed, it is evident that if this amount be added, the buildings can be so adorned, and well built, that the yearly rents and proceeds will outgrow and exceed the amount formerly produced by the said houses, by 20s., more or less, a year.

Item. On the same day, for a legitimate cause approved before the Master and three senior Fellows, permission was obtained for Mr. William Wright to be absent for a whole year, to attend the Bishop of Lincoln during the same year.

[*Page* 45. No entries.]

[*Page* 46.]

Promotions to Livings in the year 1539.

Firstly, Mr. Christopher Worsley was appointed Vicar of the Church of St. Laurence, in Old Jewry, London, on the last day of the month of October, in the year above-written.

Item. On the 6th day of the month of February, in the same year, Mr. George Cott, Master of this College, received the advowson of the parish Church of Filyngham, given to him under the College seal, by the majority of the Fellows.[1]

Item. On the same day of the same year, Mr. Thomas Parke was presented to the Rectory of Brattelbye, formerly held by the aforesaid Mr. Christopher Worsley.

[*Page* 47. No entries.]

[*Page* 48.]

A p̃sydent of a voyson of a benefice.

To all believers in Christ to whom the present writing may come, George Cot. S. T. P. and Master or Warden of Balliol College, in the University of Oxford, and the diocese of Lincoln, and the Fellows of the same College, true and undoubted Patrons of the parish Church or Rectory of Filyngham, in the diocese aforesaid, Eternal Health in the Lord. Know that we, the aforesaid Master and Fellows, with our unanimous consent and assent, have given and granted, as by the tenor of these presents we give and grant, to our beloved in Christ, Edmund Newers, Gentleman; Richard Salven, Clerk; John Coot, Yoman; the heirs, executors, and assigns of them, and of each one of them, in common, and to each one separately for himself, the first and next advowson, donation, nomination, free disposition, presentation, and our full right of the patronage of

---

[1] This entry is crossed out; and in the margin is written, *This advowson is annulled.* See p. 52. of the Register.

the aforesaid parish Church of Filyngham, for a single and the next turn only, whenever it may be; and when the said Church first and next, by death, resignation, deprivation, whether *de jure* or *de facto*, change, cession, dismissal, renunciation, or in any other manner, shall either *de jure* or *de facto*, rightly be vacant: so that it may and shall be lawful for the aforesaid Edmund Newers, Richard Salven, and John Coot, their heirs, executors, and assigns together (as above) and separately, by authority and virtue of this our grant, rightly and legitimately to present once only any able or suitable person whatsoever for the said Church of Filyngham (as aforesaid) when it becomes vacant, to the Diocesan and Ordinary of that place; or at least to present so often until one person nominated by the above-named, shall have been instituted to the said Church, admitted to, and placed in peaceable possession of the same, with all its rights and appurtenances; and to do, and exercise, all and single else which is requisite in the matter, which we should do, or have power to do, if our present gift and grant had never been made. And it shall be lawful for the said Diocesan, or Ordinary, [or to any Judge whatsoever who is competent to deal with the matter][1] rightly and legitimately to institute a proper person, thus presented to the said Church with all its rights and

---

[1] This sentence has been crossed out.

appurtenances, by the before-named Edmund, Richard, and John, or any one of them, or their heirs, executors, and assigns, or those of any one of them ; and to do, carry on, and thoroughly complete, whatever in this matter is incumbent on his pastoral office, without any impediment, disturbance, opposition, or calumny, on the part of us, or of our successors. And we, the Master and Fellows aforesaid, by these presents, will warrant and defend our presentation, advowson, and qualified donation of our right of patronage, against all men. In witness whereof, our common seal has been affixed to these presents. Given at Oxford, in the Chapel of the said College, on the 6th day of March, in the year of our Lord 1541.

[*Pages* 49. 50. 51. No entries.]

[*Page* 52.] Decrees of the Master and Fellows, and Dispensations, and other Grants, made in the Chapel of Balliol College, in the year of our Lord 1542.

Firstly. On the 17th day of October, all the Fellows being then present, the Master interrogated the Fellows, on their oath, whether any one of them would assert that he, the same Master, had laboured privately or publicly for the election of the Fellow of the county of York, from the time of the last election up to the date of the present. And each one answered ' No.'

Item. On the same day, Mr. John Smyth, Fellow, read before the Master and Fellows a submission of obedience to the same Master, enjoined upon him by the Bishop of Lincoln.

Item. On the 19th day of the same month, Mr. Thomson, and Mr. Stop, were elected Deans ; and Mr. Browne, and Mr. Broebden, Bursars.

Item. On the 20th day of the same month, permission was, with unanimous consent, given to Mr. Cosin, to be absent whenever he chooses during the whole of the year next following.

Item. On the same day, permission was given to Mr. Ffrannt, to be absent whenever he chooses during the whole of the year next following.

Item. On the 21st day, the advowson of the parish Church of Filyngham was given to Mr. George Coot, S.T.D., and then Master of Balliol College aforesaid, with the consent of the Master, and the majority of the Fellows.[1]

Item. The 21st day, the Master, in Chapel, in the presence of the Fellows, gave to the Bursars of the College, as he had been commanded by the Bishop of Lincoln, 5s. 4d., for one month's Commons.

Item. The 22nd day of November, it was agreed, between the Master and all the Fellows,

---

[1] See page 46 of the Register.

that the election to the Fellowship then vacant, be postponed till the following year.[1]

Item. On the same day, it was agreed between the Master and the three senior Fellows, viz. Mr. Smythe, Mr. Cosyn, and Mr. Thomson, that for certain reasons it was expedient that the election to the vacant Fellowship be postponed for a year.

Item. On the 10th day of December, the Master in the Chapel, in the presence of the Fellows, showed Mr. Nowell a mandate, bidding him conduct himself obediently and peaceably towards him and the Fellows, according to the tenor of the Statute.

[*Pages* 53. 54. 55. No entries.]

[*Page* 56.] A.D. 1525. Nov. 15.

On the 15th day of the month of November, in the year of our Lord 1525, at the hour of 10, all and single of the Fellows having been convoked into the Chapel of St. Catherine, in Balliol College, Oxford, the learned Mr. William Whyte, S.T.B. produced and read before all a certificate signed with the hand and name of Mr. Claiton, Notary Public, by virtue of which it was notified, and most clearly shown, that the aforesaid Mr. William Whyte had been presented to Mr. Doctor Aleyn, Commissioner General for the visitations of the most reverend Father, Thomas, by Divine Mercy of the Title

---

[1] This entry is crossed out; and in the margin is written, in Latin, *Cancelled, in the presence of the Master and Fellows.*

T

of St. Cecilia, and had been by the same rightly, lawfully, and in accordance with the Statutes of our College, admitted Master or Warden of our College : which admission we all and single, Fellows, with our unanimous consent and assent, accept, and allow that Mr. White has been thus, as aforesaid, presented and admitted.

[*Page* 57.   No entry.]

[*Page* 58.]   A.D. 1539.   November 25th.

A copie of an instrument concernyng thadmission of Mr. Doctor Cott to the maistreship of this college made by an notary.

In the name of God, Amen.   Be it evident and known to all, by the present public instrument, that on the 25th day of the month of November, in the year of the Incarnation of our Lord 1539, and the 31st of our most illustrious and potent Prince, Lord Henry VIII, by the Grace of God, King of England and France, Defender of the Faith, Lord of Ireland, and, under Christ, sole and supreme Head on earth of the Church of England, in a Chapel situated within the College, commonly called Balye College, in the University of Oxford, and in the presence of me, John Croke, Notary Public, underwritten, and of the witnesses named below, the learned Mr. George Cott, S.T.P. in person read a letter written in English by the illustrious and potent Lord Thomas Crumwell, Counseller, and Keeper of the Privy Seal to the most illustrious Prince aforesaid, and Vice-gerent, Vicar-general, and principal Officer in Ecclesiastical cases, sent to the Fellows of the aforesaid College ; which letter when he had read through, he showed to me, the under-named Notary, and publicly presented, and handed over to me, and with due persistence humbly requested that, on account of accidents which might probably happen, I would transcribe and make copies of the said letter, and guarantee, and publish the same thus transcribed, with my seal and subscription. Where-fore, considering for the aforementioned reasons that the petition of the aforesaid Mr. Coot was reasonable, I gave orders for the making of verbatim transcrip-tions, and copies of the same letter, whole and entire, with nothing omitted or cancelled, and, as far as I saw, without any mistake anywhere. Of which letter the tenor follows and is this :—

AFTER MY HARTIE com̄endations wher as by my last letters addressid vnto yow I gaue yow in com̄anndmēt in the kings maiesties name that forthw᷄ apon the recept theroff w᷄owt any cytations delayes or other like solempnyties of the lawe and notw᷄stonding the absence of any of yo᷄ company so that the more part were present yow sholde procede to the election of a cōvenient Mastre of yo᷄ howse then vacant and that of yo᷄ electon so being made w᷄owt any parcyalitie or corruption youe sholde incōtinent Ꝗtifie me to thend the same myght be ratifyed and cōfirmed as shulde appteign, and for asmoche as according to the tenor and effecte of the same yow haue assembled yoᵣsellfs to gether vpon good deliberation and advise taken therin haue elected and chosen my frend DOCTOR COTT to be maistre of yoᵣ howse like as by yoᵣ ꝑntation sealed wᵗ yoᵣ cōmune seale I am adcerteyned, Thies shalbe to Signifye vnto yow and eůy of yow that I haue ꝑvsed & examyned the same and eůy circumstaunce therof and do comēnd and allowe yoᵣ good pro-cedings therin and haue confirmed ratified and approved yoᵣ said electᵒon by thauctoritie comēitted vnto me by the kings highnes in that behallf willing and comānding yow by thies presents that yow and eůy of yow shall from hensforth repute accept and take the said DOCTOR COTT as the very rightfull and just maistᵉ of yoᵣ howse vsing yoᵣsellfs toward him in eůy condytion wᵗ suche dewtie and obedience as to the said office doth appteign as yow and eůy of yow tendre the kings highnes pleasˢ.   Thus fare yow hartely well from London the xxijᵗʰ day of novembre ᵧoᴿ LOUYNG FREND THOMAS CRUMWELL.

¹All and single of these things were done as they are written above and recited, in the year of our said Lord, the King, in the month, day, and place, aforesaid, in the presence of the Venerable

---

¹ Here the Register proceeds in Latin.

Richard Smyth, S.T.P., and the learned Mr. George Nevell, and William Hubberden, specially called and summoned as witness to the aforesaid.

And I, John Croke, by the King's authority Notary Public of the diocese of Winchester, being present in person, with the witnesses aforenamed, at the reading, exhibition, presentation, and handing over of the said letter, the tenor of which is given above, and finding the letter itself thus (as above-said) exhibited, whole and entire, and, as far as I saw, free from any fault, gave orders that the same letter should be transcribed, written, and copied, verbatim ; and that this present public instrument, in the hand of another (being myself meanwhile engaged elsewhere) faithfully written, should be compared with it, and the collation of this transcript with the original having been faithfully made, that it should be published, and put in this public and authentic form, and have signed it with my seal, name, and surname, accustomed and usual, so that as full reliance may be placed on the present transcript, or published copy, as on the original aforesaid, I having been specially called, and requested to see and attest all and single of the aforesaid. And I, the Notary above-named, made the erasures in the second line, in the word ' anno,' and in the word ' Henrici.'

[*Pages* 60–63.   No entries.]

[*Page* 64.]   A.D. 154$\frac{9}{1}$.   February 2.

Decrees made in the Chapel, on the 2nd day of the month of February, in the 31st year of the reign of King Henry VIII.

[On the remainder of this page, and on the three following pages, there are no entries.]

[*Page* 68.]

On the 2nd day of November, in the year of our Lord 1542.

Firstly. Mr. Carter's attestation concerning Frideswide, made by a Public Notary, was replaced in the Chest.

Item. Another deed, called an acquittance.

Item. An obligation between the College and Mr. Cosyn.

Memorandum. That I, William Frannt, in the presence of the Fellows, took from the Chest fifty instruments concerning Abboldesley, on the 2nd day of the month of November, in the year of our Lord 1542. *Item.* At another time fifty court rolls deposited there.

Memorandum. That all the above-mentioned instruments were replaced in the Chest of the Society, on the 4th day of the following February, in the presence of the Fellows.

Item. On the 11th day of March, with unanimous consent of all the Fellows then present, for good and honourable reasons already shown, a dispensation was granted to George Cot, S.T.P.,

Master of the College, to be absent whenever he chooses, the Statute notwithstanding.

[*Page* 69.   No entries.]

[*Page* 70.]

Decrees made in the Chapel, by the Master and Fellows, in the year of our Lord 1543, after the Feast of St. Luke.

Firstly.   It was decreed, with the consent of the Master and all the Fellows, on the 24th day of October, that Mr. Philip Crome be our agent for the transaction of all legal business, in London and elsewhere, until we or our successors shall determine otherwise, and receive an annual salary of 13s. 4d.

Item.   On the 17th day of November, Mr. Smythe was summoned before his Master, the Dean, viz. Mr. Thomson, and one of the Treasurers, viz. Mr. Brogden, and by these same the aforesaid Mr. Smythe was mulcted in one week's Commons; because, as was certified by the Master and two Assessors aforesaid, the said Mr. Smythe took for his yesterday's breakfast the Commons which rightly belonged to the aforesaid Master.

Item.   On the 14th day of December, a dispensation was granted by all the Fellows, to Mr. Cosyn, that he be not bound to pay 5 marks due to the College till the Feast of the Ascension of our Lord, notwithstanding an obligation to the contrary.

On the 27th day of the month of October, in the
year of our Lord 1554, and the 1st and 2nd of the
reign of Philip and Mary, of England, France,
Naples, and Jerusalem, King & Queen, a question
and doubt in the statute 'On promotion to a living,'
concerning which a contention arose, and which
in truth needed interpretation, was referred to the
Visitor, the Master, and two senior Fellows.   The
question was this :—whether to '*Incept in Arts*' is
to take the degree of Master ; and this the Visitor,
Master, and two senior Fellows have so determined ;
viz. that to '*Incept in Arts*' is to take the degree :
so that the Statute 'On promotion to a living' will
have force within four years after Inception.   In
proof and witness whereof the Visitor, Master, and
two senior Fellows have subscribed their names.

Jo. Lincoln.

James Gloucest.
John Smythe.
William Taler.[1]

[*Pages* 71. 72. 73.   No entries.]

[*Page* 74.]   Decrees of the Master and Fellows
for A.D. 1544.

Firstly.   It was decreed, with the unanimous

---

[1] This entry is crossed out, and a note added, in Latin.—This
Decree was cancelled and erased, with the consent of the two Visitors,
the Master, and all the Fellows, on the 6th day of the month of June,
in the year of our Lord 1575.

Ita est.   Richard Joynes,
Notary Public.

consent and assent of the Master, and all the Fellows, that if any one in the said College shall in future be Proctor of the University, both he, and all others living in the same College, who are summoned by him, or by his deputy, and the deputy, if he so desire, shall be allowed to carry any arms and weapons whatsoever, the Statute ' On things forbidden ' notwithstanding.   Given, the 3rd day of May, in the 36th year of the reign of our most illustrious Prince, Henry VIII., King of England, France, and Ireland, and Supreme Head of the Church of England and Ireland.

Memorandum.   That on the 26th day of May, were placed in the Chest, A Charter of King Henry VIII.   An indenture of the Town of Oxford, for the non-payment of tithes.   *Item.*   An indenture on behalf of the Vicarage of St. Laurence for a rent of 20s.   *Item.*   Lawrence Atkins' indenture.   *Item.*   An indenture on behalf of the University School.   *Item.*   A Charter of the King's Court of Augmentations for the rent of Canterbury College.   *Item.*   A roll for Woton, and Old Woodstock, concerning seisin and fine. *Item.*   Mr. Carter's notarial letter for the lands of Frediswyde.   *Item.*   An indenture of Evans in Woton.[1]

---

[1] The remainder (about half) of the leaf has been cut out.

[*Pages* 75 (*half-page*). 76. 77.   No entries.]

[*Page* 78.]   A.D. 1554. 2nd of Mary, Nov. 7.

On the 7th day of the month of November, in the year of our Lord 1554, and the 1st and 2nd of the reign of Philip and Mary, of England, France, Naples, Jerusalem, etc. King and Queen, it was decreed, with the unanimous consent and assent of the Master and Fellows of Balliol College, that no Fellow, Commoner, Scholar, or Servitor, be in debt to the College for his Battells after the expiration of more than fifteen days from the end of each Term, under the following penalties: if a Fellow he shall receive no Commons or stipend till the whole debt be paid; if a Commoner, Scholar, or Servitor, he shall be expelled.

Moreover, it is decreed, that each Commoner and Scholar shall have a surety bound to the College for himself.   To certify which each of us has signed with his own hand.

JA. GLOUC.[1]

JOHN SMYTHE.

WILLIAM TALER.

JO. LINCOLN.[2]

1 Oct. 1555.

ANTONY GARNETT.

BRIAN NEDAM.

ALAN HIGGINSON.

BARTHOLOMEW GREME.

---

[1] James Brooks, Master of the College, and Bishop of Gloucester.

[2] John White, Bishop of Lincoln.

A coppy of a bill of Mr. Hydes hand which is to be found in the treasurye of his owne writinge. Memorandum that I, Thomas Hyde, fellow of Baliol colledge do owe to the said colledge that I borrowed 20s. to be payd the 7th of September 1573. In witnesse whereof I haue subscribed the 26th of August *anno praedicto.*

By me, THOMAS HYDE.

[*Page* 80.]

In the year of our Lord 1556, and the 2nd and 3rd of the reign of Philip and Mary, by the Grace of God, of England, France, etc. King and Queen.

On the 16th day of the month of January, the Venerable Mr. William Wright, S.T.B., before (viz. on the 1st day of December immediately preceding) elected Master or Warden of Balliol College, was present and laid before the Fellows, who had been summoned in the Chapel of the said College, an instrument, or certificate, of his admission by the Bishop of Lincoln, Visitor of the aforesaid College, sealed with the seal of the Public Notary. Which instrument, when they had inspected and heard read, the before-mentioned Fellows of the same College took in a proper manner, and placed for preservation in the College Chest. All which was done lawfully, and in accordance with the meaning and form of the Statutes of the College aforesaid, on the year and

Manner of admitting a Master after his admission by the Visitor. Will. Wright. Master.

day aforesaid, about 6 o'clock in the afternoon of Thursday.

The same year, on the 29th day of November, the Rev. Robert Woodd, and Mr. Richard Shaghnes were elected Probationer-Fellows for the year following.

The same year, on the 11th of July, died, the Rev. Father in God, Mr. John Bell, who, a little before his death, gave to the Master, Fellows, and Scholars of our College of Balliol, the house in Clerkenwell, near London, which, before he gave to the College, he had himself occupied, and where he afterwards died. Which house the Master and Fellows leased to a certain noble, Mr. Salisburi, Knight, on the Feast of the Purification of the Virgin Mary next following, for a term of 21 years, at an annual rent of £13 13s. 4d.

Death of Doctor Bell, July 11, 1556.

Lease of houses in Clerkenwell to Sir John Salisbury at an annual rent of £13 13s. 4d.

The same year, the said Master or Warden of our College, on his first arrival, gave to the College, or for an ornament to the Chapel, what is called a ' *theca*,' a most elegant ' *Corporalis*,' called in the vernacular a ' *Corpores case*,' which we use only on the chief Feasts.

Item. The same year, it was decreed by the Master and Fellows, that the Bursars, whoever they be, shall in future receive all profits on bread, on the stipulation and condition that they be answerable for the expenses and Battells of ' Strangers,' or Commoners. This regulation was not, however, intended to detract from the force of the regulation on the payment of battells written on the preceding page.[1]

2.

.   .   .   .   .

[*Page* 81.] A.D. 1557. In the month of September, of this year, Mr. John Smythe, senior Fellow of this College, died, in the county of Kent. By his will he left to the College six silver spoons.

The same year Mr. John Tomson, formerly Fellow of our College, in token of his gratitude to the College, his most illustrious mother, gave to the Chapel a white damask vestment.[1]

The same year Mr. Antony Garnet, then Fellow of the College, gave to the same one silver spoon.

.   .   .   .   .   .

The same year, the said Mr. Antony Garnet decorated and adorned a large room near the Library at his own expense, on condition, however, that the said room be retained for him for four years after he has resigned his Fellowship.

.   .   .   .   .   .

---

[1] This entry is crossed out.

[2] At about this date the Register begins to be regularly kept ; but most of the entries are elections of Fellows, leases of houses, leave of absence, and other like matters.   Only the more interesting entries will be given here.   Some of the entries are in English : they will be easily recognized.

The same year, on the Feast of the Annunciation of the Blessed Mary, the Master and Fellows
leased to Robert Richardson, joyner, a house on the
west side of the College, called 'The Catherine
Whele,' at an annual rent of 20s. ; the tenant to be
bound to do all repairs, after the first, which is being
done almost entirely at our expense

.   .   .   .   .   .

It is decreed, on the same day of the same year
[Oct. 21. 1560.], that each day, after the reading of
a chapter of the Bible, one of the Scholars, on
whom the duty shall fall by turns, shall read some
learned, short, clear, and diligently-selected episode
from sacred or profane history ; unless the senior at
table, on account of unsuitability or shortness of
time, or for any other reason, determine otherwise.

.   .   .   .   .   .

A.D. 1561, July 18th.

On the said year and day, it was ordained, with
unanimous assent and consent of the Master and
Fellows, that no ' Stranger' residing in the College
be permitted to lodge in the City or suburbs for a
whole week, month, or Term, unless for an urgent,
good, and legitimate cause, approved before the
Master, or his Vicar, and all the Fellows in residence, if he desire to make any use of our College,
or of his position as a Commoner ; but that each
one of them shall, in accordance with the Statute

' On Strangers,' in hall, at table, and at the Disputations, conduct himself according to his degree and status, like the Fellows and Scholars.

.   .   .   .   .   .

Memorandum, that wheras we were bownd at the lettinge of the lease of Robert Joyner his of [1] vnto hym to fynd hym all stuffe towards the first reedifinge of the same as well within as without he hathe nowe had all necessaries for the same 17 September anno 1561.

.   .   .   .   .   .

certayne customes to be observed 1564.

[*Page* 92.] 1. In p̃mis the m^r oweght at all tymes at his depture frome home to appoynt of the iij senior fellowes one to be his depute (seldome it hath byn sene but that ye senior of them hath byn appoynted his vice-gerēte) & hyme he oweght to appoynt openly in the chappell *ceteris sociis p̃'sētib⁹*, & thre to delyver vnto hyme the statutes & the keyes of the treasure howse wch the m^r kepethe & not p̃vatly : to this end that the other fellowes maye than knowe to whom they owe dutie in his abseunce & of whome to requier the execution of the statute yf ned be.

2. It by auncient custome the fellowes are allowed of the colledg Everye satterdaye at night

---

[1] *Sic.*

after disputacions so muche bread to ther supper as
they wyll eate leving also to the schollers or servitors
bread according to the discretion of the m^r or the
senior wch shall be p̃sente the fellowes maye chuse
whether they will be allowed ther bread or drincke
but com̃only they have taken ther bread bothe
because the ̄schollers might have parte allowaunce
ther by, and also for other causes.

[*Page* 93.] A note of diverse customes by
report vsed 1564.

1. It in consideratiō y^t on easter evē diverse do
receaue and for that it is the begininge of the
gawdy week the felowes are allowed so muche as
w^t reasō they will spend at diner.

2. It at o^r fyrst accompt on seynt thomas day
the burser is allowed to make the felowes gawdes of
iij^s iiij^d or ther aboute.

3. It also y^t at christmas and the holydayes
folowinge easter and the dayes folowing and lykwyse
at wytsontyde the m^r and felowes shold singe after
grace an himpm or anthem together.

4. [*In Latin.*] *Mem.* That by an ancient custom of this College, the Master and Fellows are
wont to have on the table, beyond Commons, one
half-penny, or thereabout, on each double Feast ; as
they commonly say ' in eluerymesse.'

5. It alsoe in the rogaciō week in cōsideratiō
that it is a gawdye week and also for that then ther

is but on meal a day the m^r and felowes are alowed so much as they will reasonably spend at euery meale.

6. I̶t̶ alsoe apō st john baptists day, St peter advincula mary magdalin St michaell and o^r lady dayes and alhollowday w^t thapostles dayes and diverse other the felowes are allowed aboue comēs at the reasonabel discretiō of the m^r and bursers or senior at home so y^t they be not muche chargeabel to the howse.

7. I̶t̶ also at easter, christmas whitsontyde and st katherins daye the m^r and felowes are allowed breakfeast in the morning w^t stwed meat or suche other.

8. I̶t̶ on midsomer evē seynt peters evē magdalin evē and Saynt James evē the m^r and felowes wear wont by a laudabel custom to haue an hores drinkinge w^t fyne caks and good ale and wear wōt being then together to sing som himpen or anthē.

　　.　　.　　.　　.　　.　　.

m̄^d y^t the xx day off februarye in the xix yere off the Reigne off kynge henry ye viii that it is conventyd & fully agreid betwyx maist^r & fe - -¹ows off balliall college in oxforth & m̄ John lobbens m̄ off my lord . . . . & William Jonsons fremason to werke or cawse to be wroghte iij heides off wyndos

---

¹ The edge of the page, in the Register, is slightly worn ; and some letters in this, and in the following entry, are illegible.

. . . off iiij lyghtes & one off iij lyghtes off yᵉ northe
syde & the heid off yᵉ eiste wyndoe off v lyghtes
eũy wyndow to be wrowghte wᵗ wovsers & chaw-
merantes & yᵉ said m̃ lobbens to see all mañ off
stones to be cōveid and caryed in to oʳ college off
ballial sayff and sownde wᵗowt eny brekyng or bres-
sing or iff so be yᵗ any stones be broke in caryage
the said m̃ lobbens to cawse to be mendyd or to be
reparyd.   And the said maist and fellows to p . . for
the caryage off yᵉ stones.   And yᵉ said maist and
fellows to pay or cawse to be payd to yᵉ said m̃
lobbens & William Jonson for yᵉ ꝑformy . . off yᵉ
promyss xxi markes iijˢ iiijᵈ

mᵈ that the iij day of aprill in the xiij yere of the
regne of Kyng henry the . . . that m̃ wittim Eist
mason of Burfurth hath ꝑmysyde to mak iij great
wynd . . . both the soolls & hedds of the south syde
of the new capell with a litill wyndow . . . to yᵉ
vestre with corbell table & iiij corbylls & retorn the
wall at heght to lay the ioysse oũ the litill wÿdowe
& sich ston as is wᵗin the colleg yᵗ wyll sue the said
wittim to haue & all other he to fynd at hys own
charge of burfurth ston cariag & skaffold warman-
shipe & lyme, & so the said wittm hath ꝑmosyd to
maik it ꝑfit & redy to ly the tymbre warke apon to yᵉ
corñ of m̃ blonston chamber & for to haue for hys
labor xviijˡⁱ of the which he hath resauyd afore xˡⁱ &
the rest he shall reseve as yᵉ werk goth forwards.

Iniunctions ordayned by m^r Thomas Godwine Mr Lawrence Howmfrey, Doctors of Dyvinitie m^r Richarde Barbere commissioners to my Lorde of Linkoln in there visitation had in Bayly colledge in Oxon the 4. of marche A^o D^{ni} 1565 lefte to be perpetually observid within the sayde colledge and confirmed with the puttinge to of there handes in the margente.

Imprimis it is ordeined and decreed that the communion shalbe dvelie ministred and geven into the handes of the commvnicants accordinge to the order set forthe in the booke of common prayer and that all and every person and persons beinge of lawfull yeres and discretion shall at the leaste thre or fowre times in the yeare reverently receave it and that the contemners or refusers thereof shall pay every time iij^s iiij^d at the discrecion of the master to be levied.

2. *Item* that all fellowes schollers communers and others sogvrninge within the howse shall resorte to the chappell in the time of service and common prayer and then and there shall behave themselves in suche godly manner that they hinder not the worde of god to be redde or songe or disturbe others which ordinawnce whosoever breaketh shall pay xij^d and if after admonition and thrise correction he or they do refrayne to come as is above ordayned then he or they whosoever he be shalbe at the discrecion of the m^r put owte of the howse.

3. *Item* that publicke prayer in the morninge shalbe sayde in the vulgar tonge as is throwgh the Quenes maiesties dominion vsed and that every communer scholer or bacheler within the sayde howse not frequentinge the sayde prayer shall for every time so offendinge be punished with stripes if he be vnder correction or els have oune farethinge set vppon his hedde at the discretion of the sayd m^r.

4. *Item* that as well divine service as the sacramente of the supper of the lorde shalbe sayde in the chappell of the sayde Colledge to the which all the howse shall dilligently repayre and not to the parishe churche.

5. *Item* that all lattine primers not allowed by the Quenes maiestie and all other superstitiows books be nether in publicke prayer had or vsed but be browghte and deliverd to the m^r forthewithe by him to be abollished.

6. *Item* that suche bookes for divine service be bowghte and vsed in the sayd colledge as are mentioned in the Quenes maiesties inivnctions as the bible communion booke davides psalters and the bookes of homelies.

7. *Item* that all the service be distinctely and openly pronownced as it is set forthe in the booke of common prayer.

8. *Item* that the prayers at vsuall times and the graces at meales shalbe sayde or songe within the

sayde colledge withoute invocation of sayntes or prayer for the deade.

9. *Item* that the m^r bringe with him all his company to the sermons specially if the be solemne and ordinary otherwise the absente shall pay ij^d at the discrecion of the m^r, if he be not vpon resonable cawse licencid by the m^r.

10. *Item* that there shalbe a minister chosen within oune moneth accordinge to the statute.

[*In Latin*] Written by me, John Ball, Notary Public of the diocese of Lincoln, on the 10th of March, of the year aforesaid, in my own room in the College, or House of Christ, in the University of Oxford.

.   .   .   .   .   .

[The heading of this entry is mutilated.]

Feasts on which we are wont and bound by custom to offer . . . or make certain oblations in other . . .

On the Feast of St. John the Baptist, in Merton College.

On the Feast of St. Mary Magdalen, in Magdalen College.

On the Feast of All Saints, in All Souls College.

On the Feast of St. Thomas, in the days after the Feast of the Nativity of our Lord, in Exeter College.

On the Feast of Trinity, in Trinity College.

.   .   .   .   .   .

Weeks . . . of 20 d.

Christmas. Epiphany. Carnival. Easter. Ascension. Pentecost. Corpus Christi. Assumption of Blessed Mary. Catherine, Virgin.

Feasts on which we have Mass and Gaudia[1] in Chapel, for the soul of Elene Longspei, and about 40 d on the table, beyond Commons.

St. Vincent, Martyr. St. John before the Latin Gate. St. Kenelm, Martyr. St. Leonard, Abbot.

.   .   .   .   .   .

Fire in the Hall on these following Feasts and their Vigils.

All Saints. Martin, Bishop. Edmund, King. Catherine, Virgin. Andrew, Apostle. Nicholas, Bishop. Conception of the Blessed Mary. Thomas, Apostle. Christmas, and the following days. Circumcision. Epiphany. Conversion of St. Paul. Purification of Mary. St. Peter's Chair. Carnival.

.   .   .   .   .   .

Memorandum. That according to the custom of workmen, carpenters, masons, sawyers, and joiners, shall receive 5 d. a day from the Feast of All Saints to the day after the Purification; and 6 d. a day from that day to the said Feast of All Saints.

.   .   .   .   .   .

[1] To recite the Rosary. See Du Cange, *Glossarium Mediae et Infimae Latinitatis*, under 'Gaudia.'

[The following entries have been made in two columns, on a page at the end of the Register; and have, afterwards, been struck through, with several long pen-marks. At the bottom of the first column the names, John Turner, Edward Whryt, and William Whryt, are written. At the bottom of the second column is written, in Latin, By me, John Atkynson, Fellow of Balliol College, in the year 1560.]

Office of the Dead to be recited for the Founders and Benefactors of Balliol College, in the University of Oxford.

In the month of January.

Obit, with Mass the next day, of Mr. Rodolph Hamstely, on the 2nd day of January.

26th day, Office of the Dead, for Lady Darvorgulla de Balliol, our Foundress, with Mass the next day.

On St. Vincent's day, we have Gaudia in the Chapel.

In the month of February.

4th day. Obit of Mr. Thomas Harroppe, with Mass the next day, when the Master and each Fellow receives 8d., each scholar 2d.

10th day. Obit of Lady Elizabeth Longspei, with the Mass the next day.

13th day. Obit of Mr. Thomas Cisson.

In the month of March.   None.

In the month of April.

7th day.   Obit of Mr. George Nevell, Archbishop of York.[1]

On the Friday in Easter week, the Office of the Dead to be recited for the soul of Edmund Norton.

In the month of May.

16th day.   Obit of Mr. William Bell, with Mass the next day.

Gaudia in Chapel on the day of St. John before the Latin Gate.

• On the Thursday in Whit week, the Office of the Dead is to be recited for Mr. Philip Somerwell.

In the month of June.

Obit of Mr. George Nevel, Archbishop of York.

In the month of July.

13th day.   Obit of Mr. Robert Ald, when the Master and each Fellow receives 5d.

10th day.   Obit of Robert Beamond, with Mass the next day.

On St. Kenelm's day.   Gaudia in Chapel.

In the month of August.

4th day.   Obit of the Venerable Father in Christ, William Graye, Bishop of Ely.

---

[1] This entry is crossed out.

20th day.   Obit of Mr. Lawrence Stubbs.

10th day.   Obit of the Venerable John Bell.

In the month of September.

25th day.   Obit of Mr. Edward Pool, when the Master receives 12d., and each Fellow 8d.

In the month of October.

24th day.   Obit of the most illustrious Prince, John Balliol, King of Scotland, Founder of our College, with Mass the next day.

In the month of November.

On St. Leonard's day.   Gaudia in Chapel.

29th day.   Obit of Lady Anna Danvers.

CHAPTER XII.

THE eminent men, learned Clerks, great Scholars, and members of noble families, who have belonged to Balliol College, are very many. To write about them all would extend this book beyond a simple history of the College. It would become a volume of short biographies ; and it would have to treat not only of the men whose names belong to Balliol, but of those great movements, Ecclesiastical, political, and educational, which have together made up the Story of the Nation. Antony à Wood wrote three columns, three of those closely-written columns of his MS. work, about 'the writers and learned men.' Gutch, in his edition of Antony à Wood, has not followed this portion of the MS.; but he gives, instead, a bare list of Benefactors, Bishops, and Masters of the College. Henry Savage, in his *Balliofergus*, presents us with a quite characteristic List of ' Learned Persons, and others desirous of good Letters,' who have belonged to Balliol.

The first of these to claim our attention is Johannes Duns Scotus, the celebrated Schoolman ;

and the arguments to prove that he was once at Balliol, though not weighty, are not such as can be lightly set aside. To these arguments might be added the fact that some connection certainly existed between the College and the Friars Minor, in Oxford ; and that one of the ' Extraneous Masters ' was always to be a Franciscan Friar. If Duns Scotus was a member of the College, one of Dervorguilla's Scholars from Northumberland, which is not unlikely, he must have entered the Franciscan House when, according to Dervorguilla's Statutes, his Scholar's stipend at the College ceased. But this would contradict the claim advanced by Merton College. The Warden of Merton tells us, that there is ' good reason to believe ' [1] that Duns Scotus was once a Fellow of Merton. And even to-day Merton Undergraduates relate how the Ghost of Duns may be seen, in the dark of November evenings, emerging from the old archway by the Chapel, to glide noiselessly across the Mob quadrangle, and disappear up the stairs leading to the old Library. These are modern stories.

Mr. Maxwell Lyte says, ' Duns has been claimed as a fellow-countryman by Englishmen, by Scotchmen, and by Irishmen alike, and he has formed the subject of several laborious biographies. Yet all that is certainly known about his life may be summed up

---

[1] *Memorials of Mert. Coll.*, Brodrick, p. 36.

in a very few words : he was born in the British
islands, he became a Grey Friar, he lectured at
Oxford in or about the year 1304, and, after resum-
ing his lectures at Paris, he died at Cologne in 1308.

.   .   .   .   .   .

'Dismissing without serious comment the tradition that his lectures were attended by audiences of
thirty thousand listeners, we need only remark in
connection with his Oxford career, that many writers
of good repute have fallen into the strange error of
supposing that he became a member of Merton
College after having joined the Franciscan Order in
his boyhood.   Such a proceeding would have been
forbidden alike by the practice of the Grey Friars
and by the statutes of Walter de Merton.'[1]

The story of John Wyclif's life finds its place in
the history of that movement which ended in the
establishment of the Protestant Church in England ;
and it is not necessary here to discuss, or to analyse,
the doctrines of the eminent ' Doctor Novellus.'   He
was born near Richmond, in Yorkshire, in the early
part of the fourteenth century.   'His biographers
have been at some pains to ascertain the college at
which he was educated, but it should be remembered
that, in the middle ages, the greater number of
Oxford Scholars did not belong to any college.
There is reason to doubt whether the Reformer

---

[1] *Hist. Univ. Oxford*, Maxwell Lyte, pp. 115, 116.

should be identified with a certain John Wiclif who was steward of Merton College in 1356, inasmuch as a Yorkshireman would scarcely have sought or obtained admission to that stronghold of the southern faction. On the other hand there seems to have been some connection between his native place and the college which owed its foundation to the Balliols of Barnard Castle, and was chiefly frequented by Northerners. This much only is certain, that John Wyclif the Reformer was Master of Balliol in May 1360. The Mastership of Balliol was not in those days the dignified and lucrative post that it is now, and accordingly we find that, in May 1361, Wyclif accepted in its stead the rectory of Fillingham in Lincolnshire, of which the advowson belonged to the College. He probably took a year of grace before actually resigning the office of Master, and his sojourn at Fillingham cannot have lasted very long. The income of the rectory helped to maintain him as an independent student at Oxford.'[1]

Another argument might be urged to show that Wyclif was educated at Balliol. He was elected Master when Sir Philip de Somervyle's Statutes were in force; and, according to those Statutes, it would appear that the Fellows of the College were to elect a Master from among themselves. This is not explicitly stated; but it is certainly implied. The

---

[1] *Hist. Univ. Oxford,* Maxwell Lyte, p. 250.

Fellows were to elect 'him whom they know to have most knowledge, most ability, and most zeal for advancing the affairs of the House.'

Humphrey, Duke of Gloucester, and George Nevil, are names which the College is indeed proud to own: Duke Humphrey, the great Patron of letters; and George Nevil, who was ' Benefactor to our Colledge in Books, Buildings &c.' William Gray gave ' all his Books, consisting of rare Manuscripts to our Library.' And Robert Abdy helped to build the Library. Robert Parsons' life belongs to Ecclesiastical history; but his name is prominent among the eminent and learned men who have been members of the College.

Antony à Wood wrote.—

'As for ye writers and learned men, but these following haue as yet come to my veiw, viz: Rich: Armachanus before-mentioned, an irish man & one of ye greateſt clerks of his time, y^t his country euer before pduced; he was bred up here till he was Master of arts according to ye statutes of ye Colledge, w^{ch}, (as 'tis before said) allowed ye fellowes to tarry noe longer therin then till they had comenced y^t degree. afterwards (if y^t wch I haue deliued elswhere from good proofe might be beleiued) 'tis pbable y^t he became one of ye masters of the foundation of Mr Will: of Durham or at least a student therin, and at length w^n he had pceeded D^r, chancellour of of yᵉ Vniůsitie ; he was pupill to, and receiued his education from John Baconthorp as Fox in his book of acts & mon. in R. 2. yᵉ worthieſt Philosopher & Theologist yᵗ euer his, or seůall ages before brought forth, but whether in this Colledge or some hoſtle adioyning (for according to yᵉ generality of writers yᵉ said J. Baconthorp was of this Vniůsitie,) it doth not certainly appeare. the next writer yᵗ was of this house was Dr Will : Wilton somtimes chancellour also of this vniůsitie, he was authour of seůall philo-sophicall treatises in yᵉ raigne of Ed. 3. of wᶜʰ some were lately extant, in this Colledge Library : then Alexanď Carpenter (sʳnamed by some Fabricius) if yᵉ authour here quoted in yᵉ margin might be trusted ; he was a great Wickliuist and a stiff writer & Preacher in yᵉ raigne of H. 5. againſt yᵉ vices & corruptions of yᵉ church : some of his works were lately in this Colledge Library, wᶜʰ perhaps was yᵉ occasion why the aforesaid authour should write, yᵗ he had his education here as he doth upon little or noe authority of some other writers for other places ; if he had had receiued his breding here, his name without doubt would haue occurred in some of yᵉ writings books, or glasse window of this house, wᶜʰ to my knowledge doth not, but of John Carpenter often, who was Contemporary with yᵉ said Alexanď & a Benefactour towards yᵉ glasing of this Library as his name in one of yᵉ windows therin doth shew, wᶜʰ phaps might be

another reason why ye said authour did mistake . then
was there Bishop Whelpdale before mentioned an
excellent philosopher and Mathematician, and some
years after in ye same Century wherin he died,
Rich : Rotheram a Yorkshire man, D.D., Comis-
sarie and at length Chancellour of ye Vniusitie an.
dni. 1440. he wrote seuall bookes y^t were well
accepted by ye learned of his time, and perticularly
his lectures de pluralitate beneficiorum wch is in M.S.
in this Colledge library, with seuall other tracts w^ch
are either gotten into priuate hands or else quite lost :
contemporary with him was Humphrey ye learned as
well as ye good Duke of Gloucefter as diuers books by
and to, him written, doe tefttifie : some yeares after in
ye same century was bred here John Tiptoft who became afterwards ye learned Earl of Worcefter, he was
ye onlie light of learning (as Leland saith) among y^e
Nobles of his time; who as he farther addeth auoiding
ye Ciuil dissentions of his country retired to Rome
where he became a great admirer of ye virtues &
doctrine of ye learned Free, of whome I am about to
speake ; in such a flourishing condition it seemes was
this Colledge in ye raigne of H. 6. by ye retiring
therof diuers of ye Nobility of England y^t our
authour Leland is pleased thus to speak of it.   Vbi
tunc temporis (meaning in this Coll : in ye raigne of
H 6) nobilium Juuenum corona celebris renascentem
imbibebat eloquentiam. then was there about ye same

time bred up here John Free before mentioned, borne at Bristow, where, after some yeare he became Rectour of St Michaells Church on ye mount; at length hauing a great desire to see other Countryes journyed into Italy where first he studied in ye Vniūsitie of Ferrara, then read Phisick and at length became Doctor of ye same facultie at Florence and Padua, afterwards he went to Rome where plying himself to ye Ciuill Law, became D^r also of y^t facultie & soe much was he noted at y^t place for his great learning and parts, y^t Pope Paul. 2. (to whome he had wrot seūall epistles concerning ye 6 bookes of Diodorus Siculus poetically mocking) præferred him to ye bishoprick of Bath and Wells, *but* though died before consecration; this was ye man as a iudicious authour reports y^t was one of ye cheifeſt of those English men, y^t by his honest & vsefull labour, reſtored his country burdned with barbarisme, to its former estate as it flourished beyond ye thought of man while ye Romans gouerned: diūs workes he wrot wch were uery gratefull to persons in seuerall ages y^t directed their studyes to those matters wch they deliuered, of wch works, some were lately, & are now (as I suppose) in this Colledge library & others either lost or in obscure hands: about ye same time as it seemeth one John Tartays was bred up here also, he was a uery learned sophister & one y^t heaped to himselfe great admiration from ye Scolars of this

x

Vniűsitie by his quick and acute disputations, w^ch
were uery often performed by him in ye publick
Schooles : w^t learned men were here at, and diűs
years after, ye same time, appearing not, I must descend to ye raigne of Q : Mary, in whose time liued
here one Rob : Woode & Rich : Shagens both notable
disputants & sophisters, as for ye former, I know
not certainly whether he published any thing or noe,
ye other retired into Ireland at ye change of religion
in ye beginning of Queene Elizab:, where gaining
repute by his noted parts is reported by an Irish
authour to haue bin a writer ; ye next y^t appears, was
Rob: Persons ye Jesuit, soe well knowne to Theolo-
gists y^t speaking of him might be now well spared ;
then of ye reformed haue bin Dr Tho: Holland D^r
Roɓt & Dr Georg Abbots, of whome histories being
plentifull, silence of them might be also now excused.

'And thus reaɗ y^o haue with breuity those
worthyes y^t haue bin bred up here, diűs other without doubt, especially those of antient time, haue
receiued their first seeds of literature here also, but
record being deficient & therfore cannot as yet
present them to y^r veiw (notwithſtanding I haue
seűall in mine eye y^t I may with circumstance or leſſe
authority then before adde,) I must by force omitt,
till more certainly appears & in ye meane time
descend to speak of this place according to y^t method
wch I haue pposed to my selfe.'

The following account of some of the eminent men who were at Balliol before the year 1600 is given, word for word, from *Balliofergus*; but the particulars of George Nevil's ' Feast of a Magnificence unheard of in our Age ' are omitted, as being quite unnecessary detail.—

' But whatever hath been the condition of this Colledge, as being a part of the Material World : It gives way to few in relation to the Intelligible, as I may so say, It having been the Nursery of so many Learned Persons, and others desirous of good Letters : A List of some whereof I am now to exhibit.

' *Walter de Fodringheye.*

' The first Principal, who became a Dignatary, *viz.* Prebendary of *Lincoln.*

' *Johannes Duns Scotus.*[1]

' There's as much contending for the breeding place of this rare Man, as hath been for the birth of *Homer* : We conjecture him to have been of this Colledge of *Balliol*, inasmuch as he was by Country of *Northumberland*, and of *Duns* there, as might be seen not only in *Pitsæus*, but before every Volumn of his Works in MSS. in our Library, of the gift of Bishop *Gray*, but torn off in the time of the late

---

[1] Mr. Bass Mullinger says that Duns Scotus was educated within the walls of Merton College ; but he gives no authority for the statement. (*University of Cambridge*, vol. i. p. 169.)

War ; and for that in *Northumberland* was the first
Endowment of our Colledge.   He liv'd *Anno* 1300.
which was after *Dervorgilles* Statutes (but before
those of Sir *Philip Somervyle*) yet not after the time
when it was granted by the Pope that the Scholars
might live in the House after they became Masters
of Art : and therefore he might for that reason
depart from this to *Merton* Colledge.   But if this
be not current, I shall give you in exchange

' *William* Bishop of *Worcester.*

' But whether he were *William de Lynna*, or
William Whitlesey, afterwards Archbishop of *Canterbury*, I am not sure : whereof this was Bishop of
Worcester, 38 *Ed.* 3. that the 43 of *Edw:* 3. and
immediate successor of this *Whitlesey.*   I find not
either of them chalenged by others.

' *Jo: Wickleff.*

'There were two of the name Masters of this
House : The later is he of whom we now write :
He was first Fellow hereof, then Master, and was
he that gave the name to the *Wicklevites.*   His
Letter written to the Pope, is to be seen in *Fox's
Acts and Monuments.*   Whom *Balæus* commends
as liberally, as *Pitsæus* spends his black mouth upon.
He was publick Reader in Divinity in the University.
He set up the Doctrine of the *Waldenses*, who were
called *Lollards* in *England*; who being also written

Lolleards, seem to be so called *quasi Low-Lords*, that is, Levellers: who though Reformers of Religion, yet the hostile manner wherein they assembled themselves, gave occasion to the Laws which were Enacted againest them, *Temp. Hen.* 5. and of that Oath given to the High Sheriffs of Counties to persecute the *Lollards* to death : (That which Mr. *Fox* in his *Acts and Monuments* urgeth against *Alanus Copus*, in defence of Sir *John Oldcastle*, the Lord *Cobham* (that the Act of Parliament was falsified, in that the consent of the Commons was not found in it) proves only that the Commons had then no Vote in Parliament, as to the making of Laws ; but the falsifying of the Act, it proves not at all.) Which damnable Doctrine of Rebellion, *Religionis ergo*, cannot be ascribed to *Wickleff*, the University giving testimony to his great Learning and Integrity of Conversation, *Anno Dom.* 1402. And all our Colledge Records wherein he is mention'd, do speak him a Man of great Trust, in the Reign of K. *R.* 2. which things were witnessed by his very Enemies. He is said to have written 200 Volumns against the Pope : He translated the Bible into English. See the Catalogue of his Books exhibited by *Balæus*. His Bones were by the Decree of the Councel of *Constance*, taken up and burned 41 Years after his death, which Councel was called *Anno Dom.* 1414.

'*Jo: Waltham.*

' He was Fellow of this House, and Sub-Dean of *York* : He gave as a Legacy to the Colledge *Notingamum Anglum* in MSS. *super quatuor Evangelia.* Although he be placed in our Colledge Library Catalogue, *Anno* 1492. or thereabouts, yet the very writing of *Balliol* with a double *LL* in the midst of the word, shews it to be at least as antient as the gift of *Fylingham*, &c. when it began to be written ordinarily with a single *L*, (which was 1343.) as I have observed ; which variation begat writing of it sometimes *Bayly* Colledge, sometimes *Bayliolle*, sometimes *Bayly-hall* Colledge, whereby the true Founders came to be forgotten, instead whereof Men became the Adorers of Fancies. This kind of negligence, about those times, became the Mother of Ignorance, which spread it self so far, that it stirred up the Industry of after-times to correct it.

' *William Wilton.*

' Fellow of this House, Professor in his Faculty : but in what that was, *Pits* doth not know ; but it could be no other then Divinity by the Statutes of this House made by Sir *Philip Somervyle* : After which, he lived here and wrote many things ; namely,

Super Priora Aristotelis. l. 2.

Quæstiones de Anima. l. 1. MSS. Bibl.B.C.

Super Ethica. l. 10.

' He was Chancellor of the University of *Oxon*: 1373. according to *Twine Apol: antiq: Oxon:* but noted to have given Books to our Library, 1492. There were two other *Wiltons* mentioned by *Pitsæus*, both named *John* ; one lived 1310. the other, 1360. In neither of which is our Colledge concerned ; and *Tho: Wilton*, 1470.

' *Roger Whelpdale.*

' He was Fellow of this House, and afterwards Provost of *Queens* Colledge *Oxon*: as they of *Queens* would have him to be ; but of this *Balæus* takes no notice : and lastly Bishop of *Carlisle*, a great Mathematician. He wrote many Books, whereof these are to be found in our Colledge Library.

Summularum Logicalium.	l. 1.
De Universalibus.	l. 1.
De Aggregatis.	l. 1.
De quanto & Continuo.	l. 1.
De Compositione Continui.	l. 1.
De rogando Deo.	l. 1.

' According to *Balæus*, he lived in the time of *Edw.* 3. He is noted to be the first that enriched our Library with Manuscripts, besides those of uncertain donation.

' *Thomas Chace.*

' He was Dr. of Divinity, Fellow, and afterwards Master of this Colledge, Chancell: of *Oxon*, *Ireland*,

and St. *Pauls London.* He built part of our *Library*, *vid. Sect.* 29.

' *Humphrey* Duke of *Gloucester.*

' He was Duke of *Gloucester* and Earl of *Pembroke*, of the Royal Blood : for he was Son of *Henry* the fourth, Brother of *Hen.* 5. Uncle (and Protector) to *Hen:* 6. chief of the Kings Bed-Chamber. He was a great Lover of *Aretine* and *Candidus, Italians*, as *Leland* witnesseth : He was of this House, and one of the most Learned and Eloquent of his Age: He built that magnificent Structure of the Divinity School, and Library over it [though some do conjecture from the great number of Coats of Arms in the roof of the Divinity School, that this was built by a common contribution] It is said, That order was given for the taking of it down, as a thing too superbe for a Building of that nature, which he enriched with 129 of the rarest Authors procured from Foreign parts at a very great charge, besides innumerable other Books of less value. After whose Example the other two parts of the Library, which cross this at both ends, was founded and furnished by Sir *Thomas Bodely* [since which time it hath received the access (amongst others) of rare Manuscripts of the gift of *William* Earl of *Pembroke*, Sir *Kenelm Digby*, *William* Archbishop of *Canterbury* ; together with the whole Library of Mr. *Selden*, which is therein placed by the appointment of his Executors, Men eminent for their Learning, and skill in our Municipal Laws.] And this Building hath received such further improvement, as if it strove not only to fetch out, but to go beyond the Copy given by our Duke *Humphrey* : for the great Gate of the Schools, and Tower over it, is of that height and excellence, that I know nothing of that nature comparable to it, being adorned on both sides within the Quadrangle, with five Stories of double Pillars of five several orders and dispositions, *viz.* The *Tuscane, Dorick, Ionick, Corinthian* and *Italian* ; all improved by the skill of Architecture, which will not be solely espoused to the Fancies of Antiquity. Adde hereunto the Theater now on Building, begun by the most Reverend Father in God, *Gilbert* Lord Archbishop of *Canterbury*, which once finished will as far exceed all the rest, as any one part thereof now goes beyond the other. So great a promoter was this Duke of Learning as well by the pattern he left behind him, as the cost he was at, and that as well of time bestowed in study, as in money imploy'd towards the work aforesaid. He was a skilful Astronomer, and wrote,

Tabulus directionum.	l. 1.
Ad Abbatem Sancti Albani.	l. 1.
De sua donatione.	Ep. 1.
Ad viros eruditos.	l. 1.

' At length, in the Parliament at *Berry, Feb.* 24, he was stifled with Feather-beds at mid-night by the *Suffolk* Faction : His Body was honorably Interred at St. *Albans, Anno* 1447. *Temp. Hen.* 6.

' *Rob: Twaytes.*

' He was Master of this House, and Dean of *Aukland* : and more of him I cannot write, unless that he gave Books to our Library, which though many others have done, I note him as being a Dignatary, 1451, which, or any other promotion, he might hold with his Mastership by the Bishop of *Londons* Statutes, a thing which by former Statutes was not allowable.

' *John Tiptoft.*

' He was of noble Parentage, but nobler for his Atchievements, and most of all for his Inclinations to good Letters. His Father was *John Tiptoft*, a Peer of this Realm, his Mother the incomparable *Lady Jocosa* ; by both of these he was consecrated to Vertue and good Letters, born at *Everton* in *Cambridge* shire, saith *Leland*, brought up in this Colledge, wherein, saith the same *Leland, Tunc temporis & Nobilium juvenum corona celebris renascentem imbibebat eloquentiam.* He was created Earl of *Worcester*, and at 25 Years of age Lord high Treasurer (High Constable, saith *Camden*, in *Worcester* shire) of *England* : and was Beheaded,

Anno 1471.   He wrote many Orations full of Roman Eloquence.

To *Pope* Pius *the second*	l.	1.
Ad Cardinales.	l.	1.
Ad Patavienses.	l.	1.
Epistolarum ad diversos.	l.	1.
Et ejusmodi alia plura.		

· He Translated out of *Latin* into English *Publius Cornelius*, and *Caius Flaminius*

of true Nobility.	l.	2.	⎫ and other
Cicero de amicitia.	l.	1.	⎬ good
Et de Senectute	l.	1.	⎭ Authors.

' *Jo: Freus*, vulgò *John Free*, or *Phreus* in *Leland.*

' He was Fellow of this Colledge : He became an admirable Philosopher, Lawyer and Physician : He became Publick Reader of Physick at *Ferraria*, afterwards at *Florence* and *Padua*, where he was made Doctor in the Faculty.   He wrote to his *Mecænas Tiptoft* abovesaid, Earl of *Worcester*.

Expostulationem Bacchi.	l.	1.
De rebus Geographicis.		1.
Petrarchæ Epitaphium.		1.
Epistolas familiares.		1.
Carmina diversa.		1.
Epigrammata.		1.

De Coma paruifacienda.   [l] 1.

Librum   Geogra- ⎫ *Per plagiarios surrep-*
phiæ.   1. ⎪ *tos:* as Dr. *James* testi-
Contra Diodorum   ⎬ fies : but these two, and
Siculum   poetice ⎪ only these, are in Manu-
fabulantem.   1. ⎭ script in our Library.

' He translated out of Greek into Latin, these following, as *Balæus* testifies.

Diodori Siculi Bibliothecam.   l.   6.
Xenophontis quædam.   6.
Synesium de Caluitio.   1.

' And many other things wherein he imployed his Pen well ; for a Translation which he dedicated to *Paul* the second, Pope of *Rome*, he was rewarded with the Bishoprick of *Bath* and *Wells*, a Moneth after he went to *Rome* ; where he dyed before he could be consecrated, but not without suspition of Poyson from some Competitor.   1465.

· *George Nevil.*

' That great Earl of *Warwick, Richard Nevil* [who, as in a stage for some Years, did set up and depose Kings at his pleasure] had a Brother which was this *George Nevil*, whom yet but young, he promoted to high Honors : for, being Chancellor of the University of *Oxon* [where he studyed and became Fellow of this Colledge] he was consecrated

Bishop of *Exeter*, *Nov.* 25. 1455. not yet 20 Years of Age. Afterwards, *viz.* 1460. he was made Lord High Chancellor of *England*, till his Brother the Earl being sent by K. *Edw.* 4. upon an Embassy into *France*, he was put out of his Chancellorship, and another, *viz. Stillington*, Bishop of *Bath* and *Wells* substituted in his place. But afterwards, *Henry* the sixth being taken, *George Nevil* was permitted to be promoted to the Archbishoprick of *York*, and consequently Metropolitan of all *Scotland.* Three Years were not hence expired, when *Edward* was devested of his Kingdom, committed to the Custody of this Archbishop of *York :* and *Hen:* the sixth being delivered out of Prison, restored to his own again, which he had before held for almost 40 Years. But *Edward* enduring an easie Imprisonment, made, by the aid of his Friends, an escape, recoverr'd his Kingdom, took K. *H.* 6. and this Archbishop [who had formerly taken him into Custody] But mindful of former Obligations, he let him, *viz. Nevil* Archbishop forth again ; but suffered K. *H.* 6. to be murthered in the Tower. And it was scarce a Year after, but K. *Edward* committed him Prisoner again, and plunder'd him of the worth of 20000*l.* at his House at *Moor* in *Hereford-shire* (among which, is recorded a Mitre set with Gems of a great value, whereof the said King made himself a Crown) Time and death having lost him his

Friends before; He lay Prisoner after this for the space of four Years, at *Calais* and *Guines* in great want, the Revenues of his Bishoprick mean-while being sequestred for the use of the King. This his Calamity began 1472. and he was, 1476. by the Intercession of his Friends, let out of Prison; and dying of Grief, he was buryed in his own Church. *In his time,* did Pope *Sixtus* the fourth divide the twelve Bishopricks of *Scotland* from *York*, and subjected them to St. *Andrews*, which he erected into an Archbishoprick. This our *Nevil* was a Benefactor to our Colledge in Books, Building, &c. And at his Installation, he made a Feast of a Magnificence unheard of in our Age, Recorded by Bishop *Godwin* (Bishop first of *Landaffe*, and then of *Hereford*.)

·   ·   ·   ·   ·

· *Thomas Gastoing.*

· He was Doctor in Divinity, Fellow of *Balliol* Colledge, and Chancellor of the University: This may be the same with *Thomas Gasconius* in *Pitsæus*, and *Thomas Gascoign*, called also *Vasco* in *Leland*. *Hunfleta inter Brigantes nobili loco natus*, saith he. *Pitsæus* notes him to be *Anno* 1460. and that he wrote many things, *viz.*

> *Dictionarium Theologicum*   lib. 3.
> *Septem flumina Babyloniæ.*   l.   1.

Veritates ex scriptura.   l.   i.

Ordinarias lectiones.   l.   i.

Sermones Evangeliorum.   l.   i.

Vitam Hieronymo Stridonis Senioris viri
ad miraculum cum eloquentis, tum docti,
quem mirifice coluit.

Ita Balæus etiam.

' *Stephanus de Cornubia.*

' *Stephanus de Cornubia* was Fellow of this House :
He travelled beyond Seas, and became Doctor of
Physick in *Paris*, *Anno* 1460.   He hath left no
memorial of himself with us, but the gift of *Galen's*
Works to our Library ; but hath written, *Subtiles*
suas & omni admiratione dignas moralitates, viz.

In Pentateuchum.   libros 5.

In libros Regum.   l. 4.

In 12 *Proph. minores.*   l. 1. teste Pitsæo.

' *William Gray.*

' He was Bishop of *Ely*, Doctor in Divinity, born
of a Noble Family, *viz.* of the Lord *Grays* of *Codnor*.
His ingenuity and towardliness gave occasion to the
great care that was taken for his Education, which
began in this our Colledge.   Afterwards, at *Fer-*
raria in *Italy*, he was an Auditor of *Guarinus*
Veronensis, and got to himself praise by his skill in

polite Language, and various knowledge of things.
He is said to have written much both before and
after he received his Mitre at *Rome* :   Neither was
he a mere Scholar, his Wisdom making him K. *H.* 6.
his Procurator at *Rome.*   After his return thence,
he was made Chancellor of *England.*   He gave all
his Books, consisting of rare Manuscripts, to our
Library ; built part of our Colledge, and bestowed
much upon the building of *Ely* Cathedral, where he
was buryed, *Anno Dom.* 1478.   More of this Prelate in the next that here follows, *viz.*

' *Robert Abdy.*

' *Robert Abdy,* a Gentleman of a good Family, as
is evident by his Coat of Arms, was bred up in this
Colledge in the time of K. *Hen.* 6. became Fellow
here about the first Year of K. *Edw.* 4. *Anno* 1461.
and Master of the same about the 17th of K. *Edw.*
4. *viz. Anno* 1478. in which place he continued till
the time of his death.   He built half of the present Library of our Colledge.   The fore-mentioned
William Gray and he are never put asunder in
places where they are remembred, as particularly
in the Colledge Library: wherein are [as I have
formerly noted] 21 Windows curiously painted: every
Window having two Coats of Arms, with Verses in
painted Wreathes about them: In one of which Windows on the South side their Arms are placed, and

none's else [for each Window hath two only] the
Verses about them are,

Hos Deus adjecit, Deus his det gaudia cæli.
Abdy perfecit opus hoc, Gray Presul & Ely.

'And in the uppermost Window, on the North
side, their Coats likewise are with these Verses,

Conditor ecce novi structus hujus fuit Abdy.
Præsul & huic Ædi Gray libros contulit Ely.

'This *Robert Abdy* lies buryed in the Nave of St.
Mary Magdalen Church [within the Parish whereof
this Colledge stands] under a Marble stone, which
had once a border of Brass about it, signifying his
Quality at the time of his death : but it's now lost.
In the middle of the said Stone is yet remaining his
Image in a Plate of Brass, with these Verses under
his Feet.

Testis sis Christe quod non jacet hic lapis iste
Corpus ut ornetur, sed spiritus et memoretur.
Quisquis eris qui transieris tu respice plora :
Sum quod eris, fueram quod sis, pro me precor ora.
                    Abdy.

'*John Tartays.*

'He studied many Years in this Colledge, as
Balæus witnesseth, even till he became Master of
Arts ; he wrote

Summas Logicales.	l. 1	with other
Quæstiones Naturales.	l. 1	things.

which he testifies to have been in our Library.

Y

' *Richard Clifford.*

' *Richard Clifford*, supposed onely to be brought up here because not chalenged by others, and a worthy Benefactor to this House : as is implyed, though not particularized in the 7th Window on the North-side of our Library, in these Verses,

> *Clifford Ricardus Antistes Londinensis*
> *Fusis expensis tale non avit opus.*

' He was first Bishop of *Worcester*, where, having sate about six Years, he was translated to *London*, *Octob*: 13. 1407. and *Anno* 1414. being sent to the Council of *Constance*, he made a Latin Oration before the Emperor and Cardinals.   In that Council that lasting Schism had an end, and *Martin* the fifth was declared the sole true Pope.   In his Election it was, by the Authority of the Council Ordained, That 30 Electors should be added to the Cardinals, whereof one was to be our Bishop of *London*: neither were there wanting amongst them that thought of making him Pope.   Certainly he was the first that nominated Cardinal *Columna*, who, with the consent of the rest, was declared Pope, and took on him the name of *Martin*.   This Prelate dyed *August* 20. 1421. and lyes buryed in St. *Pauls*, near to the tomb of Sir *Christopher Hatton*.

· *Dr. Balc.*

' Fellow of this Colledge, and Arch-deacon of *Ely*, 1478, a Benefactor to our Library.

· *John Bell.*

· *John Bell* brought up in this Colledge Doctor of the Laws, Arch-deacon of *Gloucester* : He was confirmed Bishop of *Worcester*, *August* 11. 1539. where when he had sate only four Years, he left it, as his Predecessor had done before him. He afterwards lived and dyed in his own house in *Clerkenwell London*, which he left (*inter alia*) to the Colledge : and was buryed in the same Parish Church, where he lyes under a plain Marble-stone on the North-side of the Chancel, with this Epitaph engraven upon it.

Contegit hoc marmor Doctorem nomine Bellum.
Qui belle nexit Præsulis officium.
Moribus, ingenio, vitæ probitate vigebat,
Laudato cunctis cultus & eloquio.
Anno 1556. Aug: 11.

· *John Cotes.*

' Brought up in *Magdalene* Colledge *Oxon*, Master of this House, and afterwards Bishop of *Chester*, 1556. *Mariæ* 4. thus Bishop *Godwin* of Bishops writes, but there is some mistake in it : I find *George Coats* Doctor of Divinity to have been Master, 1539. *John Cotes* I find not at all.

'James Brooks.

'*James Brooks* was Master of this Colledge, *Anno* 1554, and Bishop of *Gloucester* at the same time, where he succeeded *Hooper*. He was a Learned Man and an Eloquent Preacher: But by delegation from the Pope he condemned to the fire those Excellent Men, and Holy Martyrs, *Cranmer*, *Ridley*, and *Latimer*, who were burnt in the Town-ditch, commonly called *Candych*, over against this Colledge.

'John Piers, and Adam Squier.

'*John Piers* was Doctor in Divinity, Dean of Christ Church, and Master of this Colledge both together: He was admitted here, *May* 23. 1570. resigned it again, 1571. He was consecrated Bishop of *Rochester*, 1576. and then made *Almoner* to the Queen. From *Rochester* he was translated to *Sarum*: at last, *Anno* 1588. after the death of Archbishop *Sandys*, he was advanced to the Archbishoprick of *York*, dyed 1594. The next Master was *Adam Squier*, D.D., and a great Mathematician. I know of nothing he has left in Writing behind him.

'Robert Persons.

'*Robert Persons* was *Socius Sacerdos* of this Colledge, commonly called Chaplain-Fellow; and consequently entered into Holy Orders when but

Bachelour of Arts [for so 'tis required of every one that is to be chosen Chaplain-Fellow] He resigned his Fellowship, Anno 1573. *Feb.* 13. with dispensation granted him to keep his Chamber and Scholars as long as he pleased; and his Commons to be allowed him till Easter following : But afterwards he turned Jesuite, received Orders from the Church of *Rome*, and became Rector of the English Colledge there, *Anno* 1587.

' He wrote

Responsum ad Edictum Reginæ Angliæ.	l. 1.
De Sacris alienis non adeundis.	l. 1.
A Christian Directory, or Book of Resolution, an excellent Piece, in two parts.	l. 1.
Novam Anglic: reip: reformationem.	
De 3ᵇᵘˢ Angliæ conversionibus. English.	l. 3.
Martyrologium Catholicum, against *Fox.*	l. 1.
Censuram Catholicam contra Hanmerum.	
&c.	l. 1.
The Defence thereof. *Anno* 1582.	l. 1.
Contra Edvardum Cocum *de antiq: legibus Ecclesiast: Angl: extat.* 1606.	l. 1.
De successione Regni Angliæ.	l. 1.
Modestam admonit. contra Fr: Hastingum.	l. 1.
De mitigatione erga Catholicos in Anglia. English.	l. 3.

' These are all reckoned up by *Pits.*

' There's a Manuscript written with his own hand
in our Library, stiled *Epitome controversiarum hujus
temporis.* By all which appears, That it was the
wisdom of the Society to use that gentleness and
moderation as they did, towards a Man of his excellent parts, wavering in his Religion, and already
wandring in his mind towards *Rome*, to the end
that thereby they might allure him to stay : which
had they prevailed upon him to have done, it had
been good service to God, and an acceptable one to
the Queen of *England*, which the events of things
proved to be true.

Christopher Bagshaw.

' About the same time was *Christopher Bagshaw*
Fellow of this House ; afterwards, likewise chang-
ing his Judgment, he travelled beyond the Seas,
and being a Man of parts, became Doctor in *Paris*,
and one of the Faculty of *Sorbon*. He lived long
after this, even to the time of King *Charles* the
first, as I have been informed, and was wont to
say, He hoped to see a reduction of *England*
to obedience to the Church of *Rome*, and then he
would come and repossede his Fellowship again
here, inasmuch as he was never expelled, nor did he
resign his place as Father *Parsons* had done.

' *Robert Crane.*

' *Robert Crane* Fellow of this House, a Man of that prudence in the Eye of the University, that he was chosen Proctor thereof, 1581. nor could it be said of him as 'twas of that Emperor *Galba, viz.* That he was *omnium consensu dignus Imperio si non imperasset* : for they approved of his government so well, that they made choice of him the Year following : and all this when Proctorships went not by Cycle but by Suffrages, and so continued to do till the Cycle was thought fit to be made as best suitable to the present time.

' *Thomas Holland.*

' *Thomas Holland* was Fellow of this Colledge, Dr. of Divinity, and *Regius* Professor, all at one time. He was chosen Rector of *Exeter* Colledge, and a great Patron of Dr. *Prideaux*, as appears by Dr. *Prideaux's* own Epistle to him, put before his Introductory Tables to the Greek Tongue, a task imposed upon him by Dr. *Holland*, whom he thus bespeaks *viz. Pietatis & eruditionis nexu, non spectabili minus quam suspiciendo viro*, D. D. Hollando, S. S. T. *Professori Regio, omnibus à me nominibus patrono venerando.* It were a sufficient Eulogy of either, to say they were Friends one of the other ; which puts me in mind of the Epitaph of

Sir *Fulk Grevil* in *Warwick Church*, *viz. Servant
to Q. Eliz. Councellor to K. James, and Friend to
Sir Philip Sidney.* He never went any Journey,
but he took solemn leave of his Fellows, with this
Benediction. *Commendo vos dilectioni Dei, odio
Papatus & omnis superstitionis.* He went beyond
others in Reading, and beyond himself in disputing.
Him succeeded *Robert Abbots.*

· *Thomas Wenman.*

· *Thomas Wenman* was Fellow of this House, and
Publick Orator to the University, 1595. He hath
left nothing, neither would he leave any thing in
Writing behind him : because that whatsoever he
had left us, must needs have fallen short of his Per-
fections, inasmuch as the best part of an Orator
dyes with him.

· *Robert Abbots.*

· He was of this Colledge and Fellow here :
from hence he became Parson of *Alhallows* in *Worcester* : from thence he was preferred to a Living
in *Leicestershire*, which had been refused by Dr.
Reynolds, President of *Corpus Christi*, and *George
Abbots* then Master of University Colledge : from
thence he was chosen Master of this House, and
then made *Regius* Professor of the University, in
Divinity, whose Patent for the place is in our Treasury, in the Box of Admissions of Masters. He was

also a frequent Preacher : He wrote all his Sermons in Latin only, and Preached them out of the Latin Copy : they were begun to be translated into English by a Fellow of this Colledge, but he receiving small encouragement from whence he expected much, went not through with the work. After that the said *Robert Abbots* had, by Writings extant, confuted the Errors of the Pontificians, he was consecrated Bishop of *Sarum, Anno* 1615. One Book not yet Printed, is his Commentary upon the Epistle to the Romans : the Original Manuscript Copy whereof is in the University Library. In this, saith B. *Godwin,* he matched the happiness of *Seffride* B. of *Chichester,* That he, being a Bishop, saw his younger Brother Archbishop of *Canterbury, viz. George Abbots.* Him succeeded in this Colledge, the Reverend and Learned Doctor *Parkhurst.*

George Abbots.

' *George Abbots* was Fellow of this House, proceeded Dr. in Divinity here, then he became Master of University Colledge ; afterwards consecrated Bishop of *Coventry* and *Lichfield,* 1609. *Decemb.* 3. and the beginning of *February* following, he was translated to *London* ; where he had not sate a Year, before, by the prudent judgement of King *James,* he was designed Successor to *Bancroft* at *Canterbury,* and Privy Councellor ; whose Learn-

ing, Eloquence, Vigilancy, and unwearyed Study in
Writing, in a Man so overwhelmed with business,
Posterity will celebrate, though I be silent, says
Bishop *Godwin.*   He wrote a Book of *Geography,*
which Dr. *Heylen* took for the ground-work of his.
Another Book called, *Look beyond Luther.*   A third
contains his Questions stated in *Vesperiis.*   He new
publish'd *Foxes Acts and Monuments,* with an addition of the Persecution in the *Valtoline.*

Lawrence Kemis.

Lawrence Kemis was Fellow of this House,
Companion in Travel, and Councellor in Designs to
the Renowned Knight Sir *Walter Rawleigh,* who
gave him his History of the World which he
bestowed on our Library.   Sir *Walter* not capable
of his advice in one thing abroad, he chose [and an
ill choice it was] rather to become *felo de se,* then
scrupling an αὐτοχειρία, to return home and become
a State-criminal.   This fact of *Kemis* was like that
of *Torquatus Silanus,* who killed himself upon a
bare accusation.   *Tac. Hist. l.* 15. c. 8. of whom
Nero said, That he should have had life granted, if
he would have expected the Judges clemency.
Here was the difference, That the Case of *Torquatus
Silanus* was better, but his Judge worse then that of
Kemis.

' *Hen. Bright*, Mr. *Moor*, and Dr. *Hyde.*

' *Henry Bright* was Probationer-Fellow of this House, and afterwards chief Schoolmaster at *Worcester* for above 40 Years before his death : and the number of Scholars under him and the Usher, were usually 300 : out of which he furnished the Universities, and especially this Colledge, with many Scholars well grounded in the Latin and Greek Tongues, 3 or four whereof were usually Fellows of this House together. A Man he was of that incomparable diligence and method in his Vocation, that he seem'd to be born to that only : this and his temperance, spoke him a Man *natum ad reformandos hominum mores.* He became Prebendary of that Church of *Worcester* (in which City he was born) seven Years before his death ; for which Prebend a Patent had been procured him before by one that had been his Scholar, and at last Lord Keeper of the great Seal of *England*, *viz.* Lord *Coventry.* At the same time Mr. *Moor* was Prebendary of the same Church, formerly Fellow of this Colledge too. And Dr. *Hyde* Prebendary of *Sarum*, once of this Colledge, Father to the Reverend Dr. *Tho: Hyde* late Chanter of *Sarum*, and sometime Commoner here.

' *Tho:* Lord *Coventry*, and *Tho: Coventry* Fellow.

' *Thomas* Lord *Coventry* was of this Colledge, a great Lawyer: who became Kings Attorney [in which Dignity he procured Mr. *Bright's* Patent aforesaid] last of all Lord Keeper of the Great Seal, wherein he lived for the space of 17 or 18 Years, which he resigned up by his death. He was born in *Worcestershire*, Father to my Lord *Coventry* who was likewise of this House; and Son to *Thomas Coventry* sometimes Fellow of this House (and afterwards a Judge at *Westminster*) see *Sect.* 31. and more in the description of *Tho:* Lord *Coventry* the second.

' Dr. *Wakeman.*

' Dr. *Wakeman* was Fellow of this Colledge, a Learned Man : but hath left no memorial of himself, besides Sermons Preached at Court, &c. Printed 1605, and a Treatise call'd the true Professor.

' Dr. *Tho. Holloway,* and Mr. *Boswell.*

' Dr. *Thomas Holloway* born in *Worcester*, and Scholar to *Henry Bright* there, Chaplain-Fellow of this House, afterwards Vicar of St. *Lawrence Jury London* ; an excellent and assiduous Preacher there : exceedingly respected of his Parishioners, which is wonder, he being presented by the Colledge : After his death, immediatly succeeded him Mr. *Boswell*

(Fellow of this House too) after his return from *Spain*, with the Earl of *Bristow* : which Mr. *Boswell* gave many Books to our Library, a Person of known equal worth and integrity with the other.

' *Edmund Lilly*.

' *Edmund Lilly* D.D. was many Years Master of this Colledge, as appears by the Catalogue of Masters.   He was an excellent Divine, universally read in the Fathers, all whose Opinions he would reckon up upon any Question at Divinity Disputations in the Colledge ; and that with such volubility of Language, and rivers of Eloquence, as made all covet to hear him, and his very Enemies to admire him.   He was Chaplain to Q. *Eliz*. and had been preferred by Her, had not his long-winded Sermon displeased Her, when State-business occasioned Her to enjoyn him brevity.'

BENEFACTORS TO THE COLLEGE.
1260- 1600.

1260. John de Balliol.—' Assigned a sum of fixed maintenance to be continued for ever to Scholars studying at Oxford.'

1282. Dervorguilla.—Rented Old Balliol Hall, for John de Balliol's Scholars ; and granted them ' all the Goods of John de Balliol,' and all

1287. the debts due to his estate.

1284. Dervorguilla. — Purchased Mary Hall, for her Scholars; and 'all the Buildings and place in *Horsmongers* street without North-gate, in *Magdalen* Parish, lying between the Land formerly belonging to *Jeffrey le Sauser* on the one part, and the Land of *Walter Feteplace* on the other': and she had the hall, kitchen, and other buildings erected. Dervorguilla gave lands in Stamfordham and Howgh, in the county of Northumberland, purchased by her husband's executors, to her

1287. Scholars, and their successors for ever.

1289–90. Richard Hunsington and Walter Hork-stow.—Two messuages: 'one call'd St. Hughs-hall, the other Hert-hall.'

1294. Hugh de Vienne.—A soke of land, and several houses, in the parish of St. Laurence, Jewry, London; and the advowson of the Church of St. Laurence.

1306–7. William Burnel, Provost of Wells.—Seven messuages in St. Aldates' parish; one in St. Martin's; a School of the Jews, and the Synagogue. Also, 'the rest of the premises, together with ten Shops.'

1309–10. Gilbert de Pomfrait, and Thomas Humble-ton.—Land in Horsemonger Street.

1310. Hugh de Warkenby, and William de Gotham.—Four houses in School Street, with the area adjoining them ; for the support of a Chaplain, for the Chapel of St. Catherine, within the precincts of the College.

1310–11. Hugh de St. Ivo, and Geoffrey de Horkestowe.—Chimers Hall.

1315–16. Richard de Hunsingoure. — ' All that Tenement, with the Houses, Curtilage, and all other the Appurtenances in the Parish of St. John de Merton, lying between Alban-hall and Lomb-hall, which Tenement he had of the Legacy of Walter de Fodringheye, Canon of Lincoln.'

1317–18. Geoffrey de Horkestow, and Richard de Staynton.—Houses and land, near the City Wall, on the site of the Divinity School.

1319–20. Richard de Hunsingoure.—Twelve acres of meadow, called Bayly-mead, in the parish of Steeple Aston.

1327. Nicholas de Quappelad, Abbot of Reading. —Money and timber, for building the Chapel of St. Catherine ; and one glass window for the Chapel.

1327. Roger Whelpdale.--(In 1327 and following years.) Manuscripts for the Library.

1340–41. Sir William de Felton.—The advowson of the Church of Abboldesley ; and the Manor thereof, including Beeston.

1341. Sir Philip de Somervyle.—'The advowson of the Church of Mickle-Benton, in the county of Northumberland, and in the diocese of Durham, together with two ploughlands of arable land, and twenty acres of meadow, in the fields of the same City.'

1342–43. Thomas de Cave, Rector of Welwick.— Left in the hands of William de Broclesby, Clerk, £100. to buy the advowsons of the Churches of Filyngham, Brotelby, and Risom, in Lincolnshire, for the College, 'that the number of the Scholars might be increased.'

1375–76. John Burton.—'The House and the Appurtenances in St. Peters Parish in the Bayly.'

1379–80. John Duke, and Julian, his wife.—'A Messuage and Shop in St. Giles's Parish.'

1386–87. Hamond Haskman, and Thomas Cinlow —'Three Tofts and one Garden, with the appurtenances contiguous to the House of the Master and Scholars of Balliol-hall, for the enlargement of their Mansion.'

1401–21. Richard Clifford; sometime Bishop of Worcester; and, afterwards, of London.— Benefaction not recorded.

1427. Thomas Chace, Chancellor of the University, and sometime Master of the College.—

Built the lower part of the Library, adjoining the hall. And, also, contributed towards the building of the hall, buttery, and the Master's lodgings.

1451. Robert Twaytes.—Books for the Library.

1455. George Nevil, Bishop of Exeter.—An house in St. Ebbe's parish. Other buildings. Books.

1460. Stephen de Cornubia. — (1460, or thereabouts) Galen's works.

1474–75. George Nevil, Archbishop of York.— Buildings. Books for the Library.

1477–94. Robert Abdy, Master of the College.— Built the part of the Library next to the Chapel.

1478. William Gray, Bishop of Ely.—Completed the building of the hall, and buttery. Rebuilt the east window in the Master's dining room. Gave rare Manuscripts to the Library.

1478. Doctor Bole.—Benefactions to the Library.

1487–88. William Kyrby, and Alice, his wife.— Gave Oddington Farm to the College.

1492. John Waltham. — Gave Nottingamum Anglum, in MS, super quatuor Evangelia.

1517. Thomas Harropp.—

1529. Laurence Stubbys.—East window for the Chapel; and, together with

1529. Richard Stubbys.—South window for the Chapel.

1538. Mrs. Anne Danvers.—Gave £30. towards repairing Rood Lane Tenements, greatly injured by fire.

1555-56. Doctor John Bell, Bishop of Worcester. —Property at Clerkenwell. And, it is supposed, built the front gateway and tower.

1556. William Wright, Master of the College.— Gave, for the Chapel, 'an elegant Corporalis'; called, a 'Corpore's Case.'

1557. Antony Garnet, Fellow of the College.—A silver spoon.

1557. John Smyth.—Bequeathed six silver spoons.

1564. William Bell, Fellow of the College.—An Horn to summons to dinner.

1564. Doctor John Warner, Warden of All Souls. —Bequeathed £20. to the College; 6/8^d to the Master, 3/4^d to each Fellow, and 1/8^d to each Scholar.

1583. Antony Foster.—£200. to the College.

1583. Robert Crane.—A silver cup.

1593. William Hammond.—£1100. to the College.

1602-3. Peter Blundell.—

PRINCIPALS, WARDENS, AND MASTERS OF THE COLLEGE.

Walter de Fodringeye .	1282
Hugh de Warkenby .	1296
Stephen de Cornubia .	1303
Richard de Chickwell	1309
Thomas de Waldeby	1321
Henry de Seton .	1323
Nicholas de Luceby	1327
John Poclynton	1332
Hugh Corbrygge .	1340
Robert de Derby .	1356
John Wyclif	1360
John Hugate	1366
Thomas Tyrwhit .	1371
Hamond Haskman	1397
William Lambert .	1406
Thomas Chace .	1412
Robert Burley .	1428
Richard Stapilton .	1429
William Brandon .	1429
Robert Twaytes .	1450
William Lambton . . .	1461
John Segden . .	1472
Robert Abdy	1477
William Bell .	1496

Richard Barningham . . .	1504
Thomas Cisson	1511
Richard Stubbys	1518
William White . .	1525
George Coote .	1539
William Wright . .	1545
James Brooks . .	1547
William Wright . . .	1555
Francis Babington . .	1559
Antony Garnet .	1560
Richard Hooper . . .	1563
Robert Hooper . . .	1567
John Piers . . .	1570
Adam Squier . . .	1571
Edmund Lilly . . .	1580
Robert Abbots . .	1609
John Parkhurst . .	1616
Thomas Lawrence. . .	1637
George Bradshaw	1646
Henry Savage . . .	1650
Thomas Good	1672
John Verre	1678
Roger Mander . . .	1687
John Baron	1704
Joseph Hunt.	1721
Theophilus Leigh	1726
John Davey	1785
John Parsons . . .	1798

Richard Jenkyns 1819
Robert Scott.   1854
Benjamin Jowett 1870

Many of the earlier dates in this list of Masters
are not the dates of their admission to the Mastership ; but only the dates of documents in which
they are mentioned as Masters of the College.
The dates of their elections have not been preserved. Some of the above names and dates have
been taken from manuscript corrections in a copy
of *Balliofergus* in the College Library.

What of Balliol now?   And what of its surroundings ?   More than three hundred years have passed
away since the Early History of the College can be
said to have ceased.   There is a Modern History
since then.   A story of the slow development of what
the College was in Mediaeval days, into what we see
it to be now : the collection of new buildings, and
new new-buildings, the sets of rooms where so many
of our English sons are gathered together.   The
House of Balliol, founded, as we have seen, for poor
Scholars, has become an Home of Learning for the
rich, and for the poor ; alike for the Lowlander, the
Englishman, and the Celt.   They have forgotten,

long ago, the old feuds of Northerners and Southerners ; and live their three or four years in Balliol,
forming friendships which, begun under the shelter
and fascination of Alma Mater, endure through the
turmoil of life's dusty highway, and remain as an
abiding honour for their old age

> 'so blest,
> That by its side youth seems the waste instead.'

Under a common roof, proud of a common name,
to-day Dervorguilla's Scholars prove that the bond
of honest work, and honest play, the home-feeling of
their College life, the common share in the College
honours, are even stronger ties than the ties of
Nationality or of Citizenship.   Citizenship stops at
the old stone walls.   Nationality is limited to our
cliff-bound Islands.   But Balliol men may be found
now among the people of that vast New World
across the Atlantic ; and among the sons of that
Older World of southern Europe and Asia.   And
across seas, through all the breadth of our 'old
green-girt, sweet-hearted earth,' the name of the
House of Balliol is known and reverenced.

We know how the Mediaeval Scholar tramped
his way to Oxford, begging from house to house,
and asking alms along the road.   We can imagine
Scholars skirting the forest of Shotover, and finding
the Horsepath which, through bramble and across
moor, led them to the East Gate of the City.   If

late in the day, the City would be dim and dusk; but the sky warm and lurid from the rays of the sun just sinking beyond the Wytham hills. While other Scholars, after receiving hospitality at the Abingdon Abbey, would be making their way along the beaten track, in the midst of the underwood and bracken of what is now Bagley Wood. Perhaps a kindly Lay Brother would walk part-way to Oxford with them, to direct their steps, and point them the Towers of Oseney, or the grey walls of the Dominican House, in the distance. They would reach Oxford in the early evening, the moon scattering ghostly rays around them, and a thick white mist rising from the river and the winding streams by Trill Mill and Preachers' Bridge.

We like to go back in thought to those first days; and fancy that we see the tenements, with their small-windowed, low rooms, and uneven roofs. They were, probably, not unlike the old Benedictine rooms at Worcester College, but not so spacious; and the buildings not so substantial as the old Hospital, or Cripples' House, next to St. Giles' Church, which must have been built at about the same time as Old Balliol Hall, St. Mary's Hall, and St. Margaret's Hall. Some tall elms now shading the garden quadrangle, were probably planted on the site, and in the line, of Dervorguilla's grove. The gravel paths across the front quadrangle, and round

the fine chestnut tree opposite the Master's house,
are indications of where she had made the 'pleasant
Walks and Groves.' The ground which Dervorguilla purchased for her poor Scholars, in 1284, has
been trod by numberless Scholars' feet since then.
The House she founded has sheltered many of her
own Scotch boys ; and hundreds of others have faced
their first conflicts, and gained their first real knowledge, within its walls. The footsteps have died
away with the centuries ; and the story of lives is
left untold.

The old tenements are replaced by modern
buildings ; the trees of the grove have died, and
others have been planted ; the Portitorium . . . .?
Lost, long ago.

Yet if Dervorguilla could revisit us, she would
find her Scholars still in the Home she founded for
them. And if, in these pages, there seems to be
much of praise given to the Mediaeval days, and but
little said about the House of Balliol now, or about
Dervorguilla's Scholars of to-day, it is because the
names and the works of to-day are too near to us to
be spoken of here.

But, what makes the years at Balliol so dear, in
memory, afterwards ? It is that, side by side with
the daily work, and the clinging friendships, came
the bright dawn of appreciation amid a world of
beautiful things. Of all the beautiful sights and

sounds of country ; of all the rare, grey buildings, suggestive of a peaceful Past, which Oxford is so justly proud of; no memory is so cherished by Balliol Scholars as the recollection of the garden quadrangle in summer Term.

> 'While overhead the burning afternoon
> Glowed as if May had caught the heart of June.'

Then it is that the Old Library is most beautiful. There is a silence in the air around it. The spirit of the Past, which has been chased from every corner of the College, has gathered itself together around the quiet of that upstairs room, where Manuscripts and books live in happy security. That is the picture Scholars carry away with them, when, Oxford days ended, they bid farewell to the House they have learned to love. There are but few words of parting ; but to each one there comes the thought, perhaps the fear, that

> 'separate or together scarce our feet
> Will find another pathway quite so sweet.'

The Library deserves especial notice. It is the best College Library in Oxford, except Queen's. Of the first books possessed by the College we know nothing ; but it is safe to conjecture that they were few, and much worn. Antony à Wood tells us about the early Library of the Monks of Durham, and the books which are supposed to have been given to Balliol. 'The Monks of Durham hauing

begun to build a colledge or studying place for their
Nouices in y⁰ north suburbs of Oxford about y⁰ year
1290 on a certaine peice of land wᶜʰ they seũall years
before had purchased, Richard de Bury otherwise
Angeruyll Bishop of yᵗ place not onely finisht &
partly endowed it but also before & at y⁰ time of his
death (wᶜʰ was 1345) left thereto all his bookes
(more than all y⁰ Bishops in England had then besides) to y⁰ end yᵗ y⁰ scholars of yᵗ colledge & of y⁰
Vniũsity might vnder certaine conditions haue y⁰ vse
of them.   After they had been receiued, were for
many years kept in chefts & in a certaine roome
under y⁰ cuftody of seũall scholars deputed for yᵗ
purpose, at length a Librarie being built in yᵗ colledge
wⁿ moft part of it was built wᶜʰ was in the raigne of
H. 4. (William Appleby & Thom. Romo being then
succefsiuely Guardians or Wardens thereof) the said
bookes were put up in pewes or studies with a chaine
to each for y⁰ vse of scholars, wᶜʰ continuing in yᵗ
manner till y⁰ colledge was dissolued by K H. 8.
were then taken & conueyed away, some to D.
Vmphreys library (though there they did not remaine
long neither) & others to Balliol Coll. library : ' [1]

No one has any knowledge of what became of
those books ; and it is impossible now to find any
trace of them.   They must be reck'oned among the
good things lost.   Perhaps they shared the fate of

---

[1] *Antony à Wood. MS.* in Bodleian Library.

the volumes in Duke Humphrey's Library. That Library 'before it had continued 80 years in its glory & the triumph of its rich treasure, obtained from moft parts in Christendome it with other libraryes in the Vniᵛsitie found Rifelers & Pla-giaryes.'[1] The splendid volumes given by Duke Humphrey to the University suffered sadly. Any that 'looked like missals, and conveyed ideas of popish superstition, were destroyed or removed by the pious visitors of the university in the reign of Edward the sixth, whose zeal was equalled only by their ignorance, or perhaps by their avarice.'[2] In the reign of Edw. VI. 'certaine Visitors came to reforme yᵉ Vniᵛsity, one of them by name Rich. Coxe Deane Ch. Ch did with some others as zealous as himselfe soe purge this place of all its rarityes especially those yᵗ had rubricks in them or sauoured any way of superftition yᵗ he left not one of those goodly MSS giuen by yᵉ before mentioned Benefac-tors.'[3] It is a grievous story ; how 'some of those books were burnt, some sold away for Robin Hoods pennyworths either to Booksellours, or to Glouers to presse their gloues, or Taylors to make measures, or Bookbinders to bind books with, & the others the Reformers kept themselues.'[3] In the reign of Queen

---

[1] *Antony à Wood. MS.* in Bodleian Library.
[2] *Hist. of Eng. Poetry.* Warton, vol. ii. p. 45.
[3] *Antony à Wood. MS.* in Bodleian Library.

Mary, the books were searched for; 'there was some inquisition made after them'; but only one was discovered. The Balliol Library, with its gift of books from Durham College, very probably suffered in like manner.

The list of the printed books, which the Library now contains, is a clue to the kind of reading followed by the Fellows, at different periods. There is a very fine collection of historical tracts, which might repay the trouble of a careful sorting and examination: while the very many volumes of medical literature, now antiquated and valueless, prove that medicine was at one time a favourite study. An interesting article in *Notes and Queries*, Jan. 22, 1881, written by Canon Cheyne, formerly Fellow and Librarian of the College, states that, 'Our collection of manuscripts is a large one, but contains few of interest except to very special scholars. Our greatest benefactor was William Grey, Bishop of Ely [and Lord Treasurer, 1454–78]. He endowed us with not less than 127 MSS., including some, exquisitely written, of works of Cicero. It is difficult to specify the important MSS. when so much depends on knowledge of subjects not those of the present writer. " One of your MSS. of Isidorus's *Etymologiæ*," writes Mr. Madan of Brasenose, " certainly supplements all published editions in several passages." But Mr. Coxe's *Catalogue* is accessible, and to his pages I refer the reader. He does not, indeed, include our most recent benefactions, mostly due to the kindness of Mr. Greville Chester. These consist of various Oriental manuscripts—Hebrew, Arabic, and Armenian (not, however, of critical importance)—acquired by him in his Eastern travels. Among our printed books I ought to mention a choice collection of English translations, and of early editions and translations generally, of the Bible ; a copy of the 1512 folio edition of the Sarum Missal, with remarkable MS. notes ; and two copies of Dean Nowell's *Small* Catechism, both of which are the only copies known of their editions. I may add a copy of an Italian translation (interesting from the name of its author, Brunetto Latini) of the *Ethics* of Aristotle, printed at Lyons anno 1568.'

The fine room, which was the dining hall before the present hall was erected, is now known as the Lower Library, or Reading Room. It is a delightful room for the purpose. But the books overflow the shelves and bookcases ; and other rooms have, also, to be used. One room, opposite to the Lower Library, contains all the Chronicles published under the direction of the Master of the Rolls, and called, technically, ' The Rolls Series.' Some old stained glass, which in former years was in the Chapel, is now inserted in the centres of some of the large windows on the east side of the Lower Library.

The St. Catherine glass, as it is called, is remarkably rich in colour ; and, remembering the vicissitudes it has experienced, is in fair preservation. 'It was found in a disused cellar,' you are told, if you enquire where it was originally. But the glass itself replies that it was the old Chapel window, which represented the life of St. Catherine of Alexandria, the Patroness of the College. On it there appear to be some remains of the black paint, which so kindly helped to save windows from destruction, at the time of the Reformation ; and there are very evident traces of the same black protection in the beautiful little bits of stained glass which still adorn the windows of the Upper Library.

Always it is difficult to bid Good-bye to the friend we value, or to the work we love ;

> 'For words are weak and most to seek
> When wanted fifty-fold.'

We could linger in the Upper Library, and take down the Manuscripts, and admire the writing, perfect and finished, in those large and small volumes ; and grieve over the pages from whence some unknown hand stole the illuminated capitals. There is Capgrave's autograph[1] Manuscript, to touch and to hold ; the *Commentary on the Acts of the Apostles*, which he dedicated to Bishop Gray,

---

[1] See, Preface to *Capgrave's Chronicle of England*, ed. Hingeston.

and which Bishop Gray afterwards gave to the College. Also a Manuscript of *Capgrave on the Creeds*, written in a large and careful hand, and corrected in many places in Capgrave's autograph writing.[1] There is an Hebrew Bible, exceptionally fine as a specimen of beautiful and exquisite Hebrew writing, with both Masorahs in ornamental style. And there is that beautiful little Manuscript Vulgate, with its closely-written lines, on vellum so thin it might be finest paper, and the writing delicate as finest print. In the glass case, is a Manuscript on vellum, a Book of Hours, Litany, and Psalms, rich with highly-coloured illuminations. A note at the beginning of the book explains that it was found in the thatch of an old house ; and was, the writer of the note thought, probably hidden there at the time of the Reformation. The old thatch did its work well. The book is in good preservation. Also a printed book, *Hore diue Virginis Marie secūdum vsū Romanū*, printed on vellum, and beautifully illuminated afterwards. And there is a splendid Manuscript, on vellum, of *Ovid's Epistles*, translated into Norman French, with the Latin text in the margin, and with gorgeous illuminations. Volume after volume we might look at, and speak about ; but we must not stay.

The Chapel is quite modern ; but some of the

---

[1] See, Preface to *Capgrave's Chronicle of England*, ed. Hingeston.

windows are the old windows, mentioned by Antony
à Wood, in his description of the former Chapel.

The Fellows' garden, the small piece of ground
on the north of the Chapel and Library, and sepa-
rated from the larger garden by a low wall, was
one of the various plots given in early days to the
College. The wide gravel path, which is parallel to
it, by the mulberry tree, was, we may quite safely
conjecture, part of the land which reached ' from the
way over against the East end of St. *M. Magdalens*
Church, to the land of the Monks of *Dunelm*, now
Trinity Colledge ; passed over by Jeffrey Sawser to
Walter Fodringheye, with liberty to give it to this
Colledge.'[1]   Or the line of the gravel path at least
marked its boundary.   Looking towards the ' Monks
of Dunelm,' we see, inserted in the high stone wall,
which separates Balliol from what was their land,
several bits of very old carved stone, probably saved
from the old Balliol Chapel : all, of stone, which now
remains of it.   There is a mutilated figure holding an escutcheon, much worn ; yet we recognize
Balliol's shield with the orle upon it.   There, on
another piece of stone, is a St. Catherine's Wheel ;
and a St. Catherine's Wheel, again, on another,
farther off.   On a rather larger stone are St. Peter's
two Keys.   They were boldly and strongly cut, and
are very distinct.   And, near, an Angel holds a

' *Balliofergus*, p. 29.

shield on which we see a carved heart, surrounded by what might, in the rough and worn stone, be a wreath of immortelles, or a crown of twisted thorns. Was it a thought of Dulce-Cor ; or did a more sacred thought prompt its carving ?[1]

These remnants of carved stones seem to bid us look back once more to the early days, and remember all that Benefactors have done for us. There comes a longing to go back to the first of all, to ' lean and love it over again,' to

> ' now forget and now recall,
> Break the rosary in a pearly rain,
> And gather what we let fall ! '

The sun is going westward ; the elm trees are in shade. And we, standing here in the Fellows' garden, within touch of the grey Library, under the solemn dome of Heaven where the blue sky grows pale, think once more of Dervorguilla, and of all her beautiful love for others ; her care for the living, her care for the dead. And we remember, again, other Benefactors. We think how each benefaction might have a story written about it, longer and more detailed than this small book gives ; which afford many glimpses into Mediaeval days, and would tell us more about the people who were ' exercised

---

[1] In the south transept of the ruined Abbey of Dulce-Cor is a carved heart, and the words ' Christus Maritus meus.'

In the College wall there are other pieces of carved stone, of equal interest, but not mentioned here.

in mind, pondering whether they could do aught for the Honour of His Name.' There is the much more, that might be told, about the Oxford Mayors and Burgesses, who witnessed deeds of gift, and have left their names and their seals to be treasured in the Balliol Archives. The Chancellors of the University, also, had always a voice and an hand in the gifts to the College. St. Lawrence, Jewry, with its Monastic associations, might have an history of its own written, which would tell something of the old Monastery at Montreuil, and its poverty and 'urgent necessity;' and how the soke of land had to be sold, and the advowson of the Church. And the account of each gift to the College, of land or house in Oxford, might be enriched with the honoured names of the ancient City families, and the Burgesses to whom such properties first belonged. An history might be written of each Hall, or School, or tenement, or toft, in Oxford, which became Balliol property by the generosity of friends and Benefactors.

Everywhere, in Oxford, as we walk by College walls and gateways, or pass by narrow Entries and Streets, and read the names which are like echoes from the Past, a voice arrests us, and bids us think of our forefathers with loving gratitude. Balliol has its history; here so faintly and so falteringly sketched. Canditch, with its Fish Ponds, and City Wall, its Prison, and its Gates, has one also.

Bocardo has perished ; but the walls of ' our Lady's Chapel' near to Smith Gate, still stand. The carving, now worn and broken, which is supposed to represent the Annunciation, is still over the door,—now the door to the book shop near the entrance to New College Lane.

The Divinity School, one of the most beautiful relics of Mediaeval Oxford, is instinct with memories of the days and the deeds, which make its history grand and pathetic. The site, or part of it, was Balliol ground once. Then, as we have read, the University took it, in exchange for Sparrow Hall. This arrangement gave to the College its original ' Old Balliol Hall,' and to the University the plot of ground, in busy School Street, which was needed for the Divinity School. It would be a long story to tell, how money was collected for building this School. How the University sent 'petitionary epistles to set all persons to contribute towards ye carrying on of ye work. The first y^t appears to haue benne written for y^t purpose was y^t to ye order of S. Bennet wch shortly after was by ye care of Edm. Kirton Prior of Glocester coll. in Oxford & others presented to ye monks of ye said order in a generall chapter of them held at Northampton, beginning thus Reuerendissimi in Christo patres et præstantissimi domini &c. written last of June 1427. or else ye yeare going before wch request of ye Vniuersity

being taken into consideration yᵉ said monks consented at length to giue them 100ˡⁱ towards yᵉ said
work conditionally yᵗ yᵉ said schoole should be free
for their order : for yᵉ receipt of part of wᶜʰ wee
haue yᵉ transcript of two acquittances viz. one dated
yᵉ last of Aprill 8. H. 6. giuen to Ralph, Abbat of
Abendon for his paying of 20 marks and another
13. may yᵉ same year to John Wethamsted S.T.p.
Abbat of S. Albans for as much. about yᵉ same time
yᵗ yᵉ said Epistle was written Hen. Chichley Archb.
of Canterbury gaue for yᵗ purpose a plentifull summ
of gold as yᵉ Vniūsities letter of thanks to him testifie.
William Gray Deane of Paules gaue another summe
of money, yᵉ Deanes & chapters of Salisbury, Wells,
Exceter & Lyncolne, others, yᵉ monks or Canons of
yᵉ order of S. Augustine a considerable summe also,
to yᵉ Presidents & Prelats of wᶜʰ order sitting in a
gencrall chapter at Northampton yᵉ Vniūsitie had
before sent their Epistle for yᵗ purpose. all wᶜʰ gifts
being receiued with moneys also from other persons
especially from Humphrey yᵉ good Duke of Glocester
(wᶜʰ were considerable, soe much it seems yᵗ he is
stiled yᵉ Founder of yᵉ said Schoole) the Vniūsity
ꝓceeded to build a storie ouer it for a Library & yᵗ yᵗ
work might yᵉ better goe forward they wrote a com-
plementall letter to yᵉ said Duke an. 1445 telling him
how farre they had proceeded in their work & how
yᵗ yᵉ place it selfe being fit for a library because

remote from secular noise offered him yᵉ title of
Founder of it, yᵉ wᶜʰ whether he accepted I know
not, he it seems took it soe kindly yᵗ he did not onlie
giue them moneys, but also two years after wⁿ he
died 100ˡⁱ more & diũs choice MSS, wᶜʰ last being
with much adoe obtained by yᵉ Vniũsitie were reposed
in yᵉ old library till such time this was finished.'[1]

They were generous Benefactors, and we like to
recognize the good Duke Humphrey among them.
There were other Benefactors, also. It is an history, rich with the names of men about whose gifts
and work more ought to be told.

The Divinity School is empty now. Not an
echo of the old Scholastic Disputations breaks the
silence. A young boy loiters near the door, to tell
visitors to Oxford that it is, or was, the Divinity
School; for, otherwise, they might not know it. And
he adds that it was used as Council Chamber, by
Charles I., when Oxford was a centre of civil discord. The Divinity School has its older and better
Past than that. And it has its sadder history also.—

'To conclude, all yᵗ I shall further adde concerning this place, is yᵗ it suffered yᵉ same fate in yᵉ
raigne of Ed. 6. as yᵉ Schooles of arts did. It
suffered in its roof & gutters of lead wᶜʰ being not
repaired for seũall years great dammage followed,
It suffered in its furniture, part of it being taken

---

[1] *Antony à Wood. MS.* in Bodleian Library.

away by Mechanicks, in its windows adorned verie
curiously with ye pictures of Apostles Fathers &
armes of benefactours, most of them being then
broken downe & ye lead wch Joyned then to other
glasse taken away.   furthermore also not onely
nettles bushes & brambles grew about ye walls
(soe disused was it & ye other schooles adioyning)
but a stinking pownd for cattle erected close &
joyning to it all wch being beheld with sorrowfull
countenances by ye Romanists w^n their religion was
restored, were taken away & all things relating to
ye schoole it selfe put into good order 1557.'[1]

School Street clamours to have its story told.
It would be an history of the Schools, and the
Teachers; and of the men who listened, and learned,
and went out into the world, owing all that they
most prized to the lectures and Disputations in those
small and crowded tenements.   Though so central,
time has been merciful to School Street.   It is
quiet enough now; and, opposite, the grass is green
around the Radcliffe Reading Room, and on the
north side of St. Mary's Church.   In School Street
there was Balliol ground also; the four houses,
with the area adjoining them, which Hugh de Warkenby and William de Gotham gave to the College,
for the support of a Chaplain.

[1] *Antony à Wood.   MS.* in Bodleian Library

So we might wander through Oxford, and recognize ' Balliol ' in almost every Street.

There are still rays of light upon the spire of St. Mary's Church. The Statues we look up to are clearer now, in the evening light, than when the midday sun shines full upon them. There is St. Cuthbert ; and there St. Hugh, the ' Venerable Brother,' mentioned in the Legate's letter to the Burgesses of Oxford. St. Cuthbert looks towards Durham. St. Hugh, also, looks north, to his Cathedral at Lincoln. For centuries those sightless eyes have been bent on the old home, where his body was laid to rest. Our eyes follow our thoughts. What do we see ? The Cathedral, which was his Cathedral ; where, also, Oliver Sutton was Bishop ; and others, who wrote letters, and granted Licences to the College. Bishop Oliver witnessed Dervor-guilla's foundation deeds ; and wrote that beautiful and pious letter, which gave permission to Balliol Scholars to have the Divine Office said in their own Chapel or Oratory.

We look farther north, and we see the ruins of Barnard Castle, where John de Balliol and Dervor-guilla lived in great state ; and where, in happy days, they entertained Prince Edward. Farther still, to Durham ; and we remember John de Balliol's penance, and the poor Scholars he was to maintain at Oxford. And we think about Bishop Richard, and his love for books.

Very little farther north still, we see the ruins of Dulce-Cor, the Abbey built by Dervorguilla, in memory of her husband ; and where his heart was placed, in the wall near to the High Altar. At Dulce-Cor, also, Dervorguilla's body was laid, when her spirit passed from this life. We look in vain for her tomb, or any trace of where she was buried. There is no stone left to mark the spot : no ruined shrine, no broken carving, no time-worn words. There is nothing but the ruin, to tell of her who built the Abbey, and whose body sleeps there.

But the memory of Dervorguilla de Galwedia, Domina de Balliolo, will live for very long in the Home of her Scholars at Oxford.

INDEX